Dances *of the* Heart

Connecting with Animals

D0768124

Sally Morgan

Praise For

Dances of the Heart
Connecting with Animals

Animals are complete; man is not. We have much to learn in order to become complete in a world full of difficulties. Animals are here to be our teachers and healers. As Sally's stories in *Dances of the Heart—Connecting with Animals* show us, we can learn from the behavior of animals and from the unconscious messages that they share with us. Sally's book gives us all the opportunity to learn from her experience and from that of her animal teachers and healers. The animals are our role models and help us all survive. Whenever I am in a difficult situation I say to myself, WWLD? Or, What Would Lassie Do? So, as Sally shows us in her book, find your role model and live the message so you can be almost as good as your animal role model.

– Bernie Siegel, MD author of *Buddy's Candle*, *Smudge Bunny*, and *Love, Animals & Miracles*

This beautifully insightful journey through Sally's life weaves her powerful experiences with an amazing group of animal souls and deep wisdom from visionaries in the animal world who continue to influence our world today. She sees the animals through the eyes of her heart as sentient beings who not only share our lives but teach us in profound ways. She shows us how true listening to the animals and living a life of connection with them evolves and transforms our lives. Let her words stir your heart and inspire you to be in right-relationship with the four-legged beings in your life.

– Tracy Vroom, CST, EBW, CEMT, CCMT, Equine Craniosacral Instructor, Shaman

With heartfelt respect for animals as fellow beings, Sally Morgan relays with honesty and intense feeling her gripping adventures with animal companions. In a life dedicated to perceptive listening in learning to help and heal animals, her understanding and practical wisdom widens and inspires. What a joy to be carried along with her captivating accounts linking different species as partners in life's deep dance! Sharing the author's ocean of knowledge and healing awareness of our animal friends is guaranteed to warm your heart and enlighten your life.

– Penelope Smith, Founding Animal Communication Specialist, author of *Animal Talk*, *When Animals Speak*, and *Animals in Spirit* www.animaltalk.net

I have had the great fortune to see Sally Morgan work her magic for the past three decades. Her ability to understand and provide the best physical therapy required by each animal is amazing. Having attended her classes in TTouch and Craniosacral Therapy, I can attest to her in-depth knowledge of the field of hands-on work with animals, and her ability to connect deeply with all animals. Her work has produced results that might seem beyond reach, but the stories she reveals in her book are true testaments to the powers of healing that lie within each individual. Her journey of deepening her understanding of animals will inspire all of us to enrich our relationships with our own animals. A wonderful read that will leave you wanting more!

— Judy Morgan DVM, author of *From Needles to Natural, What's for Dinner, Dexter?*, and *Canine Kitchen Capers*, www.DrJudyMorgan.com

Sally's approach, as both a practitioner and writer-storyteller, is truly sensitive and insightful. She blends her extensive professional experience in multiple healing modalities and training techniques, with deep, intuitive wisdom to tap into and address animals' needs and wants. Sally's perceptive, multi-sensory stories of her experiences with the animals in her life are deeply moving. This book will engage both your heart and mind, and help you strengthen the bonds between you and your animal partners.

— Sandra Mendelson, Animal Channel, author of upcoming book *We Walk Beside You*

Sally Morgan joins the ranks of authors in the TTouch family who share their experiences of TTouch with animals and their people.

On the plane from Los Angeles to Washington, D.C., I had my first chance to take a peek into *Dances of the Heart—Connecting with Animals*. OMG! I was hooked from the introductory sentence onward and could not stop reading. It gave me a warm fuzzy feeling like being curled up around a crackling camp fire on a warm summer night by a lake, enchanted by Sally's heart-warming stories of her life with animals, told with humor and passion and a deep appreciation of life as a cancer survivor.

Not only do her stories elicit deep emotions, she drops informative tips throughout the chapters, like the banana chips she uses to leash-train her bunnies. Sally brings a unique perspective to the human/animal connection, combining her experience as a teacher, a physical therapist, a craniosacral therapist for animals and people, and Tellington TTouch practitioner for humans and animals.

She began her adult life as a school teacher and has been a Tellington TTouch teacher for horses for nearly 30 years, introduced by her problem horse Burgers. She began applying TTouch for companion animals in the 90's before we had a certification training program.

I love the way she weaves training tips she applied to her beloved corgis who have inspired her to explore many healing and training modalities for dogs and horses. TTouch inspired her to pursue a career as a physical therapist for humans, and that led to CranioSacral therapy with the Upledger Institute where she was invited to develop a program for CranioSacral therapy for animals.

All of this knowledge is deepened by her sharp intellect and passion for constantly learning, enriched by her lifelong love of animals shared by her mother and her close connection with her sister, a holistic veterinarian. The blessing she received by attending monthly cancer-survival support groups with the legendary Dr. Bernie Siegel will speak to many survivors. This book will be one of my book club choices and is an absolute must-read for all of you who love animals!

– Linda Tellington-Jones, author of *Dressage With Mind, Body, and Soul* and *The Ultimate Horse Behavior and Training Book*

Dedicated To All Of The Animals

Dances *of the* Heart Connecting with Animals

TABLE OF CONTENTS

The Animals Who Have Shared the Dance With Me

THE DOGS

Toby, 1958-1971, a cocker spaniel mix, my mom's dog

Dandy, 1967-1974, an English Llewellyn setter, family dog and my friend in exploration

Jack's Winsome Winston, (Winnie), Aug. 1986-Nov. 2001, Pembroke Welsh corgi, my first dog

Foxy Rosé (Molly), 1988-2003, Pembroke Welsh corgi, Jack's best friend

Sally's Charismatic Comet, (Comet, Mit), Dec.1999-Oct. 2015, Pembroke Welsh corgi, my second dog

Sally's Intrepid Trystan, (Trystan, Biscuit), Nov. 2009-present, Pembroke Welsh corgi, my third corgi

THE RABBITS

Easter Bunny, 1972-1973, New Zealand white rabbit, found pet rabbit

Agatha, 1980-1989, black Netherland dwarf rabbit, my first rabbit

Hershey, Eileen, Candy, three of Agatha's bunnies who found homes with my friends

Leo, 1980-1990, Siamese Netherland dwarf rabbit, Agatha's daughter

Lily, 1984-1991, Himalayan dwarf rabbit, pet store adoption and Leo's beloved friend

Rufus, 1990-1999, gray Siamese Netherland dwarf rabbit, my last house bunny

THE CAT

Saffron Sugarspot, (Kitty), 200?-2005, ginger marmalade female short-haired cat

THE HORSES

Buttercup, pinto Chincoteague-type pony who belonged to my friend Kathleen

Blaze, mixed-breed dark bay pony assigned to me as a camper

Phantom, black Quarter horse cross who I rode as a camp counselor

Prince Charming, palomino Quarter horse cross who I worked with at a CHA camp

Spooky, 1950?-1974, flea-bitten gray mixed-breed grade pony, my first horse

Goblin, (Diamond) 1969-1974, chestnut Thoroughbred mare, my second horse

Sir Richard of Harlech, (Richard pony) 1970-1990, chestnut half-Arabian gelding, my third horse

Boca Kay, (Bokey), buckskin gelding, my sister Judy's first show pony

Auto Pilot, (Rocky), 1985?-present, American Quarter horse, my sister Judy's show horse

LHM Night Hawk, (Hawk), 4/1982-1990, black Morgan gelding, my fifth horse

Smokey, ?-2010, gray cross-bred pony, my niece Gwen's first pony

Lucky Star, 4/2000-present, gray miniature horse, first Gwen's then my mother's horse

Ten Penny Moonshine, (Burgers), May 1979-July 2008, mahogany bay Morgan gelding, my last horse

Foreword

Dancing With Animals: How It Began

I shared a special bond with my horse, Burgers, and my corgi, Comet.

" ... I used to think it silly for people to speak of dogs as "family" or other animals as "friends." Now I feel it's silly not to ... I'd underestimated the intelligence and sensitivity of other animals."

— Carl Safina, *Beyond Words: What Animals Think and Feel*

" ... having a special trust that I feel when I put my hands on a horse for the first time. It is with a sense of honor and gratitude and respect for the heart and mind of that individual. I feel a cell-to-cell and heart-to-heart connection, without words."

— Linda Tellington-Jones in *Strike a Long Trot*

This book is the story of my path with the many animals with whom I have shared my life. It is the story of how I found a deep connection with them through learning how to listen to them. In this time of the popularity of horse whispering and positive dog training, we are so focused on how to impart our wishes to our animals that many of us have forgotten the importance of listening to them.

Our animals have much to tell us through their posture, breathing, stance, and what they pay attention to, which we would hear if we could only step outside of our human biases long enough to appreciate the world that they live in and see it from their perspectives. The animal-human bond is boundless, if we learn to listen with open hearts.

I learned how to make soul connections with my animals through careful observation, and by giving up what I thought was right about training—or what I had been told was right—in order to understand what my animals were showing me. As Frédéric Pignon, originator of *Cavalia*, describes:

> ... you must observe the horse; listen to him, make the horse confident, trusting, and relaxed ... An even more vitally important thing, you have to *believe*. Without losing hold on reality you have to believe that you can communicate with the horse and that one day, with persistence, you will have such close communion that you may be able to change leads at every stride with no detectable instructions ... You must believe that you can continue to improve communication between yourself and the horse, and if everyone shares their discoveries then the day when we really understand may arrive sooner rather than later.

Many of us are coming to a time when indeed we want to understand the animals in our lives and improve our relationships with them, and find more subtle ways to communicate with them. The insight and guidance animals have to share with us is infinite.

As you will see, it took many horses and people to show me insights about the limitations of conventional training methods, including lunging my horses. And with my dogs, I had to recognize them beyond what I, as a human, perceived as their desires, to see gentle shifts in them that were not simply about wanting food, but wanting to help me earnestly in anything I was doing. With my rabbits, seeing them as individuals and opening my life to them—as most people do with dogs—allowed the rabbits to play with me, travel with me, and share their lives with me in meaningful ways. The cat I knew closely showed me that some cats can be more like dogs than most people imagine, with clear opinions, needs, and dreams, just as I saw in all of the other animals in my life.

For me, being with animals is not about dominance, control, or demands. Animals in my life are given guidelines about how to live in my house and with me, so that we can explore life together as partners in a beautiful dance, each following the other's lead as we interact with the world that surrounds us. Animals can enrich all of our lives in ways we have too long overlooked.

My friend Dr. Bernie Siegel, who shares with me a deep appreciation of animals, suggests solving situations in life by asking the question, "What would Lassie do?"

Lassie consistently made the right choices, heroically arriving in a time of need, acting with compassion and love, demonstrating intelligence and understanding, all while continuing to embrace life with play and joy. Linda Tellington-Jones, my mentor, believes that Lassie is no fantasy. As I do, she feels that all dogs—and all animals, for that matter—can be like Lassie if we allow ourselves to see their brilliance and beauty. My dogs and my horses have done extraordinary things in their lives; I just needed to learn how to recognize what they were telling me. They even have shown me that they were capable of skillfully working with me in healing sessions for other animals and people. I learned to see all animals with my heart, not just my eyes.

I hope that the stories of my animals will inspire you to make deeper connections with your own animals—the dog who shares your house, the horse who explores trails with you, or the birds who flock to your feeder each morning. When we come from a place of respect, compassion, and love, animals will show us remarkable qualities that would have been otherwise lost to us, allowing us to transform our lives. Animals all around us are trying to communicate with us, to make profound connections with us, if only we can shift our understanding of them and ourselves, in order to find ways to truly listen to them, to share the dance with them.

Chapter 1

Dogs and Their Dance of Devotion
Toby and Dandy; Morphic Fields

From right, Judy, Toby and me celebrating Christmas.

*"Once you have had a wonderful dog,
a life without one is a life diminished."*

— Dean Koontz

The little red cocker spaniel mix pushed his nose through the cracked window of the parked sedan—there was that smell—home! He pawed at the window, scrambling over the hand-crank with his back feet, and the window inched down slightly. The dog pawed more vigorously until he could just wedge his head and shoulders through the opening, and then he pushed with his back end. He was free. He collapsed onto the hot summer pavement in a heap, amidst the blaring of car horns and yells of passersby. He zigzagged his way through the cars, safe until the stoplight changed and the traffic started on. Honk! He did not even break stride when he felt his rump brushed by the bumper of a passing car, and then sprinted forward, determined to get to the smell of home.

Once across the street, the dog trotted easily along the sidewalk, following the rich fragrance of home. The humid summer air only intensified the smell of Chanel No. 5, his own silky red dog hairs, the soapiness of the freshly bathed little girls, his home, the smell of his home. As he came closer to the red Rambler station wagon, he could see the windows were all open. He picked up his pace and loped to the car, jumped smartly into the front seat, wincing a bit at the slight ache in his rear end. He curled up on the floor in his accustomed space and waited for the driver to return.

Having finished at the bank, my mother checked her pocketbook to make sure her sunglasses were tucked inside, as she had a habit of losing them several times during the summer. She tapped along in her high heels and scooted into the front seat, putting her pocketbook next to her. She tied the thin chiffon scarf around her hair to keep the bouffant from blowing down as she drove home. She didn't notice the sleeping dog on the floor behind the passenger seat as she turned up the volume on the radio to hear her new favorite song, "Downtown," and began singing along.

She pulled into the driveway, switched off the ignition, grabbed her pocketbook, and paused to untie her scarf before she slammed the car door. The little red dog squirmed out behind her in that moment, padded up the back steps, and sat looking up at my mother, the woman who was his world. As my mother stepped forward to unlock the door, she saw the dog— "Toby! Now how did you get here?" she said. Toby wagged his stump of a tail, smiling and looking up at her. He was home.

Toby came back to my mother more than once after she had been forced to give him away rather than risk having to "put him to sleep." The neighbor boys threw sticks at him and hit him when he was tied out on his line in the back yard. He had growled more than once in self-defense. A nip would be the end. My mother cried and missed her dog almost as much as she would have if someone had taken one of her daughters from her. Fortunately, the last time Toby came home, he got to stay home, because we were moving away from that area. Originally, he was supposed to be my dog, brought home when I was just an infant as a companion for me. But he was always my mother's dog. All I know of the depth of love for an animal, I learned from my mother's heartfelt connection with Toby, who always knew how to find her.

She had gotten him from a nearby farm family, who implied he was a purebred cocker spaniel, after her other dog, a lovely English setter, had died from a badly managed case of distemper. In her grief, the little red puppy was exactly what my mother needed. Toby followed her around the house, licked up food I dropped, and took rides in the car when my mom went out shopping or doing errands. He was her constant companion and her best friend. She could not imagine life without him, and it was only to save his life that she had found him a new home when it was not safe for him to stay with us anymore.

Toby was a little brother to me and my one-year-younger sister as we grew through our toddler years. He suffered through wearing our clothes, walks on a leash around the yard and the house, exotic gourmet dinners we made for him with our childish cooking skills, and endless love and hugs. He liked to chase squirrels and rabbits and cats, but he never ran away. When my sister and I were in elementary school, we skated with Toby trotting behind us on the frozen lake behind our house; he chased sticks on the ice and then sat patiently once inside while we pulled the snowballs out of his fluffy leg feathers. By this time, we were in a suburban New Jersey town where people just let their dogs outside. Generally, the group of dogs would travel in the area of a block, following the neighborhood children in their kickball or baseball games.

Me, Mom & Judy with Toby around 1964.

One winter day, Mom had first let Toby go outside while we bundled up before going outside as well. My mother looked out the big picture window in the kitchen and screamed, "Toby!" We looked out to see his red body half submerged under the ice, about fifty feet from shore. We raced outside to rescue him, running through the back yards next to us to save our dog. By the time we got to him, Toby's frantic paddling was just breaking the weak ice ahead of him and he could not get out of the water. He was headed out to middle of the lake in a panic, though he turned his head towards my mother's desperate calls. It was far too cold and dangerous for us to go into the water.

9

All at once, we saw the neighbor's rowboat, and the three of us ran and slid the boat onto the ice, using the oars to break the ice and follow Toby. It took an effort from all of us to reach him, and my mother finally scooped him up into the boat. He probably weighed 35 to 40 pounds, and my mom is petite, so this was not easy. But she loved Toby completely and would do anything for him.

Once in the boat, Toby was shivering heavily and my mom wrapped him in her coat. My sister and I rowed to shore, heaved the boat over as it had been, and followed my mom as she carried Toby back to our house through three back yards. After we were inside, we dried him with towels while Mom called the veterinarian. He advised her to dry him thoroughly, warm him slowly, keep him warm, and call again if there were any problems. Mom made a big fire in the kitchen fireplace. We piled blankets over Toby and the three of us snuggled up around him until he stopped shivering. An hour later the phone rang. It was the neighbor whose boat we had borrowed, irate with Mom for taking the boat. Mom explained that she had to save her dog, and the neighbor did not care at all about that. We were not to use her boat. My mother, to this day, cannot understand that neighbor's lack of kindness or sympathy. Ultimately, Toby recovered just fine and moved with us again, this time to Virginia.

A view of our lakeside back yard with Judy and Toby in our rowboat.

At this point Toby was getting very old, over thirteen, about the same age as me. He still followed my mom around the house, and we still lived in an era when people just let their dogs go outside without a fenced-in yard. One raining, cold night, Mom let out Toby for his before-bed "business." Mom soon called him in and he didn't come. The dark and the rain made it hard to find him, and Mom walked around the yard with an umbrella, calling him. Toby was very elderly—blind, deaf, and losing his sense of smell. About an hour after he went missing, the phone rang. My sister and I knew something bad had happened, as Dad had left by himself in the car. Mom was crying. Apparently, a doctor had accidentally hit Toby with his car in his driveway and killed him. He tried to save the old dog, but Toby was beyond help. All the doctor could do was call the number on Toby's collar. He lived directly across the golf course from our house, a place we had never gone with Toby. I didn't understand then that when dogs are lost they often go to houses with similar smells or looks to their own homes. Dad buried Toby in the back yard, next to the doghouse he'd never used, came inside extremely solemn, and gave Toby's collar to Mom. I had never seen anyone so overcome with grief as my mother was that day.

Judy, Mom, and me with Toby at Christmas.

I don't know what became of his collar. I do recall my mother saying, when we moved back to New Jersey a few months later, that she was relieved not to look out through the kitchen window and see Toby's house and his grave. I was of the opinion that we were abandoning him, but Mom knew the physical dog she had loved was gone forever.

No family picture was complete without Toby.

We poured our love onto our second dog, Dandy, a liver and white Llewellyn setter. Once we returned to New Jersey, we also spent time with Lucky, Dandy's son, black and white, who lived with Dad's parents. Lucky was a fine bird hunting dog. Dandy was not.

Dandy was my dog, although he was to have been Dad's bird dog. He ran next to me on my bike, followed me on my expeditions through the woods, took rides with me in our rowboat, and sat close to me while I was reading or doing homework. He had come to live with us about two years before Toby fell into the ice. While Toby was a contented house pet, Dandy loved to run. He did not stay within the one-block radius of our house, but ran to the next subdivision, chasing kids he didn't even know and running with dogs I had never met. He often would run away, and I would ride far on my bike, calling him. Once he saw me, he always trotted home behind me. We finally built a dog run with a doghouse in it, surrounded by high chain link sides to contain him. No one I know would think of putting a dog in a place like this now, or tying a dog out on a line as we had done with Toby; Dandy was really only in the run to do his business.

Dandy was a beautiful, leggy dog with a broad head, caramel eyes, and rabbit-soft fur behind his ears. I think we had an understanding. Like him, I loved to run in the woods, stay out too long and too far, and longed for the wild places on the earth. Dandy was probably my first spirit animal, and we were deeply connected.

Dandy with his Christmas present, 1971.

Sadly, he just vanished one night when he was outside. He knew how to come home from far away, so something must have kept him from us. We hope someone maybe took him home to be a hunting dog. He was about ten when he was lost to us. Every day after school, I looked for him to have come home. When we rode in the car, my sister and I searched the expansive fields in our rural area for our brown and white dog.

This time was the beginning of my learning to see animals beyond the fur and bones in front of me. I could sense Dandy and I did not feel his death until years later. I silently called to him to come home. For years, I was never in the woods near our house without calling to him in my mind, wondering if he had ever come back to the places where he and I had played.

Since this time, my mom has had an Irish setter, a Doberman, and two standard schnauzers. The evolution of Mom's care for her dogs follows the changes in our culture in how people see their dogs. Now she walks her dog daily, has a fenced-in yard, has a chair for the dog to sit in and watch television with the family, and the dog sleeps next to her bed on a special orthopedic pillow-bed. Some of the most contented moments in my mother's life are when she is snuggled next to her big schnauzer on the sofa for an afternoon nap. Her dogs eat extremely high quality foods and have excellent medical care provided by my sister, Dr. Judy Morgan, who is a holistic veterinarian. Finally, Mom is able to live with her dogs the way she has always wanted to, with the dogs fully integrated into family life. She is like many, many pet owners who freely love and enjoy the companionship and understanding of their animals.

The connections we have with our animals are deep and profound and defy attempts at explanation. Rupert Sheldrake has written about the connection between animals and their owners in his book *Dogs Who Know When Their Owners Are Coming Home*. Known for his simple experiments designed to enlighten us about seeming coincidences, he describes how many animals will wait at the door no matter how far out of routine or unexpected the owner's return may be. He even tried to rule out telepathic communication between the owner and animal as an explanation by having the people completely unaware themselves when they were escorted home without notice, as hidden cameras observed the dog or cat's behavior. Dogs still waited in the usual place for their owners' arrival. Sheldrake's brilliant work is a reminder of why we have animals in our lives, and of the depth of the relationships we can form with them.

Sheldrake uses the term "morphic field" to describe a bubble of energy that surrounds each of us and our animals. Our morphic fields, or energy fields, overlap one another when we are physically or emotionally close to another animal or person, like a Venn diagram of overlapping circles, and they stretch when distance grows between the person and the animal. Morphic fields can connect individuals of a social group, or two related beings. Sheldrake describes miles of distance between people, or people and animals, where a measurable connection still exists. Perhaps this is one explanation for Toby's returns to my mother, beyond his sense of smell. As the overlapping connections of my mom's and Toby's morphic field bubbles stretched across miles like energetic elastic bands, he used his canine "sixth sense" to follow his connection to my mom back to his home with her.

Sheldrake writes, "I propose that these bonds are not just metaphorical but real, literal connections. They continue to link individuals together even when they are separated beyond the range of sensory communication. These connections at a distance could be channels for telepathy." The phenomenon of morphic fields, or our overlapping energies when we sit close to our animals and feel a connection to them, may be one way we develop deep relationships with our animals.

Chapter 2

Finding the Dance With Connection
The Ways of the Rabbit

Lily and Leo—bunny best friends.

"And rabbits scuttle through the maze of elfin paths"

— Frances Stephenson, *Poem on Skokholm*

I remember the rabbit; well, not a specific rabbit, because wild ones generally look very similar. But I spent several summers and many evenings after school watching a rabbit in the woods three houses up the street past my house. It was a sacred, quiet place, that place of the rabbit. There was a fallen tree about two feet in diameter, a perfect place for me to rest my childhood angst. There were red ferns surrounding the clearing by the lake that ran behind all of the backyards of the homes on our street. Sunlight filtered in such a way that it appeared misty even on a clear day, creating magic pockets of light on the forest floor, where small grasses grew. The rabbit would gently hop from green place to green place, nibbling on the grasses.

She would allow me to come very close, maybe three feet from her, if I moved very slowly and carefully. Sitting cross-legged on the forest floor, my eyes would melt into her deep brown eyes, and I felt all things rabbit in those moments. I brought my tears and loneliness to this rabbit and she quietly befriended me. I would watch her eating for hours, until darkness carried one of us away. No matter when I ran down the street, past the paved road that turned to gravel and past the last house with the white dog in the yard, across the bit of meadow to the forest entrance, where I slowed and proceeded with quiet and care into the forest clearing, I had only to wait a minute or two for the rabbit to appear and meet my gaze.

So many hours were spent communicating with this rabbit, with feelings and thoughts, no words. She sustained me for years with her peaceful presence.

One day after my family moved to another place and I was about to start high school, my sister and I spotted a white rabbit grazing under the cedar trees in our yard. It was a large rabbit, with pink eyes, reminiscent of our first white hamster. We corralled our dogs and gradually herded the rabbit into the empty two-car garage. He hopped ahead of us, devoid of enthusiasm or fear. While my sister ran into the house to get our mom, I scooped up the rabbit, finding him incredibly calm except for a few frantic scratches with his front paws as I lifted him up. We cradled him on the kitchen floor, and soon we discovered a terrible bloody mess in the hair on his hind leg. My mother, a farmer's daughter wise in the ways of nature, carefully inspected the site, wielding a pair of tweezers.

As I held the rabbit and my sister steadied the hind leg, my mother removed a large wormy creature, a maggot, from the hole in the rabbit's leg. We were disgusted, but quickly we realized that the maggot had likely saved the rabbit's life by eating all of the infected tissue around the wound. We cleaned the injury, wrapped the leg in gauze, and made a cozy spot in the garage for the rabbit. Our garage had never housed any cars anyway, so it was an easy choice. We named the rabbit Easter Bunny because we supposed that he had escaped from the neighbor children's yard, as Easter was a few months behind us. The rabbit recovered and lived in our yard for two years, using the back door of the garage to come and go, until eventually we simply did not see him anymore. He was a large and gentle rabbit. At the time, I did not understand that this rabbit should have lived ten years or more, and that horse feed and hay were not a substitute for the nutrition of food made for rabbits.

Years later, I moved to Harrisburg, Penn., replacing the polluted lake of my early childhood with a nuclear power plant that had erupted the year before I got there. I lived in a spacious apartment, and wanted a pet, since animals had always been in my life. I first got two hamsters—there were rules forbidding dogs and cats. The hamsters escaped and created a drama for the woman downstairs, who feared her apartment was being invaded by giant rats. The hamsters, captured by the plumber, went to live with his daughters. I returned to the pet store and saw a rabbit, shiny and black, a Netherland dwarf rabbit. Our eyes connected, and I knew that Agatha would become my companion bunny.

A pet store rabbit is a fierce animal. Agatha was prone to biting me or thumping me with her back feet. Mostly she hopped around the apartment, eating the Swedish ivy vines and sampling all of the antique book bindings within her reach. As I was writing for a farm magazine at the time, I often worked with 4-H kids, and they suggested I find Agatha a suitor and have some baby bunnies, which, yes, are indeed referred to as bunnies, or kits. I took Agatha in a box to the rabbit farm, one and a half hours away, where she was courted by a glorious golden and white rabbit. Just over a month later, she had four bunnies, three Hershey bar chocolate colored ones—appropriate, as we were within a few miles of Hershey, Penn.—and my favorite, Leo, the color of a Siamese cat. I named them for my friends. All of the chocolate bunnies had girls' names, but later I found them to be male rabbits. The female, Leo, lived up to her name in many ways—she was the undisputed queen of the household, astrologically she was a Leo, and when she yawned, her giant rabbit teeth bared, she looked like a roaring lion.

I saw no reason why my rabbits couldn't do anything a dog could do, so I taught Agatha and Leo to wear thin leather cat harnesses attached to woven nylon leashes, which they found delicious for nibbling. Indoors, I gently tugged on the leash and harness to familiarize them with that feeling, and then, after laying a trail of their favorite banana chips, I followed them, holding the leash so they could get used to the feel of it behind them. Eventually we went outside and I could safely allow them to hop wherever they wanted to go, leash trailing behind them, and easily catch the leash when it was time to come back inside. They loved the dandelions, pansies, and naps in the warm sunshine, stretched out in the cool grass. I took the rabbits for rides in the car, and they learned to come when I called their names, to get a coveted banana chip. Leo had some tricks she did as well. I taught her to sit before getting a treat, as our pet dogs had done. Next she learned to sit up on her hind end, an easy stance rabbits often use when grazing on tasty vegetables in the garden. I also taught her to stretch out on the carpet, similar to a dog's "down" position, luring her body into position as she followed banana chips until she could simply follow hand signals.

I saw an intelligence and communication that I never had anticipated with a rabbit, as so many other peoples' pet rabbits I had known were confined to cages. Easter Bunny had lived free to come and go in our garage, and as children with many pets, we did not spend the time with him to see the extent of his ability to play games with us. There seemed to be limitless potential in Leo's ability to learn tricks, solve maze puzzles I made for her with cardboard, and genuinely enjoy being with me. I am so grateful to Leo for showing me that the only limitation animals have in their abilities to relate to us is our presuppositions of what they can do.

One of my favorite rabbit games wasn't really a game at all, but rather a chance for my rabbits to show me their particular choices. I would arrange a row of their favorite foods—dandelion greens, romaine lettuce, carrots, rabbit food pellets, alfalfa hay, banana chips, papaya chips, dried pineapple, mango chips—and then let each bunny choose what was most appealing that day. I loved to see how each bunny had their own desires, and that they generally chose the same treat each time. All of the rabbits loved banana chips the most, preferring them by far over a piece of fresh banana. So seldom do our animals get to make choices, and realizing that my rabbits had preferences impacted me deeply, adding to my understanding of them as beings with unique personalities.

Leo Bunny became my best friend. I taught her how to play Frisbee with me with a gallon milk cap she tossed sideways with a quick neck motion. I made frozen water bottles for her to lounge next to in the heat of the summer. I learned to stroke the fur on her cheeks as she made the quiet, crunching sounds of rabbit "purring." I noticed how she crossed her ears flat against her back when she was content and happy. Together, we drove all over the mid-Atlantic to interview farmers in my barely-running Chevette. She perched on my shoulders or my head as I drove, and scrambled across the stick shift if the drive was taking too long. The farmers were uncomfortable enough as it was talking to a woman about their beef businesses, but when Leo hopped out behind me in her harness and leash, they were so taken aback they stumbled over their greetings. After I explained what to them was a bizarre story of needing an inconspicuous pet in a pet-free apartment building—as I was, after all, the daughter of a farm girl—they warmed up to us. When I went to interview the Dairy Queen of Pennsylvania, the young woman's mother made Leo a beautiful salad and put it in a crystal bowl on the kitchen floor while the rest of us had a huge dairy-filled meal at the table.

Leo hiding in the stuffed bunnies, 1983.

Eventually Leo moved with me to a boarding school in Massachusetts, where I taught English and married Jack, who grew to appreciate rabbits too. When we got our first puppy, a corgi named Winston, it was Jack's idea to put Leo into the tiny puppy's crate to keep him company so he wouldn't cry at night. Winston became very fond of rabbits, and as a herding dog, he could be relied upon to herd our rabbits back to us if they strayed into the woods on an adventure when we brought them outside.

Later, when we had a few more rabbits, Leo fell deeply in love with Lily, another pet store Himalayan rabbit who was fiercely defensive—the two rabbits kissed through their cages for a long time before Jack and I realized they should be together. They snuggled close, licked each other's cheeks until the fur was worn thin, and scampered across the living room floor doing "binkies," the exuberant leaps of happy bunnies. Lily used to enjoy long naps on Jack's lap, nestled in the folds of his wide wale corduroy pants. More than once, Jack was rudely awakened to Lily's bites on his thighs, demanding to be put into her shavings to relieve herself. There is a photo of Jack in his bathrobe and topsiders, at 6 a.m., watching Lily and Leo and Winston having their morning walk. There is a running joke between us that no other man would be seen walking two rabbits and a dog in front of a dorm of prep school freshman boys.

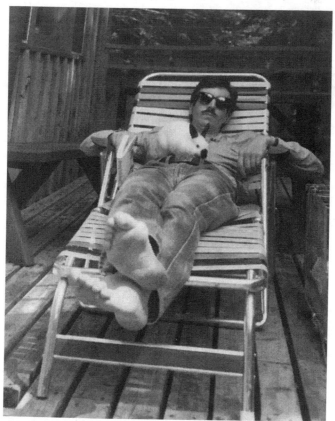

Jack lounging with Lily bunny.

The day Leo died, she had been sick only a day or two, and she collapsed, panting, on the floor of her cage, Lily sitting quietly by her. I raced her to the only vet in the area who would see a rabbit, crying hysterically in the car, barely able to keep it on the road, much less in my lane. Leo lay heaving for air in a box on the floor of the car. The vet, who I had never met before, came out of his office as I lay under a blanket of tears on the floor, gently reaching for my little rabbit. He looked down and quietly sat next to Leo's box. He said, "This rabbit is suffering. Her time has come. Do you want to come with me into the back?"

"No," was all I could mutter between sobs.

A few minutes later he came back, caressing Leo in his arms and he handed her to me. "She went peacefully," he said.

I thanked him and he refused payment. He hugged me as I held Leo, and walked with me back to my car.

It was a cloudy, damp, dark day in the early spring. Jack and I found a secluded spot for Leo, and brought Lily with us at sundown. We took turns digging until the hole was deep enough. Jack had gotten flowers somehow, for a proper burial. Leo was wrapped in a pretty little blanket in a box. Jack found the poem "Epitaph on a Hare," written by William Cowper when his own beloved pet rabbit had died in 1783. Jack soberly read the poem as I held Lily, still weak with the terrible loss of Leo bunny, my companion for nearly ten years. We sat with her for a while before we all got back into the car to return home. Lily was inconsolable—even the company of our other rabbit Rufus did little to awaken her from her quiet resting and depression. When the spring came and she was able to go outside again for hours, her spirits did revive with the warmth of the weather. Still, it was only two or three months more before she went to the same place where Leo had gone, across the rainbow bridge. In spite of our divorce, Jack met me where Leo was buried, once again bringing a bouquet of flowers and herbs particularly appealing to rabbits. This time I read the poem, and Jack held our last small gray rabbit tightly against his chest.

A quarter century later, Jack handed me a birthday card with what appeared to be a postcard of the Eiffel tower tucked inside. As I looked more closely, I saw in the foreground a dapper older gentleman holding a thin ribbon of leash. At the end of the leash was a leaping white rabbit. I looked up at Jack as I burst into laughter. "See, even Frenchmen walk their rabbits!"

Each spring, for many years, Jack and I placed some flowers or carrots around the marker in his backyard where our last little gray rabbit has rested for nearly twenty years. Sometimes one of us would read the rabbit poem. We would always wish the little gray rabbit, and all rabbits, fields of clover and meadows of dandelions.

This is how I learned the ways of the rabbit.

The postcard of a Frenchman and his rabbit.

Chapter 3

Invitation to the Dance
The First of the Horses

Spooky.

"In riding a horse, we borrow freedom"

— Helen Thompson

One of my most distinct childhood memories is of my mother reading Anna Sewell's *Black Beauty* aloud to me and my sister as we dozed off to sleep each night. My mother loved all animals, and had told us stories about her brother riding a heifer on their childhood farm since there was no place there for a pony for the kids, or for any animals who did not earn their keep. She jokes sometimes that my first words were "I want a pony," because no one in our family can recall a time when all of my childhood wishes were not for a pony. She read *Black Beauty* to us aloud at least twice, and I still have her own copy with her eighth-grade homework assignment tucked into the pages. The words of the horses in the story have stayed with me my entire life, whole passages coming back to me at times. In spite of how much the world has changed for horses and people, even now we don't always treat animals with the care and respect the book encourages.

My first horse was a small gray mare, flea-bitten with brown spots. She had luminous blue eyes and a pink muzzle, and you could easily see a wide white blaze from her younger days when she was steel gray, with four white socks to match. Mom had driven us into the country to a horse dealer. Fortunately, her charming ways and upbringing as a farmer's daughter convinced the man to sell us a gentle horse for a fair price.

Dad named her Spooky, a name he had wanted to give a bird dog, but the little white horse took the name. It turned out that she was everything except spooky. She never shied away from anything or took a misstep in all of the time we had her. She was my first pony, mine for only a month and a half before Mom, feeling sorry for the little mare to be carrying both me and my sister, drove us back to the horse dealer to get a second horse for me. Sadly, Spooky's two-year-old filly had been sold, so we bought a horse who resembled her, a leggy chestnut mare. We named her Goblin to match Spooky, which always bothered me because she had a perfect diamond between her eyes and a second diamond between her nostrils. It was very clear to me that her name was Diamond, and always had been Diamond.

She was everything Spooky was not. She was very young, probably ridden only a few times before she was my horse. She was fast, apt to run away from anything, long-legged and sleek, probably at least half Thoroughbred. She had a longish mane and tail, and like Dandy and the rabbit of the woods, she had a wildness about her that matched me perfectly. She was the first horse with whom I journeyed alone through the woods and fields with no trails, bareback, for hours, exploring the places where the forest creatures lived. In the woods, she was bold and trustworthy. Riding her like this, I began to understand what it is to be so fully aware and connected to a horse that the two of you become one being.

Before we owned these horses, Mom had taken us riding at places where horses were rented by the hour. We went at least three times every summer for many years. Mom was a good rider by our standards at the time, and she was always given the horses for more experienced riders. Once, when the three of us were out on a trail ride, Mom's big paint gelding turned sharply on the trail and galloped full speed back to the barn. My sister and I managed to control our mounts and trot slowly back home behind her. As we came from the woods into the field surrounding the barn, we saw Mom's horse galloping as fast as he could, puffs of dust rising from his big hooves as she clung to the saddle horn, not even trying to stop him. The horse swung around the riding corral and slid to a dead stop at the water trough, and sank his head in, drinking deeply. Mom, owing to her small stature, just managed to stay on as he stopped, and then she quickly jumped off. We were all horrified that he was so thirsty that he resorted to this crazed behavior, and we never went back to that stable.

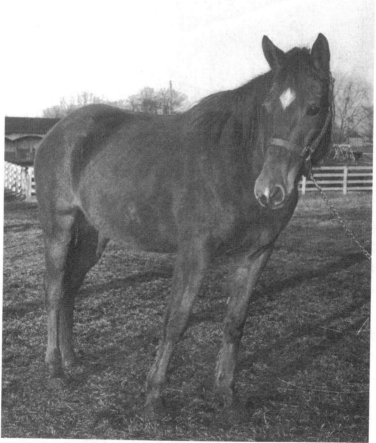

Goblin.

Fortunately, I befriended a girl at the end of my street who had a chestnut and white pinto pony named Buttercup. Kathleen was generous sharing her pony with me, although she insisted I learn to mount bareback before I could ride. After many tries, including one time when I rolled right off the other side of patient Buttercup, I was able to ride the small mare bareback through the woods. Kathleen's elderly father had been in the Cavalry, and he loved to share his tales of horse wisdom with Kathleen and me. I remember him telling us how he fed tobacco to horses to kill worms in the gut. And I recall the McClellan saddle he had kept for decades after his time in the Cavalry.

Used for over a hundred years by the military and favored by endurance riders for many years through the 1970's, McClellan saddles were quite well balanced. It would be years before I would so easily feel the balanced shoulder/hip/heel alignment in any other saddle. Kathleen and her father showed me how to properly groom a horse, tack up a horse, care for leather and other equipment, and what to feed a horse. Her father explained all of the different feed options, pointing out which was best for horses doing different types of work. He taught us about hay, showing us the fragrant clover, the rich alfalfa, and the grass hays he had stored for Buttercup.

Kathleen shared her books about horse management with me, including some of the old books her father had read. Her father quizzed us about horse confirmation, lameness, and diseases. One day we watched as he saved Buttercup from a serious colic by putting oil down a tube from her nostril into her stomach to loosen the impaction in her gut. He showed us how to trim her hooves, giving us a chance to use the rasp across her toes. Together we lay daydreaming about horses on Kathleen's front lawn as Buttercup, loose in her halter, grazed near us. These experiences with Kathleen and Buttercup were the foundation of my knowledge of horse keeping.

When I was old enough, I went to Girl Scout horse camp. Although one of the younger campers, I was one of the best riders. We rode different horses every day, and like many pre-teen girls, I fell in love with a few of the slim, tired camp horses and dreamed of bringing one home at the end of the summer. My parents, having no confidence in my riding skills, promised to get me a horse if I won a ribbon at the camp show, and if we moved to an area where it was easier to keep horses.

In my first show outfit with Goblin.

On the day of the camp show, I drew from the lottery of horses a dark bay mare named Blaze to be my show mount. She was the only horse I had not ridden that summer at the camp. She had a club foot and a very rocky gait. We were riding Western at this camp, and sitting her ungainly trot was difficult. In our class, we were squeezed into a corner on the rail, and dear Blaze stumbled so badly that she went down on her lame knee. She pulled herself up as I closed my inside leg around her, and traveled on. I won third place in equitation on her, and to this day, that white cardboard ribbon with a yellow three written on it and yellow bunting streamers stapled to the bottom is one of my treasures from childhood. Blaze did not get a home with our family, but when we moved to Virginia the next summer, Goblin became my horse.

Goblin was boarded at an old dairy farm—at one time the Bellona Civil War arsenal—surrounded by hundreds of acres of grounds where we raced all of the other riders up steep hills, winning most of the time. She was fast, and the only thing keeping her from winning every race was my fear of letting her gallop as fast as she wanted. I took her swimming in a murky pond a few times and enjoyed the seemingly endless acres of woods and fields to explore with Goblin. As more horses were boarded at the barn, our adventures turned to jumping, and learning to ride in an English saddle.

On a late summer day, Goblin was grazing as I sat bareback, leaning back over her rump, relaxed, feeling her breathing under my arms. I barely saw the long black snake slithering past her muzzle. Suddenly and slowly, she reared up, skidding to the right, and I slipped off of her back onto my left arm, breaking the humorous distal to the growth plate, just below my shoulder joint. Immediately I was pale and sick, but I had to lead Goblin back to her stall and feed her, as Mom was afraid of her. I was curled in the backseat on the way to the hospital, trying to convince my mom that Goblin had done nothing wrong and we did not have to sell her.

I should have thanked Goblin then because I was excused from gym class for two months. But I was riding her Western within a week, being careful to just meander around the pasture close to the barn. Goblin's life before I had her was one of deprivation and abuse. She must have come from a herd situation without much food, as she became dangerously violent at feeding time. We had to lock her in her stall and run around to the front of the stall to drop the hay and grain from above. She fiercely bit and lunged at any horse or person who came near her or her food, even whirling around in her stall tossing food over the door if a horse was led down the aisle while she was eating.

While I was recovering from my fall, my mom took on the chore of feeding her. One day she made the mistake of trying to run into the stall quickly, dump the grain, and run out the door, rather than waiting until Goblin was in the stall to pour the grain through the special trap door outside of the stall. Goblin, hearing the grain spill into the bucket, broke loose from where she was tied waiting for dinner, and violently attacked Mom. She fell onto my mom with her whole weight, teeth bared, slicing my mom's back and knocking her to the ground. Thankfully, Mom's farm-girl-fast reflexes made her get up immediately and leave the stall, locking in Goblin. She was incredibly shaken and had to rest a long time before we drove home. She was forever afraid of Goblin after this, and all of the work for her care became mine exclusively. We never told my father about this incident.

When we moved back to New Jersey a year later, Goblin and Spooky lived at an extremely rundown farm that was close to our house—my sister and I could paddle the canoe across the lake into the back pasture. I spent long, hot afternoons leaning over Goblin's neck as she grazed in a nearby hay field on alfalfa and clover, watching the blood red sunsets above the DuPont chemical plants just over the bay in Delaware. We were comfortable together, my chestnut mare and I. From atop her back, I shared with Goblin my dreams of horse shows and endless summer days of riding.

At the new farm in New Jersey we had no stalls for the horses, which made feeding Goblin more dangerous. Additionally, this was the kind of farm she had come from, where many starving horses would push down the rickety barn walls to try to get the food we had for our horses. Because Goblin was so difficult at feeding time, we tied her to a rail and had to come behind her with the bucket—her bites were far worse than the slight chance of her kicking us. Spooky's kind presence calmed her marginally.

One day, unable to find the halter fast enough, I just looped some twine around her neck while my sister ran to get the halter and lead line. Goblin, nervous about the other horses clambering behind her, turned to lunge at them, pulling back on the twine severely. The twine closed tightly around her throat, and my mom, sister, and I looked on in horror as Goblin struggled to pull back even more, gasping for air, her throat impossibly small. She went down on her knees as I tried desperately to loosen the twine. Someone ran to get the farm owner who ran out of the house with a very long knife. Quickly and expertly, he cut the twine, releasing Goblin and saving her life. She shook her head as she got back up, and dove into her dinner pan. The farmer was so skillful that there was not a drop of blood on Goblin's neck where he had cut the twine. We all thanked the farmer, who was in many ways a nice man, but too poor to have so many horses that he could not feed or sell.

We soon moved the horses to a better farm, but the owners liked to buy and sell horses at the auction to make money. Sadly, they purchased a sick filly, a carrier of the very contagious disease of equine infectious anemia, the disease that led to the Coggins blood test that is required before transporting or showing horses to this day. My first horse, sweet Spooky, became sick and died in the pasture next to the muddy stream at the base of the hill. We saw her body there. Without the Coggins test, we did not know why she had died. Our vet conjectured that it was her advanced age, much older than the twelve years we were told when we bought her.

We were somewhat consoled for her loss by supposing she died of natural causes, and my mother decided we needed to get a new horse for my sister Judy. We went to the better of the two horse auctions in our area and my sister got a spirited palomino we named Cinnamon Dandy. He was young and gorgeous, but he soon became sick as well. Goblin and Cinnamon both perished from the disease that had claimed Spooky and others in the herd. Later we would learn that our herd was the second largest one lost to the disease of EIA, and we were devastated that we had unknowingly brought Cinnamon into a sick herd. My sister and I mourned our losses at the end of the humid mid-Atlantic summer, unable to go back to school with any enthusiasm. We were uncertain if our parents would let us get new horses. We were uncertain if we even wanted new horses after the sadness and loss we had struggled through with our first horses.

Children dream of horses for Christmas, and that year we were no exception. We had casually looked for new horses in the fall, and I was considering another chestnut, this time a two-year-old Arabian, while my sister was looking at retired show horses who could jump and still show a few more years. By the time it was Christmas, I was second-guessing my choice of this horse after seeing how happy my sister was riding the senior schooled horses so nicely. I would have to train him absolutely from the start, though his owner had given me a leg up onto him bareback at the farm when I went to see him. Holding the halter, the owner walked the horse in tight circles, telling me that I was the first person to ride him, so he must be my horse. The second telling sign was the horse's registered Arabian name, Sir Richard, my father's name. This won the horse a place in Mom's heart, if not yet in mine.

Sir Richard on Christmas, the day that we became a pair in 1972.

That Christmas my sister and I opened the usual gifts of socks, books, new clothes, and then, working our way deeper into the pile, we discovered new halters and lead lines, new wool blankets for horses, new saddle pads. We were still unaware that a horse for each of us would be added later that morning. As we sat with grandparents at the feast Mom prepared each year for Christmas breakfast, an envelope was tucked under each of our plates. Grandparents urged us to open them together. We both were shocked to find cleverly written poems telling us about the new ponies waiting for us at a very nice farm, a working dairy. Our parents were more excited by their cleverness than we were, as it seemed so unbelievable to us. But that afternoon, we drove out to the farm and Judy rode her handsome buckskin pony around the riding ring, as my mother, much braver with Richard than she had been with Goblin, led me around bareback on my second chestnut horse. Richard had four white socks and a wide blaze, as Spooky would have had in her younger days, and a long flaxen mane, chestnut and cream, not like Goblin's black and pumpkin colored mane.

I had learned a lot training Goblin, encouraging her to jump, changing to English riding, teaching her how to be a kinder horse, one who could see humans as friends and companions rather than torturers. But I had not learned enough to teach a two-year-old Arabian. I tried to trot Richard on a long lunge line in circles, and he would pull the line away from me, escaping to run about the pasture. He was fine wearing a saddle and bridle once he was old enough to do that, but all of the steps leading up to riding were challenging. I did not yet know about the deep intelligence of Arabians, that it is much better to do things correctly and carefully the first time with an Arabian, or that they quickly learn a routine and prefer no changes in it. This horse wanted to be my friend; my problem was that it would be many years before I would learn how to understand what he needed and asked from me, and how I could tell him the same.

I rode Richard bareback close to the barn, and in a saddle through the fields and cow pastures of the large farm. I also quickly learned that Arabians are afraid of many things, or at least they react to noises in the leaves, cows suddenly trotting in a big group, dogs barking across the street. One day Richard was startled by the cow herd moving towards him and he galloped to the barn as fast as he could go, at least a mile, while Mom stood at the barn door remembering her own race to the barn on the rental horse. Richard did not slow even a bit until he skittered across the concrete surrounding the water trough, leapt up to try to jump the six foot aluminum gait but couldn't possibly do it, and turned sharply and fell, leaving me to slide onto the concrete, damaging my tailbone. I had to sit on an inflatable round cushion for several weeks after this—my second horse accident. Only once have I fallen from someone else's horse, although I was a professional trainer for many decades. Today, I can count each of my personal horses by the bones they broke in my body.

As our interest in going to horse shows grew, my sister and I moved our two ponies to the nicer barn where other girls our age kept their ponies, where many horse shows were held, and where we had good quality riding lessons from a man who had polio as a child and became a winning pony sulky driver later on. Mr. Bell was an old-fashioned horseman who had always known what horses were trying to tell him. He spent all day watching people ride and had an excellent eye and a kindly way of teaching all of us to ride better. At last I had someone to teach me riding who had a genuine understanding of horses. He would lead groups of three or four horses across the street to big pastures, holding the lines inside his car window, and none of the horses ever broke loose or started a fight. He was a genuine horseman, like the retired jockey played by Mickey Rooney in the movie *The Black Stallion*. He had three quarters of a century of wisdom to give to us.

Richard was bred to be a show horse, and Arabians were popular at this time in our area. We were close to many big regional shows for Arabians, and my sister and I took Richard to some of these shows as he became increasingly well schooled. We showed at the county 4-H shows in our area, and found local riding school shows to fill our summer weekends. Gradually, Judy's pony, Boca-Cay, was winning jumping classes, and Richard, a lovely mover with his long, floating Arabian gait, was getting ribbons in pleasure classes and "suitable to become a hunter" classes. He won his first blue ribbon in a pleasure class at farm called Sharlot Stables. I had a very nice ride and was proud of him, and when they called our number first, I hugged him as tears dampened my face. Richard and I had learned a lot together, and this was our first recognized accomplishment. He went on to win every flat class that day and was champion of the pleasure division. Ever after that day, when we pulled into a show in our borrowed trailer, other riders sighed at the competitors they would have later that day.

Sir Richard, winning an in-hand class at the Salem County Fair show when he was three.

One spring, the 4-H leader asked if anyone wanted to participate in an endurance trail ride to be held in the fall. It was a twenty-five mile ride, with a few judged trail obstacles such as steep hills, streams to cross, small jumps, and twisting turns through small, thin trees. I was sixteen or so, and the chance to spend time in the woods with my horse again could not have come at a better time. I read books and talked to Mr. Bell about how to condition a horse for a long ride. He drove his car around the area, pointing out places to practice hills and back roads for long trots, and I spent months alone in the woods with Richard, riding for three or four hours on many days of each week.

As an Arabian, Richard was made for this sport, trotting easily beside a railroad track for miles and miles under the humid south Jersey summer skies. I gradually saw the courage he had in the woods and fields, no longer shying as he did sometimes in the ring, and he finally had no problems trotting past the large herds of dairy cows on one of our routes. We shared water from my Girl Scout canteen, his lips nuzzling my fingers as he slurped from my cupped hands. We waded through hidden streams, rode past busy roads, and found passages in and out of hay fields miles away from our farm.

Richard was always nervous in the horse trailer, and when we arrived for the trail ride competition, he was very flustered after the long ride alone. I tied him to our assigned tree, and Richard was spinning around the tree and whinnying loudly to the other horses. That was when they did the pre-ride vet check. Still so excited from the trailer ride and the new place, he measured much higher in pulse and respiration than would have been his normal resting rate. I tried to explain this, hoping they could come back later to get an accurate baseline pulse and respiration to compare to his rates at the end and the check stations during the ride, but no one seemed to think his excitement was a concern.

I carefully brushed his flaxen mane, whispering to him about the wonderful things we would see on our long ride that day. Gradually, as I stroked him, he calmed down. I planned to stay away from the other horses and riders as much as I could, so that it would be just like our long rides at home.

Richard and I had a glorious ride. We trotted through streams, opened rope gates, trotted down roads and across fields, and trotted through miles of Jersey pine barrens on sandy trails. We were coming in a little early for the optimal return time, so we stopped for a break. I took off his saddle and let him graze while I brushed him with a small bristled face brush I'd carried in my pocket. After our ten-minute rest, he did not have any sweat marks on his coat and he stood quietly while I replaced the saddle and mounted for the last two miles of trotting back to the finish line. Owing to our rest stop, and our conditioning program, Richard did beautifully at the final vet check. His pulse and respiration were below what they had been at the start where he was spinning around the tree, and he was, as always, completely sound.

We returned to our tree to untack and rest awhile before we loaded Richard into the trailer for his ride home. My mom was taking him back to the farm, and our 4-H leader was staying with me and another competitor from our club for the awards dinner that evening, where we would see how we had done. I was so happy just to have had such a good ride, and to see that Richard and I could do a twenty-five mile ride successfully. I barely heard my name when they announced that I had earned sixth place that day as well as an award for conditioning. I brought Richard an entire bag of carrots the next morning to celebrate. Sadly, I was to go off to college the next year, and we could not pursue our endurance trail riding career.

Richard at the Woodedge Stables show, the year after he won his first ever blue ribbon in a Hunter Under Saddle class.

While my sister continued to ride and show Richard, I spent summers working as the head riding instructor at a Girl Scout camp in south Jersey, the same camp where I had ridden Blaze. I had a staff of three instructors, some from Europe, and over twenty-five horses to train and have ready for the campers. The campers came for either one- or two-week-long sessions, including a one-night sleepover trail ride for the advanced riders. Before camp, I spent a week riding the horses, giving them names, sorting out bridles, saddles, and halters for both English and Western riding, and sprucing up the barn, tack room, and corral. I rode the horse I had chosen for myself, a black mare I named Phantom after one of the horses in Margaret Henry's books, and clipped branches, moved logs, and made the trails around the camp clear enough to accommodate beginning riders. Some of the horses were steady and kind for the beginners, but some were difficult for even my staff to ride. All of them were thin, and we went through quite a lot of hay since we had no pastures for them.

I created a long manual for my students that included diagrams of horse conformation and anatomy, labeled pictures for the parts of the saddle and bridle, essentials of horse care and grooming, and basic information gathered from my 4-H handbook and other books. By this time I had been on the 4-H judging team and Horse Bowl team—based on the popular College Bowl competition, where our team of four girls answered detailed questions about horses after racing to press a buzzer to beat the other team. Hours of memorizing facts and practicing at our coach's house prepared my sister, our team mate Susan Sisco, and me for the state Horse Bowl Championship, and for later careers in the animal world. (Our fourth team member, Patience, has been a lifelong friend and dog lover.) Thanks to Horse Bowl, I had a breadth of material to choose from for my camper manual. And taking a cue from my own experience with the handmade ribbon I won with Blaze, my mom, my sister Judy, and I put together six ribbons for each class at my weekly horse shows, some of which were judged by my sister.

The girls came to the barn once a day for a riding lesson, sometimes longer to include a trail ride, and once a day for study of equine knowledge. The advanced students helped with the feeding and care of the horses, but much of the work fell to me. We had electric fencing set up around the corral and in some grassy areas next to the riding ring to give the horses more room. One night during a thunderstorm, I woke up to the sound of hooves galloping down the dirt path between my tent and the barn area. I scrambled out of bed to find half of the horses had escaped from the corral gate and were fearfully running from an area behind the barn where lightning had split an old pine tree. The Waterfront Director, who shared my tent, woke up as well, and together we managed to get the horses back into the corral with the sounds of feed and fresh hay to entice them, as well as some expert herding by us.

The next morning when I arrived at the barn, bleary eyed, I saw a disturbing sight. A tiny, perfect baby horse was nearly covered by the mud next to the barn. It was a two month old fetus. My beloved Phantom had been in foal and had lost her foal in the commotion of the storm. Fortunately, I was with my best student that summer, a girl also named Sally who had her own Appaloosa stabled at her house a short drive up the road. She said she'd like to take the tiny foal home and preserve it, as she was hoping to go to vet school in a few years. I drove Sally to her house so she could get her mother to help with the project, and I gave Phantom many weeks off after this event.

Sometime after this, the horses once again escaped. Later I learned that one of my assistants had been going to the barn without telling anyone to see a horse she had adopted, and she had left the gate ajar. This time, the Camp Director woke me in the early morning, shining a flashlight over my face, to say that the farmer next to us had called to complain that horses were ruining his soybean crop and galloping over his fields. I sprang out of bed in boots and pajamas and ran to the barn. I grabbed the first bridle I could, saw that not a single horse was in the paddock, and continued my jog down the dirt road of the camp, following the main road to the farm where our horses were trampling the farm crop. Sure enough, in the moonlit dawn, I saw my herd grazing and trotting in small groups around the field. My only hope of getting them back to the barn was on horseback.

I quietly approached Phantom, offering her the carrots in my pockets, and though the other horses galloped off, she paused a moment and came to me. I slipped the bridle over her head, managed to climb up bareback and began the job of gathering the horses into one group. Unexpectedly, Phantom stopped, mid-trot, head erect, ears pricked to the horizon line of the trees at the back of the field. I followed her line of sight and saw a crop duster plane swooping low, heading right at us. Having read Rachel Carson's *Silent Spring*, I knew that being covered with pesticides would be very bad for the horses and me. There was no time to escape—I buried my face in Phantom's mane and urged her to gallop into the trees behind us. We watched as the other horses raced in circles, snorting, and she and I coughed and choked from our place in the woods.

After the thick gray cloud passed, Phantom and I managed to gather the horses and get them down the main road—where thankfully no cars were moving at that hour—and back to the camp. My morning feed helpers had piles of hay and buckets with grain in the riding ring and corral so that the horses did not hesitate to return to the fenced-in areas. Ironically, the horses never left our slipshod electric fenced areas, only escaping from the board-fenced paddocks. The girls spent the morning giving all of the horses a bath, to try to rid them of the chemicals from the crop duster.

By the end of the summer, I was able to send at least five of the horses to good homes with hope that the training the others had gotten would help them to find homes as well. The director recruited me for the next year, adding that a new requirement would mean that I would go to a big equestrian camp to obtain a camp instructor's license prior to the next camp season. I agreed, excited to be able to meet other camp riding instructors.

Right after the spring semester, I drove to the camp where I would stay for a week to earn my Camp Horsemanship Association license. Although I was nervous about how my riding skills would measure up, I quickly found that my time with Goblin and Richard and the camp horses from last summer had put me far ahead of my fellow instructors. I was surprised to find that the detailed manual they gave us included much of the same information I had given my own campers.

We were each assigned horses that week. I was fortunate to be given a palomino Quarter horse gelding who I named Charming, as he was like Prince Charming, handsome with his golden coat and eager attitude. He was three, and I was the first person to ride him. I spent many spare hours with him, talking quietly and stroking his body, becoming good friends with him as I watched him grazing at the beginning and end of each day while I held his lead line. Little did I know then that this gentle "bodywork" and quiet time with him would shape the rest of my life with horses.

We had daily lessons in both English and Western riding, and had to do presentations and lectures, take written tests, and take riding tests. There were several levels we could attain based on our test scores that would qualify us for different levels of equestrian camp jobs. I was concerned about Charming's lack of training, given the rigors of the advanced riding tests, but as the week unfolded, I could see that his innate balance and lack of inexperienced prior riders was actually of great benefit to me. He easily learned his canter leads, or more accurately he was never out of balance to begin with, and so he never got the wrong lead. He learned to jump over small crossrail poles and even higher jumps. He could change gaits easily and smoothly, and calmly stand for me to mount and dismount. He even tolerated my less than ideal bareback mounting skills and my even worse flying dismounts from both sides. I loved him and wished that I could take him home, but as a college student, I could not have another horse.

By the end of the week, Charming helped me score the highest on all of the exams, written and mounted, of everyone at the camp. In fact, my scores were some of the highest anyone had achieved in a one-week course. To this day, I treasure the time I spent with this horse and his gifts to me that late spring.

After another summer at the Girl Scout camp, I returned home in August to ride Richard for a few weeks. My sister Judy had been riding him for over a year. She won many awards with Richard at Arabian shows, showing him in the hunter division at some larger shows. We have an oil painting of Richard lightly crossing a jump at the Devon Horseshow grounds at a big regional Arabian show, with the "Devon—Where Champions Meet" sign above the grandstands behind him. Judy even took Richard to Rutgers University, where he worked for a short time on the mounted security patrol with her, quietly walking on busy city streets and through groups of students on the campus, no longer fearful of rustling leaves or cows chasing him across the pasture. He was a dependable horse. My sister found several retirement homes for Richard— looking pretty on someone's lawn, doing lead line pony rides for grandchildren, giving lessons to new riders—until he finally came back to me one late summer when he was well into his twenties, somewhat lame, carrying himself like the proud Arabian he was.

I have a few pictures of Richard meeting my new horse, Burgers, at a vast farm in Connecticut, looking small and red next to my large, deep bay Morgan, muscled from high level dressage work. I wondered if they talked in the barn about me at night. Each horse had generously and patiently participated in my journey to become both a teacher and student of horses, and not simply a horse trainer. They had many common experiences as they taught me about the language of horses. Burgers, like Richard, was only a two-year-old when I found him.

Richard became a very good hunter pony.

Promise of the Dance

His Name Would Be Burgers

Ten Penny Moonshine, age three, at Percy's farm, the month before we became a team for life.

"A woman's relationship with a horse is an encounter between the intangible—the spiritual, the mythical, the ethereal—and the very tangible: the physical, everyday realities of riding, horse keeping, and life itself. In my life and in the lives of many women, the two extremes meet and merge seamlessly, contrasting and explaining each other in a way that makes both realities more clear."

— Mary D. Midkiff, *She Flies Without Wings*

When I was in graduate school, a friend suggested we go for a trail ride one fall weekend. I had not ridden much in five years except on school breaks, and at a few Intercollegiate shows. Once I was assigned my mount, a little bay Quarter horse tacked in a western saddle, I held the reins and climbed into the saddle, trying to land lightly on his back. The farm owner, a well-known horseman in the area, smiling with twinkling eyes said,

"Maybe you should come and work for me. You're a good rider." Thinking he was joking, I laughed it off, and continued on my ride with three or four other people.

The trail was wide, at times rocky, winding through woods and fields. My horse, Ace, was nothing special, but he was responsive and I had a good ride. I came back to ride him three or four more times, and the farm owner, Percy, made good on his promise and hired me to lead trail rides at his farm. I spent two or three months that fall leading rides in the glorious red and gold New England foliage. One Saturday, when I got to the farm, I could not find Ace anywhere. I thought maybe someone could have him out on a ride. The farmer sold horses often, but I was sure that he could not have sold my best trail horse. He came out of the barn and I asked where Ace was. He flat out said he had sold him, very matter of fact. I was shocked and saddened, thinking, I suppose, that I would be riding him for years. Giving me no time to react, the farmer led me into the barn and said, "Why don't you ride one of my Morgans? I need someone to ride this one."

I peered between the wooden boards of the dark stall and saw a blackish horse, grumpy, his ears back, not coming over to see us. He said, "His name is Moonshine, maybe he walks like he's drunk," as he exited the barn.

I looked into the stall for a few minutes, recovering from the loss of Ace a bit. I slowly opened the stall door and stood waiting for the horse to come to me. He had no interest; he was dozing, snarling when I moved closer to him in the stall corner. I made my way up to him slowly and he was clearly uninterested. I could see that like my second horse Richard, he would be a challenge. I put a halter on him carefully as he shook his head at me in warning, and led him out of the stall. He was a deep mahogany bay with a white moon on his forehead. Of course that was how he got his name, because he had a moon under his black forelock. He looked me over warily, not particularly interested in people, or even a handful of grain. Little did I know in those moments that my relationship with Moonshine would span over three decades, and he would transform me from a fairly skilled amateur into a professional horsewoman with a depth of skills and training that would earn us national rankings and recognition.

Moonshine, as Richard had been when I got him, had just passed his second birthday. The farmer, Percy, came back into the barn and helped me saddle him. We tacked up Moonshine in my very antique Stubben jumping saddle and one of Percy's bridles, and led the horse to the riding ring across the street. All of the farm help, a group of teenaged girls and an older man who worked as a farm hand, gathered around the ring to watch. They knew this routine and had watched Percy with his fine Morgan filly, China Doll, pulling a jog cart in the ring, or loose prancing around the turnout area. Percy gave me a leg up, and Moonshine barged off, rushing forward. I gathered the reins and walked him around the ring both ways, trotted both directions with a figure eight across the center, and even did a short canter one way of the ring. The onlookers dispersed as the show was over. I rode him a few more minutes as Percy gave me directions on how to "talk to him with the reins," an idea that reminded me of Mr. Bell's words. Due to his young age, I only rode him a few minutes, dismounted, and returned to the barn to take off Moonshine's tack.

One of the weekend girls soon came to me and said, "Well, that wasn't what we expected." I asked, "What were you expecting?" She replied that everyone else who had tried to ride Moonshine had been bucked off. Since I was the expert rider in the group, they had expected a humbling show for me, but instead Moonshine seemed to like me and did not offer any bucking or skittering around at all. I realize now that in fact my good saddle was a big help to me—it did not pinch him and allowed plenty of room for his long sloping shoulders to move when he trotted. And the back of the saddle stayed put when I posted at the trot. And perhaps I can also give Ace some credit for helping me get my riding legs back before I even met Moonshine.

As I did with Richard, I believed it was a good idea to work a young horse on a lunge line, walking, trotting and cantering in circles around me as I gave "voice commands" (command is a word I would never use today in reference to animals) to literally put the horse through his paces. Moonshine had no interest in lunge lessons. Like Richard, he pulled the line out of my hands, or short of that, pulled me around the ring. And, as with my chestnut Arabian, Moonshine especially did not like the snap of the long whip I used to urge him forward, instead bolting straight away whenever he heard the crack, or even when I raised the whip off of the ground. It was maybe two weeks into my time with him, and Moonshine was being particularly difficult with his lunge lessons. In frustration, I pleaded with him, "You had better be able to do this for me, or someone might make you into horse burgers! Is that what you want, to be horse burgers?" Immediately, Moonshine stopped and turned towards me, watching me, his unusually big ears pricked forward.

"Burgers?" I said again. "Is that what you want?" He walked over to me, put his head against my body, scratching a bit, pushing on me. "Well, that's it, you can be horse burgers," I said to him through giggles. And Moonshine chose his new name that day, the name that he would carry for thirty years or more, the name people would wonder about after they saw him perform in the show ring, the name I would say to him on his last day on earth, the name I still invoke when I am working with a horse and I need his wisdom.

Soon enough, Burgers was my trail ride mount, escorting beginners through the wooded trails, clearing new trails with me, and exploring roads and forests surrounding the farm property. I rode him daily all winter and into the spring of my last semester of graduate school. Burgers and I became friends, and gradually he began to trust me. Now when I approached his dark stall, he greeted me with his ears up and eyes bright, wondering what we would do together each day. And, happily for him, there would be no more unmounted lunge lessons ever again in his life. He was still unsociable around other horses, except the red bay Morgan in the stall next to him, Sky Bird, whose owner I rarely saw. Sometimes Percy would let the two geldings out to play in the barn area, where they raced, bit hocks and thighs, groomed each other's necks, and stood under the apple tree swishing flies from each other's faces. Percy always said he would drive them together, as that was what he loved most to do, but the two were hardly a pair, with Burgers over a hand taller with a huge-strided trot, and Sky Bird high-headed with the lifted knees of a show Morgan in his gait. Sometimes I would ride Burgers down the road next to Sky Bird when Percy took him out for a drive. A few times, Percy would harness Burgers and we would ride together on the back roads, our wooden Meadowbrook cart speeding behind Burgers with his big trot.

Burgers at Percy's, before I brought him to Ardun's Farm.

Later I learned that one of Percy's daughters had bred Burgers from what he called "a big western-bred mare, Doverdale Bambi Jean," to be a dressage horse. His father was a Vermont Lippitt type of Morgan, small and square, who was a good log puller, and who bred some draft mares in the fields at his home. I knew only a little of what the discipline of dressage entailed at that time, having once shown Richard in a "suitable to become a dressage horse" class, when he won fifth place. It was the early 1980s, and dressage was not nearly as popular in the United States as it is now. Carolyn, Percy's daughter, had two geldings to choose from that year, and her mount became a black named Destiny, with a full, long mane and tail. She always said he was prettier than Moonshine, and she thought he was a better mover. I wasn't so sure; I could see Destiny's long back and shorter legs and less-sloped shoulder, and I wondered how that would make him a good dressage horse. The horses I had seen had long strides and skipped with lead changes across the ring. I was glad she left Moonshine for me, as we were developing a bond that winter.

Burgers had a particularly helpful skill at the time. When I would ride him alone in the woods, he would sometimes stop short and paw at the ground. Each time I would look down and find money on the ground, twenty dollar bills, fives, tens, maybe some change, which had fallen out of the pockets of the trail riders, I presumed. No one else ever found money this way, and as I was a graduate student struggling to buy equipment for my horse, I was counting every penny. I was very grateful for Burgers' special skill, which continued throughout his life. He always helped me find ways to pay his board with riding lessons for fellow boarders, bodywork sessions for horses and riders at the barn, or helping me teach other riders the skills he had gained over the years. Anyone who has ever had a horse will attest to the value of a horse who can find money!

That first winter, I continued my daily rides into the autumn and then into the winter woods. I recited the Frost poem "Stopping by Woods On a Snowy Evening" to the rhythm Burgers' hooves: "Whose woods these are, I think I know ..." I was aware that the "little horse" in the poem was indeed a Morgan. I wondered if I was related to the famous Justin Morgan, though I grew up in New Jersey, not the Vermont of Morgan lore.

Burgers was leery of water on the trails. If the stream could possibly be jumped, he would leap over it. If he leapt and a hoof or two touched water, he'd leap forward again. Frozen water was to be avoided at all costs. There was one wide stream in the woods that became mostly frozen, with just a narrow strip of moving water running through the middle of it. The stream was one of the first challenges on the trail, blocking the way to miles of wooded trails across the back of the large property. It was not possible to go around it, and the way into it was a carved ditch from all of the many trail horses going that way.

It was cold winter day and I was riding with a friend. Both horses refused to cross the stream and we contemplated going back, as the sun was setting fast. But I really wanted a quick trot in the woods through the new snow. I urged Burgers to cross the stream for over fifteen minutes, using my crop, and he would get one, two, three hooves across and then fall over himself backing up, never quite making it over. Finally, losing patience, I really insisted. Burgers had three and half hooves across, and the ice made a cracking sound, even though the stream was only a few inches deep and nearly frozen solid. Burgers threw himself backward, turning on his haunches and slipping on the iced sides of the trail ditch. He fell onto his side, onto my right knee, and was stuck in the hollow of the ditch. He had his legs curled under him behind, and one foreleg was in front of him. My leg was not crushed, owing to the muddy sides of the banks, but I could not get out from under him. My friend tried tying him to the other horse's tail. My friend tried to push him from behind. My friend tried pulling on the reins. But Moonshine seemed content to rest in the ditch of the trail.

Finally, with tremendous urging from me, he groaned and pulled himself up, while I was still on him. He shook himself off, and began a leisurely stroll back in the direction of the barn. He seemed completely fine except for the thick mud and ice on his right flank. My right knee was hurt, making the ride home difficult and, thankfully, brief. I was on crutches for a few weeks with injured ligaments in my knee, but I continued to ride nearly every day, although I had to use a tall mounting block after hobbling up to it with my crutches.

Many years later, Burgers fell into a patch of quicksand in the woods. Perhaps remembering this ice experience, he similarly was relaxed with no signs of panic while I considered my options. Dismounting was out of the question, as I was surrounded by quicksand. But Nature provided me with a large tree next to the quicksand, with many branches reaching over the patch. I reached up and ahead for a big branch, holding it with both hands as I hugged Burgers with my legs, pulling him up a bit and urging him forward. With a groan, he simply lifted himself up with his body and threw his forelegs up and ahead onto the forest floor, pulling us both to safety. By that time, he and I both knew how to trust each other on our ventures into the woods.

Continuing what I had pursued as a young rider, I wanted to train Burgers to be a hunter. I knew that the most successful hunters were Thoroughbreds and crossbreds, but I also thought Burgers could learn to be a jumper since we were starting out so early in his life. Unlike Goblin's first jumps over brooms propped up on two buckets, Burgers could use the few real jumps and poles Percy had in one of the riding rings that the summer camp kids used each year for riding lessons with his daughters. I started trotting Burgers over poles on the ground and graduated to small crossrail jumps. He quickly learned to trot up to the jumps and quietly hop over, a feat that is more impressive when I look at my own position in those early pictures. I am leaning far forward out of the saddle over his neck, which threw him completely out of balance and made it hard for him to land without essentially falling forward on the first stride off the fence. Still, he did what I asked and was soon jumping four crossrails around the sides of the ring, never once refusing a jump, something I was proud of at the time.

That first winter I knew Burgers, we rode through the woods and the deep snow on trails going for miles behind the farm where he lived. On a frosty almost-spring day, Percy burst into the barn and asked if he could take Burgers while I was getting ready to ride him. He had a group coming for a hayride and the sled was stuck in the ice. His Belgians would not pull against the seemingly immobile runners. I helped him to quickly harness Burgers and watched as he drove him up the hill to the riding ring, running behind him. Once Burgers was attached to the sled, Percy pulled out a very long whip, and before I could say, "Don't hit him!" he cracked the air loudly. Burgers jumped forward, pulling the sled and knocking Percy down. He galloped out of the gate and stood puffing at the end of a small snowy slope until I caught up to unhitch him. Percy loved to tell this story, and when I met the owner of Burgers' sire, this impressed him more than all of his show wins and exhibitions. Burgers' father was a small Morgan stallion who pulled logs in Vermont, working in the woods every day. In the spring, he ran with the Belgian and draft mares, creating strong crossbred offspring to do farm work.

Burgers continued his jumping practice, and it seemed possible that I could take him to a horse show sometime in the summer. I had tracked down my high school friend and Horse Bowl captain Susan Sisco, who was then a professional trainer in Pennsylvania. I had heard she was showing Morgans in hunter classes at big shows, including hunter hack sidesaddle at the Devon show. I had been thinking of ways to buy Burgers after seeing so many Thoroughbreds with lameness problems that were in my price range, and I was not at all sure I could even afford to have a horse. Susan asked about Burgers, and I told her that he was just over 15.3 hands tall, a dappled dark bay with a big stride, although he was not a pretty horse. She told me that there was nothing a Thoroughbred could do that her Morgans couldn't do just as well, and she loved the temperament of her Morgans. She added that in her opinion, the most important factor in having a show hunter horse was not the type of horse, but the quality and skill of the rider. She had almost convinced me that buying Burgers might be a good idea.

And then one day, during the weeks of the end of the last semester of my graduate work at the University of Massachusetts, I drove up to see Burgers, and Percy broke the news when I arrived at the barn saying, "I sold that horse today."

I was immediately in a panic—how could he do this? I had spent months training him and no one else could even ride him. He would buck and cow kick when anyone else tried to get on him. He said a professor from the college wanted to make him a dressage horse, which in fact was what he had been bred for. I implored him to sell him to me instead. I had a job in the fall teaching at a boarding school, and the school Headmaster had promised to help cover my board for a horse since I would be the equestrian coach. Percy managed to get an extra five hundred dollars from me for Burgers, and then sold another, quieter Morgan filly to the professor. Years later, when I saw the professor at the Morgan shows competing in training level dressage with her mare, she would remark to me how glad she was to have her horse, and would compliment me on Burgers' skill and training in upper level dressage, saying she could never have accomplished all of that with him. I used money left from my graduate school loans to buy him. I had no idea then that buying Burgers would make profound changes in my life over my many years with him.

Percy persuaded me to take Burgers to the regional New England Morgan show that summer. He was three or four by then. Percy really wanted to show him in the Justin Morgan class: five competitions for pulling a stone weight, a trotting race, a hunter hack class with two jumps, a pleasure driving class, and a galloping race. I did not think I could ride him in a galloping race, so I declined. Percy loved that class, and this horse surely was a good prospect to win it, as he was strong and big-strided.

Percy was a long time Morgan lover, like many New Englanders, and he always wanted to own a winner at the big shows. Later, he did have lovely driving pairs of chestnut Morgans, and a nice filly he showed in pleasure driving. That summer, I convinced Percy that Burgers should be shown in the hunter-under-saddle class.

In the weeks before the July show, Burgers got many baths and Percy and I struggled to clip the hair around his hooves and ears, which Burgers hated. I also discovered that my Burgers was terrified of Velcro. When I tried to put his new Velcro shipping boots on him, he absolutely panicked, kicking and pawing and jumping over me so that I could not get near him. Thankfully, I had some old-type exercise wraps with long strings on the ends that could be tied in a bow. It would be a few years before I learned ways to teach Burgers not to be afraid of Velcro, since at that time I knew only to try to feed him something enticing to distract him, which did not work. I pulled and trimmed his mane and sorted out his long black tail. Our class was on a Wednesday afternoon. I arrived at the barn early in the morning to braid Burgers' mane with navy blue yarn, and braid his tail with a neat tuck at the bottom with a few more ties of blue yarn. I had not braided a mane in seven or eight years, but it still looked impressive, showing off Burgers' arched Morgan neck. I had lots of help cleaning my tack and boots, and on show day, Burgers quietly followed Percy into the trailer for the short drive to the New England regional show.

Burgers at his first New England Morgan Championship show in Hunter Under Saddle.

I had never been to the regional Morgan show, but I did have many years of showing behind me. I knew how to find a good place alone on the rail, and how to engage the judge's attention. Everyone from the farm was there to help me tack up Burgers, polish my boots, and give me advice as we warmed up for the class. Burgers was excited, going very strongly and pulling the reins. I could see there were thirty or more horses in my class, with many riders clearly having backgrounds in saddle seat riding, not hunt seat. This gave me some confidence. Everyone wished me good luck as the announcer called our class to the ring and the gatekeeper opened the big gate.

Burgers trotted in with his long trot until I found my perfect place on the rail. We did our walk, trot, walk, canter, reverse and went the second way of the ring. Burgers was pulling, but I knew not to make any issues during the class. I just hoped he'd get all of his leads and that they would ask for extended trot, as that was his best gait. Sure enough, after the second canter, the judge called for the extended trot, and I let Burgers stretch his top line and move into his big strides. We passed some of the other horses, who barely showed a change in stride length from the trot. We came back to a walk and lined up facing the judge for our back up. Burgers very politely backed, though he went a bit sideways. The class was excused to the far gate to wait for the placing.

They called in reverse order, starting with eighth place, seventh, sixth. They called our number—sixth place! Our fans screamed and jumped at their end of the ring as if I'd won first place. I gave Burgers a big pat and we trotted out with our green ribbon tucked into his bridle. Everyone patted him and fed him carrots as I dismounted, listening to their stories of what they saw in the class. I was so proud of Burgers, and I also knew he could do a lot better next year, and for the next twenty years after that. We drove home and I undid his mane, telling him how wonderful he was, and that one year we would win. Percy took us all out for ice cream to celebrate.

Chapter 5

Dedication to the Dance
Burgers and I Set Out on Our Own

Burgers winning his class at the New England Morgan Show in the three and a half foot Hunter Division.

"Real riding is lot like ballroom dancing or maybe figure skating in pairs. It's a relationship."

— Temple Grandin, *Animals in Translation*

A month later, Percy drove Burgers to the Berkshires, to Ardun's Morgan Farm, where he would live for the next ten years. This was a large breeding and showing farm with a spacious new indoor arena where the students from the boarding school where I was teaching English would be having their riding lessons. A woman there, Susie, would be teaching the beginning riders, and I would be coaching the team. Susie loved horses and all animals, so we quickly became friends. I asked who in the area I could take hunt seat riding lessons from, and she said that she took lessons with someone who taught eventing, but she knew of no hunt seat instructors in the area. I agreed to try some lessons to share travel costs for her teacher, and did some reading to learn more about eventing. Eventing is a three-phase or three-day sport, including dressage, cross country jumping, and stadium jumping. This sport is very popular in New England, owing to the many active Pony Clubs in the area and the perfect terrain for cross country jumping.

Burgers in Handy Hunter at the New England Morgan Show, 1986.

The next week, I watched Susie's lesson on one of the farm's Morgan mares, and then it was my turn with Burgers. The instructor spent a lot of time correcting my position, lengthening my stirrups, and explaining to me what a dressage horse should do, as that was a big part of eventing work. We did some small jumps and she immediately corrected my terrible position over fences. Her advice was invaluable. She implored me to almost get "left" to feel my bottom on the cantle of the saddle, to get my hips over my heels when Burgers was in the air over a jump. During the months of our first year, she had me ride with a riding crop between my forefingers and thumbs to steady my hands, riding for hours with no stirrups, and learning about some of the mechanics of a correct riding position that was different from what I had known in my previous hunter equitation riding. As my position improved over fences, our jump courses got bigger and harder, and Burgers was very good at making quick turns and taking big strides to jump courses set up for the long-legged Thoroughbreds. With his close-coupled body and strong haunches, he was a perfect match for handy hunter classes.

I went to many horse shows in the first two years of my work at the boarding school. Burgers was often second or third in his hunter classes, usually behind an expensive Thoroughbred. My first summer at the school, I went to Vermont with my soon-to-be husband, Jack, who was starting graduate school. Burgers and I spent the summer riding with Peggy Blish, a wonderful jumping instructor I had met at some shows. She mostly taught young girls, so I was in a group of agile teenagers with expensive horses. We had lessons on the flat and over fences every day, including on the long cross country course with big log jumps on the hillsides around the barn. She had a young man working at the farm cleaning stalls, stacking hay, and putting the horses in and out of paddocks. This fellow loved horses. Thanks to his patience, Burgers finally learned to stand quietly for fly spraying, to allow the sound of Velcro near him, and to wait patiently for ear clipping.

Burgers and me at one of our first Combined Training shows.

Peggy was a creative and gifted instructor. In one lesson, she met us in the ring for our jumping lesson, and put our stirrups up as short as they would go, even wrapping them twice. We joked that we looked like jockeys, but in fact, our stirrups were not quite that short. Then Peggy walked with us to the cross country course and had us go over two jumps with the very short stirrup length. We were laughing about it, but indeed, we all saw the horses jump with greater freedom, jumping even bigger and higher jumps with the riders more in balance. Then Peggy had us take turns around the entire mile-long course of jumps. We were reluctant, feeling like we could topple over on some of the step-down jumps. But everyone did beautiful jumps. Peggy smiled at us afterwards, listening to our comments about how we felt. Then she made her point, "So don't you think you may want to put your stirrups up more than a hole or two for jumping next time?" Our group went to several shows that summer, and Burgers and I won some classes, including a championship in a very large adult hunter equitation division. I had spent many years learning to be successful in the hunter world.

At the end of the summer, we returned to Ardun's farm with new confidence. Our lessons with Susie's instructor continued, and she convinced me to begin dressage training with Burgers and to prepare him for some one-day events for the next summer, and some two-phase shows that fall. I found Louise Wilde's invaluable book *Guide to Dressage,* with detailed instructions and drawings of proper hoof placement to perform renvers and travers, shoulder-in, half pass, and leg yield. The instructor gave us a bit from a riding school in England, a Fulmer bit, instead of the eggbutt we had used for hunters. Burgers and I struggled to understand and find the kind of balance the instructor tried to explain to us. She suggested I go to someone for bodywork, as it might help my riding.

Burgers at the New Jersey Morgan Show.

The boarding school is in the far southwest corner of Massachusetts, and I had to go to Chatham, N.Y., about forty-five minutes away, to find someone to work with my body alignment and muscle imbalances. Fortunately, I found Marge, who had been an active Pony Club leader, a member of the fox hunting group in her area, a lifetime rider, and was now in her later years, a realtor and a Feldenkrais and Alexander practitioner. She knew shiatsu and other manual techniques as well as having some background in Jungian therapy. Her understanding of riding and body mechanics was an ideal combination for me. Thanks to Marge, I was beginning to understand that I was out of balance in my beloved Stubben jumping saddle, purchased with summer job money when I was just starting high school. It was a very old, well-made saddle, but I have quite long thighs and the saddle just did not fit me.

I consulted with my instructor, who was happy that I decided to get a new saddle, as she had been urging me for some time to get a dressage saddle. I tried her Kieffer and felt out of balance, behind the motion, and very uncomfortable. She and I perused the catalogues and ordered a new type of French dressage saddle named for one of the top riders at the time. It made a big difference in my balance—finally my long legs fit and I could get my heels under my hips. The saddle, however, did put me ahead of the horse's movement too much, and in a year, I sold it and got another version of a Kieffer saddle, one that is no longer even sold in the United States. It has fit every horse I have put it on, and it is the saddle I rode in to train two horses to the highest levels of dressage.

Burgers in Hunter Under Saddle at the National Morgan Show.

With my new saddle, learning dressage made more sense to me as I experienced moments of balance with Burgers that I had not had before. I took Burgers to some shows and won blue ribbons in training level dressage, two-phase shows, and even some jumper shows. The next summer, with a new trailer and Suburban, Burgers, and my new husband Jack, I set off to the Morgan shows, some shows in Vermont we had been to the last summer, and even as far south as the New Jersey Morgan show held in Pennsylvania. There I got to see Susan Sisco ride her Morgans in training level dressage tests, hunters and jumpers, and watch her students ride the Morgans in equitation. Susan coached me before my classes, and we did very well.

By this time, I was riding in the upper training level classes, and even some first level classes, so Burgers could show off his lovely extended trot, ("lengthened trot" as it was called then). After we waited for about an hour in the hot sun for our turn to ride in a hunter class where every rider seemed to do a perfect round from Jack's perspective, he said, "I don't see the point of this. They all look the same; it's never clear who wins, and we have to wait such a long time to go into the ring. I think dressage is better—at least you have a time to appear, and you get a paper with your score and comments. It just makes much more sense to me." I could not deny that he was right. That would be my last summer showing in hunter classes.

That fall, Susan suggested that we bring Burgers along with her horses to the National Morgan Show in Oklahoma City. It was a twenty-five hour drive from her Pennsylvania farm, which she liked to do all at once in her big van. She asked me to drive Burgers to her farm a week or two early, and then she would bring him to the show and meet me in Oklahoma. Susie, my lesson partner, found a horse for me to ride at the farm while Burgers was away. Burgers had some lessons with Susan Sisco in Pennsylvania, and I couldn't wait to see him in Oklahoma. The show was held at a huge fair ground, with the more popular saddle seat and driving classes held in a big indoor coliseum. The dressage and jumping classes were in out-buildings with open sides, metal roofing, and the red dirt footing common in that state. I couldn't wait to ride Burgers and get ready for our classes the next day. Our first class was our dressage class. Based on his scores and national rankings among Morgans and all breeds, Burgers stood a good chance of winning the national championship at this show.

He was, however, a nervous wreck. He was shying at things in the ring, the lack of sidewalls on the arenas terrified him, and the proximity of the whips, equipment, and loud voices of the traditional Morgan trainers added to his anxiety. He was not listening to me, something I had said about him since that first show, something I was still a long way from understanding. It didn't occur to me yet that I was not listening to him. Susan yelled at me in our schooling time, rode him herself, and we did our best. When I was doing his braids the next morning, struggling with a place Burgers had rubbed a bit in the trailer, I grumbled that it looked good enough. Susan piped up and said, "If you are not going to do the best braids of your life here, where are you going to do them?" I fixed the braid, hoping that sometime I would be at many other places where beautiful braids mattered.

Burgers ended up having probably the worst dressage test of his life, but he earned fifth place. I was disheartened, and Susan scolded me saying, "You still have a lot of classes over the next few days. You have to forget about this and focus on the job you have to do here." I called Peggy Blish and told her how Burgers was acting and her first question was, "What are you feeding him?" She immediately said to stop giving him the high energy grain Susan had switched him to for the trip, and to give him some hay without alfalfa in it. I was able to get some new hay that afternoon, and within a day, Burgers was much calmer and more manageable. I rode him to reserve champion hunter behind Susan's horse, and she rode him in the last of his open jumper classes for him to win third in the division, behind her horse and another rider who was a professional jumper rider with a small, bright red Morgan stallion. Burgers had to do many rounds of jumps higher than three and half feet, and Susan came out of the ring telling me what a job it was to help him be brave enough to do it. I believe she really cared about him, and she was cranky with me for making it harder for him because I was not a better rider.

Our trip to the National Morgan show was a success in many ways, but for many years I regretted that we had not had a better ride in the dressage class there.

Burgers won his first Hunter Championship at New England Morgan in 1986.

Chapter 6

The Dance of Faithfulness and Loyalty
The Corgis Come

Jack's Winsome Winston, eight weeks old.

"When a dog gazes into your eyes, he melts your heart."

— Frances Wickham

The love of Susan Sisco's life was an ancient corgi dog named Arnold, after the pet pig on the television show *Green Acres*. She had gotten Arnold when we were in high school, and even then I did not see the appeal. Our family had hunting dogs, long-legged with silky hair, not short dogs without tails. Arnold was not at his most handsome during this show, and Susan pointed out that he had had a major surgery every year of his life during his older years. He was overweight and needed a lot of special care. One morning at the show, while we were cleaning bridles, I asked her if Arnie had been a cute puppy. She said, "Oh, Sally, there is nothing cuter than a corgi puppy!" Her sisters also had corgis and she clearly loved them. I said, "What do they look like when they are little?" and as she began her answer, a man walked by carrying a basket of corgi puppies with pink and blue bows on them, selling them to people at the show. Susan said immediately, "Sally, you have to call your husband and get one. Aren't they cute?" Of course, they were adorable. Susan, her riding student, and I looked through the basket and picked a big male to be my puppy. I asked the man, Jeff, to hold him until I checked with my husband. As he walked away, one puppy with a white nose scrambled out of the basket and up Jeff's shoulder, giving me a long look. I said to Susan, "I think I picked the wrong one." She said, no, we had picked the cutest one.

Jack was skeptical, being a man who had never lived with dogs, only with Siamese cats in his family's New York City apartment. He was already living with a few of my rabbits in the apartment at the boarding school where we worked. He asked what we might call him, and I said I didn't know. He suggested, "Can we call him Winston, after Churchill?" Jack actually knew more about corgis than I did at the time, owing to his family's love of all things British, including the Queens's corgis.

"Sure," I said, knowing that a name meant we could have the puppy. I wrote a check and collected the puppy. He was with us for the last two days of the show, and Susan's student, having already finished her equitation classes, became the pup's caretaker. He played with the not-amused Arnold, who was luckily very tolerant of the playful nips at his elderly ears and legs. The little guy was a good luck charm, as we finished the show with a truck cab filled with ribbons, coolers, trophies, and tired people. The puppy slept peacefully on the student's lap for the twenty-six hour drive to Susan's farm. I flew home to Massachusetts, planning to pick up Burgers in a week. Susan would keep the puppy with her until then.

Jack was so excited about the new puppy. He asked me lots of questions about his color and size, obviously more interested in the dog than the horse show. He had told everyone at the boarding school, including the students in the freshman boys' dorm where we lived, that we were getting a puppy named Winston. The day of my return, I taught my classes and riding lessons, and was grading papers with my rabbit Leo next to me when the phone rang at nearly nine p.m.. I said to Jack, "That must be Susan— home with the horses."

I picked up the phone, hearing Susan's distraught and tearful voice telling me that the puppy was dead. She had put him in a stall with Arnold to be safe while she took care of the horses. Just after her student had gone home with her mom, Susan's Labradors had tried to jump into the stall, biting her badly, and managing to leap in and kill the puppy. She said she was sorry, but the horror of the situation was overwhelming for both of us. I hung up to tell Jack, who was on dorm duty at the end of the hall. He immediately began to cry, and many of the students also cried at the loss. It was two hours earlier in Oklahoma, so I called the breeder, Jeff, and asked if he had a puppy left. He did! One red male. It was the one with the white nose, the one who had looked at me so long as Jeff had walked away. He said he could send him out on a plane the next morning, which he did. This is how I learned the difficult lesson that sometimes our animals pick us, and we have to be aware of when that time comes.

After I hung up the phone, Jack said quietly, "Winston's coming home after all."

Jack holding Winnie and Leo bunny.

Jack drove the hour and a half to the airport to get Winston. The puppy was in a little plastic dog crate, with note taped to it from the airline people saying he was adorable, had a walk at this airport or another, had some water here and some food there. He was charming. Jack put the little fellow on some scraggly grass at the airport, where he peed and peed amidst Jack's praises and treats he had packed for the trip. That was Winston's house training—he never ever had an accident in the house. When Jack returned, it was late, and we did not have much time to acquaint Winston with his new home. We put a comfy pillow in his crate, deciding to do "crate training" with him. We put a ticking clock near the crate, and positioned it so Winston could see the two rabbits. Winston was inconsolable, crying and squeaking, and Jack and I could not bear to hear him. Jack and I decided to put Leo bunny, my beloved Siamese colored dwarf rabbit, in the crate with him. Winston fell asleep quickly, snuggled close to the much larger rabbit, who was taken aback about the whole situation.

Winston, who we quickly nicknamed Winnie, was the runt of the litter, so tiny that my five-pound rabbits towered over him. We gave him tied-up old socks to play with, and Jack bought him a squeaky carrot, which was always his favorite toy. He was supposed to keep Jack company in the afternoons while I was at the barn unless it was soccer season, when he would go with Jack to help coach. However, it soon became clear that Winston was my dog, and he loved being at the barn with me, playing with the Jack Russell my friend Susie had, and the mini-schnauzer Adolf, who belonged to the farm owner.

Winnie, nine weeks old in 1986.

Once he was older and bigger, Winnie loved to follow me as I rode Burgers. I explained to Burgers that under no circumstances could he hurt the puppy. When Winnie was still very tiny, I would leave him in the stall while I rode. Once, someone put Winnie in Burgers' stall when the tractor came down the aisle, hoping to keep him safe. However, no one noticed that Burgers happened to be in his stall as well. When I went in to check on Burgers, who was eating his dinner, he was standing with one front hoof held up, a sleeping puppy next to his other front hoof. Burgers proved to be trustworthy with Winnie.

Winnie was a great favorite at the boarding school. When he was a tiny puppy, Jack and I would play "catch" with him, sitting on the floor with a pile of treats each, calling him us so he would learn his name, and "come." He also learned "find it" this way, and eventually he learned the names of over twenty of his toys: squeaky carrot, purple bunny, flat bunny, Mr. Snowman, and many others. He would bring the one you asked for right to you, so that he could then enjoy his favorite game on earth, "fetch." Sometimes he came to classes with me or Jack, but that was somewhat frowned upon by the other faculty. More than once, Winston escaped from our apartment to wander the classroom building in search of me or Jack. And at least twice, Jack was called to the Dean's office to pick up Winston, who had received a demerit for wandering about campus without permission.

As with my rabbits, one of my favorite games to play with Winston was to arrange a variety of foods and treats for him, and to let him select which one he liked best, so I could learn about his preferences. He liked cheese—which must be given sparingly to dogs—but chicken was his favorite. Jack was an avid cook, and Winston got the benefit of developing a broad palate of tastes for many foods, including seafood, vegetables and fruits. We also liked to heap his toys into a big pile each night and observe which one he picked out to play with first each time.

When Winston had just turned two, we had a big snowstorm in the Berkshires, with two feet of snow, causing school to be canceled for the day. As head of our dorm, Jack had to be extra vigilant to keep the boys out of mischief during the time off. Suddenly, we heard thumps against the front of the dorm—the boys from another dorm were throwing snowballs at our dorm, trying to even throw them inside open windows as our boys called out to the others. Jack was beyond furious and went stomping outside to yell at the older boys, telling them to stop hitting our building with the snowballs. He urged them to throw snowballs at each other, but not at the buildings. The boys stared back, loaded with snowballs waiting for a target, and without a word, fifteen boys all launched their snowballs at Jack, knocking off his hat and glasses, covering him with snow. He could not speak, he was so angry, so he groped in the snow and recovered his hat and twisted glasses, minus both lenses. Fortunately, he usually wore contact lenses.

A few days later, I was out with Winston for his mid-day break, and he was pawing at the snow. I said, "Find it, find it, good boy!" wondering what he was looking for. I bent over to help him, scratching at the snow, and found to my surprise, one of Jack's eyeglass lenses. I patted Winston, snuggled his cheeks, saying "Well done, Winnie, good boy, good boy!" Jack was delighted with Winston's find and gave him lots of extra treats, though he did point out that one lens was not enough for him to be able to use his glasses again. And then, maybe two weeks after the snowball slamming, Winston was outside, barking to call me over, about twenty feet from where Jack had been standing during the snowball fight. There, in the mud and snow under Winston's front paws, was Jack's second lens. Winston had put Jack's glasses back together! Winston got extra treats from both of us, and a dinner with some of Jack's roasted chicken in it. This was just the beginning of my understanding of Winston's remarkable intelligence.

Winston not only learned the names of all of his toys, but also words for his many beds, his blankie, and phrases like "let's go for a walk," or "do you want to go to the barn?" As we added new toys to his collection, we played with the new toy for hours the first day, reinforcing the name of the toy until Winston knew what each one was called. He knew at least twenty-five names for his toys, and delighted in bringing them to us when we asked for a particular one. He also learned to play hide and seek with a toy, a trick that had so impressed me when my grandfather's dog, Lucky, demonstrated his skills. Jack and I were so taken with Winston that we loved spending time with him teaching him many words and typical dog tricks, shaking hands and the like. Today, there is a border collie named Chaser known to have a vocabulary of more than a thousand words, and there is much research into the intelligence of dogs.

Winston, like all of my corgi puppies, was curious and intelligent.

Chapter 7

The Dance of Motherhood
Molly Corgi

Molly and Winston playing when she was a year old.

"There is no psychiatrist in the world like a puppy licking your face."

— Bern Williams

Jack was lonely when Winston and I left for the barn, and Winnie was spending less time on the soccer field after the first season, so we struggled to find a second corgi for him. Once again, the first puppy we found did not work out, biting at Winston and the students. We had to exchange her for another pup from her litter, who was smaller and kinder. Molly loved Jack as much as Winston loved me. She loved to take an afternoon nap, sprawled across Jack's chest like an otter on her back with paws dangling limply on her chest, which earned her the nickname "Tater." She became an expert soccer player, great as a goalie blocking balls with her chest, and using her nose to dribble the ball down the field. From the start, she much preferred soccer to a trip to the barn. Molly was shorter than Winston, and very cautious around the horses, even though she had come from a horse farm.

Winston, about a year older than Molly, loved romping with her around the living room and playing tug with her with the rope toy. She did have a habit of delicately taking one piece of carpet in her mouth, and then pulling gently to unravel whole patches of the carpet. Winston sometimes came to tell us about her misbehavior; other times he simply left the room, wanting no part of this bad behavior. Molly loved Winston and followed him everywhere, happy to have a big brother.

Winston with Molly when she was a puppy, both of them climbing on Jack's leg.

Because Molly was considered to be from an excellent bloodline, the breeder insisted that he choose a top show male to breed her with, so that he could keep the puppies to continue his breeding program. We agreed, since Jack had fallen in love with her immediately upon meeting her, uncertain of how we would later part with puppies we had raised. When Molly was old enough and in heat, Jack drove her to Maine to meet her suitor. It proved to be a harrowing experience for both Jack and Molly.

The male was much larger than Molly, and she did not like him at all. She tried to defend herself from his advances, and Jack had to leave since it was so clear to him that this was the wrong thing to do, but he felt helpless to stop the process. He drove home with Molly snuggled near him, regretting the situation, trying to focus on the puppies she would have. We dutifully brought her to the vet we liked for her checkups, and she grew to be round, clearly soon to be a mother, a relief, as we could not endure breeding her again. And then it was a day after she was due. Our vet assured us this was not uncommon in first litters and that Molly was fine. But then she was three days overdue. Susie at the barn was a vet tech, and she knew something was terribly wrong.

She was very upset and drove to the school to pick up Molly and bring her to her vet for a thorough examination.

Susie called me at the barn from the vet office, and said to contact Jack and get him to the office immediately. Jack raced there, signing papers for Molly to have emergency surgery. Sadly, the unborn puppies had died—all of them—and she would be in grave danger herself unless she was spayed immediately. Apparently, the large puppies just did not have enough room. The skilled veterinarian and Susie's quick actions saved Molly's life. We had legal issues with the breeder who had sold Molly to us, as he did not believe our story, thinking we had sold the puppies and cheated him. It was a very difficult time for Jack, whose love for Molly deepened as he cared for her in her recovery, taking her for short leash walks until she got well. Winston was clearly subdued around her, not enticing her to play tug or chase the balls with him.

Jack spending quiet time with Molly in 1989.

Molly recovered fully, lovingly following Jack around the boarding school campus, enjoying belly rubs from the students, and in later years, working with Jack as a real estate lady, accompanying him when he showed houses or met with clients at the office. When she was a senior dog, she also raised two children in a family that took care of her while Jack was at work. Some people claim that animals don't remember animal friendships, but I have only seen animals recall and delight in their relationships with other animals. Always, when Molly and Winnie met for the rest of their lives, they romped and played together, obviously thrilled to see each other again.

Jack with a senior Molly in 2003.

Molly and Winston, lifelong friends.

Chapter 8

Dancing Beauty
Hawk, My Black Beauty

LHM Night Hawk at his second New England Morgan show, where he was Training Level Dressage Champion.

"The essential joy of being with horses is that it brings us in contact with the rare elements of grace, beauty, spirit and freedom."

— Sharon Ralls Lemon

"I have seen things so beautiful they have brought tears to my eyes. Yet none of them can match the gracefulness and beauty of a horse running free."

—Author Unknown

Winston accompanied me to the barn every day and presided over riding lessons with me for many years. He liked to sit near Susie's instructor when she came to the barn to give us riding lessons. After some successful show seasons, the instructor suggested I get a second horse to increase my riding time each day, and to have a horse better suited to the higher levels of dressage than she believed Burgers to be. She was, and still is, quite an expert at matching horses and people. After driving all over New England, looking for a serious prospect dressage Morgan, she suggested I try a horse that was about an hour from home in someone's back yard. He was seven, recently gelded, and his owner had been hoping to make him into an event horse. He was 16 hands tall—huge for a Morgan—and perfect for me to show in dressage.

I got out of the car behind the tack shop operated by the horse's owners and saw a truly beautiful black horse waiting in the riding ring. He had a lovely, long, arched neck, small, alert ears, an expressive face and head, and two of the most crooked front legs I had seen on a horse. He had sired some palomino foals, had been driven a little, and needed an experienced rider. My instructor rode him to show me what he could do, and then I placed my saddle on him and gently sat on his back. He had an even longer stride than Burgers, and his canter was extremely rhythmic for a Morgan. His trot seemed very bouncy, but the instructor pointed out that this was because of the elevation in his gait. He appeared to be floating over the ground, but in a different way than my Arabian had done. As I held my cheek next to his very soft muzzle, I told the owner that I would like to buy this horse.

There is an old saying in the horse world that beginning riders should have well-trained horses, and beginning horses should have well-trained riders. All of my horses were ridden very little by other people before I had them. And I was not an extremely experienced rider when I got any of them, except Night Hawk. I could indeed call myself a horse trainer by the time I met him.

After a thorough evaluation by my veterinarians, a top group in the area who worked with very expensive horses and later for the USET, he was given a clean bill of health, my vet saying, "Well, his front legs are not straight, but he spent six years growing up in a pasture, so they are very strong. I would not suggest him as a jumping horse, however."

Night Hawk became my second Morgan. He was spectacularly handsome and everyone admired him. It was June, and I hoped to show him at the New England Morgan show in July, where Burgers was showing in first and second level dressage classes, and even some hunter classes with one of my boarding school students. The instructor made extra trips for lessons, as Hawk had one big issue—he had huge, dramatic bucks. I now know this was due to prior ill-fitting saddles, needing chiropractic work, and the rider asking him to "collect" more than his muscles were ready for. At the time, the bucks seemed unpredictable, and I was somewhat afraid of riding Hawk after I saw him bucking with the instructor on him. He rarely bucked when I rode him, and with my long legs, I was not at all unseated by his bucks. Yet they were spectacular to observe.

Hawk shown in hand by a friend at the New Jersey Morgan Show held in Pennsylvania.

At the show, Burgers did very well and became the first and second level dressage champion, winning a large hunter-under-saddle class with my student and several jumping classes. I felt fine riding Hawk around the show grounds and in the warm up areas, but I did not feel confident enough to show him, so the instructor took him in his classes. He earned respectable scores and some ribbons, and the show photographer managed to catch a picture of an enormous buck in one of the classes. Hawk also attracted a fan base of his own, owing to his beauty—especially with his neat white-taped braids accentuating his arched neck.

We finished out the summer going to other Morgan shows and some open dressage shows, and Burgers even carried me safely through some novice level events with seemingly huge cross country jumps. His high dressage scores insured that we were always in the ribbons, and at the end of the summer, I decided to focus my riding only on dressage. I had begun a friendship with Janet Moulding, who had purchased Burgers' half brother shortly before I bought him, and she was now successfully showing her horse, Action, in third level dressage. She had been taking Action to Maine for many years for lessons with soon-to-be Olympian Lendon Gray.

Lendon had wide acclaim at the time for winning Grand Prix championships with a little Connemara named Seldom Seen. Sadly, Seldom Seen turned up lame only one day in his life at the selection trials, so he was not to be her Olympic mount. Because Lendon was known to work with Arabians and other breeds, Janet knew she was a good fit to give her lessons with her Morgan. Lendon had moved from Maine to a town in New York State only a few miles from Ardun's farm, where I kept Burgers and Hawk. When Janet came to take lessons with Lendon, she would sometimes stop in and give me lessons on my two horses, and I was impressed with the clarity and thought she had about riding and training. Hawk looked so much like Action that everyone thought they were brothers.

In addition to lessons from Janet, I took Centered Riding lessons with Sally Swift, who was fortunately working out of a farm just north of me in Vermont, where she had been for years. She really helped me find a better balance in the saddle, feeling the connection from my hips to my heels. She loved Morgans, and thought Burgers was "delightful." I had not heard many people refer to him this way, and her words caused me to look at him differently. Her Centered Riding exercises, combined with the Feldenkrais and Alexander work I was doing, helped me begin to make the connections between holding in my body and tension in my horse's body. It was also at one of these clinics that I heard someone talking about Tellington TTouch® Training Method and the work of Linda Tellington-Jones. Janet had brought one of her horses, a chestnut Thoroughbred mare, to work with Linda Tellington-Jones in a demonstration at Hampshire College in 1981, and was very impressed with Linda's work. (In her living room today, Linda has a picture of herself working with Janet's mare, with Feldenkrais students gathered around.)

Thanks to Centered Riding and my lessons with Janet, I was beginning to have moments in my dressage riding when I felt a deep connection to my horses, just as I had in the woods riding bareback with Goblin, or riding home on a dark trail at night, perfectly attuned to Burgers' breathing and hoof steps.

The first fall that I had Hawk, he had been under saddle about six months, and he was continuing to have unpredictable episodes of bucking. By mid-September, he was becoming much calmer, as he was settling into his life at the Morgan farm. He was turned out with Burgers, though they never really seemed to get along. What appeared to be play was really Burgers making a serious effort to kick Hawk, and Hawk running away from him. In spite of his bucks, Hawk seemed to rarely shy or bolt, which made him a nice horse to trail ride. My parents planned to visit me at the boarding school that October, and I thought it would be nice to take a trail ride with my mom, though I was not sure which horse she should ride. She was eager to meet the beautiful black horse she had seen in pictures.

That Friday afternoon, I decided to take Hawk around the big field next to the property where he lived. It was several miles around the border, and fenced in. He was calm as I saddled him, and waited quietly by the mounting block as I got on him in the big field. I started around the pasture outside of the indoor ring at the walk, but he broke into a jog and then a big trot. I could feel that something was not right with him, so I urged him forward into a canter, knowing that if he was moving forward, even his big bucks would be more like a lofty gallop. As we started down the side of the field next to road, he began to buck and lunge as I urged him to continue forward, forward. We made it all of the way around the field and back to the end of the indoor, and I was feeling glad to still be on him.

Hawk on a misty morning at the New England Morgan Show.

But then he lost his footing on the slippery mud coating the concrete apron outside of the arena. He scrambled and bucked and went down onto his left side, pinning me under him briefly. He leapt up, still bucking, and raced to the gate at the end of the barn where his stall was, which formed an "L" with the arena. I was motionless, the wind knocked out of me, and there was severe pain in my left shoulder and back. I was not sure that I could get up, and it was growing dark and cold. I called Winston, who had waited in the barn. He came running out. I knew that as long as he would come to me, I would not get hypothermia and could probably keep myself from going into shock. I called him weakly, and he trotted towards me part of the way. I called again, and instead of coming to me, he turned around. I could not believe that my beloved dog, who had always shown extraordinary intelligence, was ignoring me.

Instead, he chased Hawk back and forth by the gate to the barn. The two young colts in the adjacent field came to the fence, and Hawk snorted and squealed at them over the fence. They ran around the field leaping and snorting and ran back to Hawk. This time, Winston chased Hawk back towards the barn, barking furiously and loudly.

As I lay on the ground, I was imagining how I could explain to Jack that we shouldn't sell Hawk, and wondering what would happen if I could not walk. Could I get a carriage and drive the two horses as a pair? Who would harness them for me?—could Jack do that? I could wiggle my toes, so I tried not to panic in the twilight as the stars began to illuminate the sky. The night barn check was not until ten o'clock. I tried to call Winston, but still he ignored me.

Sometimes a dog, especially one like Winston, does something remarkable that no one could predict. Thanks to his barking and chasing Hawk, the farm owners in the house nearly half a mile away could hear that something was not right at the barn. I saw a series of lights coming on, and then the headlights of a car coming down the driveway towards the barn. The farm owner, Beverly, saw me on the ground and ran into the barn to call Susie, as well as an ambulance, and Jack. Susie caught Hawk and tucked him in for the night. Winston finally wanted to come to me after Hawk was in his stall, but Susie captured him so that Jack could bring him home later.

The ambulance driver was a rider from nearby, and immediately knew I had broken my left collarbone. She whispered to me that she thought Hawk had kicked my back, owing to the hoof print on my coat, and that she did not think anything was broken, so I should be all right. Thankfully, once I got to the hospital and had some X-rays, she proved to be right. After my back was iced for an hour, I was able to feebly walk out of the hospital, and Jack and Winston drove me home. Winston was a hero, as the farm owner said she would have never noticed my car in the driveway, and it was only his barks and the hoof beats of Hawk running the fence line that got her attention.

I was in a lot of pain, so Jack propped me up with many pillows on a soft chaise lounge in the bedroom. I could not sleep much, and that night we had over a foot of heavy, thick snow that covered the trees and power lines. My parents were staying at a bed and breakfast up the road, where a fallen tree branch damaged the roof of their new car. The boarding school was closed for a few days due to power outages in the main building. I often wonder if this unusual weather was not partially why Hawk was so unmanageable that afternoon. Needless to say, my mother and I did not take our pleasant autumn trail ride in a land now buried in snow, but the next day Jack drove me to the barn, and Susie led Hawk out to show him off to my parents. My mother, nearly afraid to touch him, did remark how soft his coat was. Susie brought him up to the side of the car, and he ever so gently placed his nose in my lap—was this his apology? He looked deeply at me, motionless, and it was clear he was concerned.

It took nearly two months for me to recover, and I rode Burgers for weeks before I rode Hawk again, using neck reining to direct Burgers and keeping my left arm folded against my body, not leaving the indoor ring for the rest of that winter. Susie kindly led me around on Hawk once I could safely mount using my left arm, and she did this for over a week before I would walk him once around the arena without her. We both knew that having her lead me really couldn't stop him from bucking, but the security of her presence helped both me and Hawk. Trying to find our relationship again, I would stand in his stall, stroking his neck, where the hair was as soft as a rabbit's, and he would gently nuzzle me and circle his neck around me.

Gradually, I was able to ride him by the springtime at the walk, trot, and canter, first in the indoor arena, and finally back in the small field at the front where I had set up some dressage letters. He'd had some months off as I recovered, and with his gradual return he was much more comfortable, even though he still sometimes had remarkable bucks. If only I had known then that he was desperately trying to tell me that his back was hurting him.

Chapter 9

Dancing With Cooperation
Riding to Music

Ten Penny Action and his one-year-younger brother Ten Penny Moonshine, nicknamed Burgers.

"Dance is the hidden language of the soul."

— Martha Graham

One of my favorite classes in dressage was the musical freestyle, as it was then called. It had been introduced at some of the bigger regional shows for horses at all levels of dressage, not just at Grand Prix. I could not wait to ride Burgers to music, as he was solidly showing at second level. I found a woman in the area who could help me make a tape of music that matched his gaits. She had been showing at third level with a nice imported warmblood. She came to my house, in that era of less technology, and with a dual-tape player from Radio Shack, we patched together a master tape of German polka and Strauss music that matched Burgers' steps at the walk, trot and canter as we watched his gaits on a video tape on the VCR. We were laughing as we tried to get the record button to start at exactly the right place in the music. She and Janet helped me design a choreography that would highlight Burgers' fabulous big extended trot, his smooth lateral work in leg yield, and his good square halts.

Burgers and I set off to the NEDA (New England Dressage Association) Freestyle championships with a few copies of our tape. As at the big Morgan show in Oklahoma, Burgers was very nervous, prancing out of the trailer. Maybe it was my own nerves he was showing me. We rode in the warm-up ring next to some of the nation's top riders on big, impressive horses. Burgers, a tall Morgan at 15.3 hands, felt small and quick next to such robust horses. At the sound booth I met Fred Smith, who would later make much better tapes for my rides. I gave Burgers plenty of time to rest before it was our turn in the ring, walking him over the grounds and waiting in the shade a bit. When it was our turn, we stood at the side of the arena, and walked strongly around the side and up the center line, stopping with a near perfect halt. He loved his music, his big ears switching to the sides at the changes in tempo, and we flew up the center line with our final lengthened trot to G, with a square halt right at the judge's box. People clapped as I heard them say, "What a cute horse"—my horse, cute?

We won fifth place, the highest placing horse with a lower level ride, in the freestyle championship class earning a beautiful plaque. That would be the last time Burgers walked out of a musical ride class without a first-place ribbon fluttering from his bridle.

Hawk needed to get to first level to do his freestyle performances. I had no idea what type of music suited him. The music could not have vocals and generally classical music was preferred. Jack was a huge *Star Trek* fan, and he insisted that music from *Star Trek* and *Star Wars* would be the best music for Hawk. He was absolutely right. The judges loved the music; it matched Hawk's tempos perfectly, and the audience enjoyed music they recognized. Hawk's freestyles became well known around New England, and like Burgers, he nearly always won his class, owing to his fluid strides and striking beauty, as well as his good dressage work.

Janet and I had the idea to perform a musical *pas de deux*, a dance for two, for our two horses. We had her friends help us with choreography, as Action was at third level and Burgers at first/second level at the time. We wanted to show off Action's skills as well as work the two horses next to each other. We planned to perform in an exhibition at the New England Morgan Show, and in preparation, at some smaller dressage shows in our area. Burgers and Action were not exactly friendly with each other as Janet and I rode side by side, our stirrup bars clinking together. Our horses had amazingly matched strides in spite of differing levels of training and two different sires. In their white braids and leg wraps, they were even more similar. Janet advised me in buying a proper dressage coat with tails, in deep navy blue like hers, which looked best with our dark horses, and a new top hat. Neither of us knew of anyone else doing a *pas de deux* in dressage, although Lendon had done a demonstration of dressage riding her Olympic warmblood performing with a rider and his advanced reining horse. Two days before our performance, we were even featured in a television newscast, where the reporter spoke the portentous words, "*Pas de deux*. That's what these two brother Morgan horses do, dance together."

Janet began giving me more lessons as we prepared for our performance, and I was beginning to see many discrepancies between her approach, reflecting her training with Lendon Gray, and what I was seeing with my instructor. It was gradually becoming apparent to me that what I had been learning was not true of dressage in general, and was just one person's approach.

The night of our performance arrived, and Janet and I had our horses spotlessly clean. Burgers had won the first and second level dressage championships at the Morgan show already, and Hawk had been the champion in the training level division. It was the final night of the show with the formal park championships featured at the end of the evening. There was an orange and yellow sunset across the fair grounds' horizon, with the automatic street lights just coming on as we warmed up for our performance.

Burgers and me with Janet and Action at one of our Pas De Deux demonstrations.

Jack's parents, lifelong riders and horse lovers, were visiting from New York City to see the show and visit with Max Gahwyler, a dressage judge and a friend of theirs from his days at the Ox Ridge Hunt Club. Max was instrumental in bringing dressage to the United States, and his book, *The Competitive Edge: Improving Your Dressage Scores in the Lower Levels*, was quite popular. He had inscribed my book "Keep smiling in the face of adversity and unappreciative judges. The certain thing is that you and your horses have fun." Max helped my riding so much at his clinics, and thanks to his lessons, I had learned to feel Burger's hooves stepping under me to perform flawless walk pirouettes, and later canter pirouettes. I was very grateful for all I had learned from him.

Max, Jack and his parents Dedie and DeWitt, Susie, and the owners of the farm where I boarded, Bob and Beverly were crowded into their box seats. The only previous dressage demonstrations had been performed by Big Bend Doc Davis, a petite FEI level Morgan who had inspired me to do musical freestyle rides with Burgers. Janet pointed out that we were not being judged, so there was no need to be nervous.

Janet's husband, Dick, had prepared a professional tape for us with music from *Carmen*, and both horses stood alertly at the gate as the big sound system played the energetic music. Our horses entered at the trot, perfectly in stride, our stirrup bars rubbing and clicking next to each other in time to the music. We cantered ten-meter circles together and apart, half passed coming together and apart; Action piaffed his trot in place, and together they did canter pirouettes. We did extended trot together up the center line and halted with a sharp salute to both sides of the audience, timed perfectly simultaneously. The announcer clapped, as the audience gave us a standing ovation. Someone brought Janet and me a bouquet of flowers, wrapped in ribbons of the show colors, green and blue. Our Morgans were celebrities. Later, owing to Janet's choice of *Carmen*, an opera and Morgan lover from far away in New York state hired us to perform in his beautiful indoor ring, made to replicate a famous opera house. We also were hired to be entertainment during the lunch break at some regional dressage shows. The next year, we added our friend Chris Hickey (now a professional dressage trainer) riding Hawk, and did *a pas de trois* at the New England Morgan show, and at some other dressage shows. To this day, we know of no other riders who have performed in a pas de trois. Janet and I always had to explain to people that Burgers, not Hawk, was indeed Action's brother, as Hawk and Action looked much more similar.

Our Morgan Pas De Deux was very successful.

Chapter 10

Clarity in the Dance
A Better Way With Alexandra Kurland

Burgers and I shared a deep bond over nearly thirty years together. Photo by Helena Sullivan.

"The problem is not making up the steps, but deciding which ones to keep."

— Mikhail Baryshnikov

I knew I needed more lessons to succeed in dressage, and while she had helped me enormously, the instructor I shared with Susie was becoming increasingly frustrated with Burgers, feeling that he was limited in his potential, disobedient, and difficult. Hawk, with his lovely gaits, was a favorite for her, but she did not appreciate how I was riding him. At one lesson in mid-September, she was at the boiling point, riding Burgers and trying to get him to be more collected and lift his back, mercilessly using the whip, pulling on his mouth and neck, yelling at me and Burgers, until he simply fell into the shavings pile in the ring, and she continued to use the whip on him. She jumped off him, still furiously hitting him and yelling at me, before she stomped across the ring and said to me, "I can't work with this horse. Go work with Lendon Gray or Linda Tellington-Jones or whoever you want, but this horse is hopeless!!!" and she strode up the aisle and left the property. That was my last lesson with her, and it would be years until I fully realized my gratitude to her for this moment. Her words changed my life and the course of my work with animals forever.

I took care of Burgers, crying and apologizing to him, and drove home in despair. Jack listened to my story and said in a matter of fact tone, "O.K., let's call those people and set up some lessons then." Between classes the next day, I called the Tellington TTouch Training Method office in Santa Fe and found out that Linda Tellington-Jones was going to be teaching two weeks of clinics, one for riding and one for advanced Tellington TTouch Training Method, in New Hampshire in about a month. I could sign up for them, but I would need to learn enough to be admitted to the advanced class since I had no prior work with the Tellington Method. I ordered many video tapes to study. The woman on the phone, Carol, referred me to a nearby practitioner, Alexandra Kurland, an hour away from me. She said that if I worked with Alexandra and sent some documentation to verify that, I would be permitted to take both classes, and I could bring my horses!

Sally Swift, far left, teaching an unmounted portion of her clinic at Lucy Bump's house in Vermont, part of my Centered Riding Instructor training.

Alexandra was an absolute gift who came into my life at a perfect time. She had worked with Bettina Drummond and knew classical dressage training incredibly well, from both the French and the German perspective. She had been doing Tellington

TTouch Training with horses for many years to help with her young Thoroughbred who had Wobbler's syndrome, a neurological condition. Like Janet, she had a clarity in her words and thoughts that made sense to me. And she appreciated Morgans, seeing them as another version of the Iberian breeds she knew so well from Bettina. She was devoted to her job helping me prepare for the clinic, spending hours and hours at the farm, staying in our guest room sometimes, teaching me TTouch bodywork, ground driving, in-hand work, and Tellington-Jones' Riding with Awareness.

The farm owners offered to let us work with some of their two-year-olds as well, to start them in ground driving and basic handling. Some of these horses were very challenging, but Alexandra was never unnerved by their behavior. One little filly had been injured, being pushed into a stall door by another horse in the scramble of horses coming into the barn one night, and she had not been handled much at all. The first day we worked with her she cowered in her stall, too afraid of us even to eat. Alexandra stood quietly day after day for a half- an hour each time until the filly came to her. She said that taking a lot of time then would make everything else safer and quicker when we did more with her, and she was right.

A few weeks later, we were ground driving the filly in a small paddock near the huge field where the herd went out each day. We had two long nylon driving reins attached to her halter, and a surcingle around her girth with rings to hold the reins so that we could walk next to her or behind her, giving her cues as if she were pulling a cart. One of us walked near her head to steady her and give her signals as needed. This was my introduction to the alternative to lunging a young horse.

As it was in the early evening, it was close to feeding time, and suddenly the entire herd of fifty or more mares and youngsters came galloping towards the barn. Alexandra was not strong enough to hold the filly, as she leapt and bucked, hooves flying over Alexandra's head, and then bolted out into the field to the herd, lines trailing behind her. Alexandra simply said, "She is learning a lot about ropes today," as we watched breathless, hoping the lines did not tangle in her legs. She whirled around the corner to the barn with the herd, and came to a halt before the door. Alexandra spoke to her, and the filly calmly turned and came back to us. We quickly took off her driving equipment, she shook, snorted, and calmly walked into the barn to wait by her stall for her dinner. That filly grew up to do mounted search-and-rescue work and was a very reliable horse.

Alexandra was quite skilled with in-hand work, and she showed me how to walk close to Burgers with the reins around his neck, working at his shoulder as I had seen the Lipizzaner trainers do years ago in Philadelphia. She showed me how to properly collect a horse this way, not by driving them forward into a closed hand, but instead using many aids to compress the shape of the horse to achieve collection. She explained the history of dressage, French and German traditions, and the differences. She worked with Hawk in hand, not even flinching when he did an enormous buck right next to her. She quietly said, "Oh my, so let's look at your back and hind legs, and see why you needed to do that." Finally I would learn about Hawk's back pain and how to help him.

Alexandra showed me which TTouches to do on Hawk's sore back and legs. We lifted each leg and rotated it in a circle, a small, tight circle for him, while Burgers had much more mobility in his legs. I did TTouch python lifts on his legs, gently holding the skin, lifting it slightly, and releasing it slowly, slowly down. I did circles with his tail in both directions, and flat lying leopard TTouches down his spine. These seemingly simple circle and a quarter TTouches down his back created an obvious change in his posture and released tension in his muscles, as he became more relaxed. Each day as I did these exercises with him, I noticed the muscles were softer, and the leg circles were easier for him than the day before.

Alexandra also attended the advanced Tellington TTouch Training Method clinic, and after we arrived and I made my first contributions to the group conversations about the horses at the clinic for the week, it was clear to her and everyone that her time with me was equal to many weeks of training. Fellow students asked where and when I had taken my other courses, and I replied, "Just an intensive month or so with Alexandra!"

This was the beginning of my understanding that a horse's behavior *is* his communication with us. All of this time, I had complained that Burgers was not listening to me, when in reality, I was not listening to him, or Hawk, whose dramatic bucks clearly had so much to say.

Sally Swift, left, coaching as riders explore their balance (Marcy Baer, second from right).

Chapter 11

The Dance of Touch
Linda Tellington-Jones Dancing With Horses

Linda Tellington-Jones on her wedding day to Roland Kleger in 2000. My friendship with Linda spans over thirty years. Photo by Gabriele Boiselle.

"I feel that today many dressage riders don't have a real sense of what riding with 'feel' entails—an intricate interweaving of the physical and emotional sensations inspired by the horse's movement and state of mind. True feel ... involves an intuitive ability to know the horse's actions and reactions as intimately as you know yours, and to move in sync with them as easily as you would your own."

— Linda Tellington-Jones *Dressage with Mind, Body and Soul*

Linda Tellington-Jones was teaching the clinics with her sister Robyn Hood. Tellington TTouch Training was still in the early years of development. When I arrived, Burgers was solidly at third level dressage and Hawk was moving into second level work, the middle levels of dressage work. I was running into difficulty with flying changes for Burgers, and for Hawk, everything seemed effortless and balanced. He was showing me already the joy of working with a horse when you are a more advanced rider, and I was thanking Burgers every day for putting up with my efforts to learn. Hawk was showing me how far I had come. His flying changes were clean, and his lateral work was very good. I was excited to learn about the Tellington Training Method, but also feeling despair over my previous instructor's tirade.

On the first morning of the class, Linda asked, "Why do we have horses? To put them on the bit, or to dance with them?" She explained that our time with them is not about the destination, but about the journey, learning to dance with our horses, both on the ground with them and under saddle.

This was exactly what I needed to hear. As much as I had been very successful with my horses in dressage, and in jumping and hunters with Burgers, what I loved most was watching them in their stalls crunching on hay at the end of the day. Or just exploring the woods with Burgers on a quiet summer afternoon, knowing that we were one being. Or feeling the plush, soft hair on Hawk's neck against my cheek on a cool fall day before our ride.

I had long held deep sympathy for my horses and for all horses, recalling always my mother's voice reading the words of *Black Beauty*. Even so, I misunderstood my horses and lacked the knowledge to adjust to what would have been best for them. Goblin had to carry a western saddle so heavy that I could barely lift it onto her back. Richard tried so hard to float with his Arabian trot, and I tried so hard to make him into a hunter type pony. And Spooky, our first horse, carrying my sister and me together, carefully stepping when our mom rode her—she was so generous and yet we so often unfairly compared her to fancy ponies bred for the show ring, and saw too often her lack of better conformation. Mom loved animals so much that it was impossible for my sister and me to view them as lacking intelligence or emotions or memories from long past days. And yet the riding world we were in at the time did not treat horses with understanding and sympathy. Affecting equine behavior was mechanistic, bribing horses into trailers with grain with no effort to see the genesis of their fears, making something uncomfortable so that they would respond in a stimulus-response manner.

The week with Linda Tellington-Jones was the beginning of my new understanding of horses, and of all animals. Up until then, I was in a horse world where common beliefs were that horses did not always make an effort, that they were generally lazy and would prefer to be grazing, and that what we were asking horses to do for us was "work," which implied that it was difficult and distasteful. Later, I realized that just calling riding and training "work" pulled in all of our own beliefs about that word, and smothered our horses with worry and exhaustion. Seeing riding as a continual dance to connect with our horses so that we could better understand them, and they could understand us, changed everything I had been taught about riding.

Burgers showing in-hand at the New Jersey Morgan Show.

As the students in the clinic introduced themselves around the circle, I met Bonnie Reynolds, who with animal communicator Dawn Hayman would later found Spring Farm Cares, a prominent rescue organization, and Peggy Cummings, who went on to develop her own Connected Riding technique using principles of Centered Riding, Tellington TTouch Training, and her own insights. I was already friends with Alexandra Kurland, one of the pioneers in clicker training for horses. Wendy Murdock was in our class, and she, like Peggy, has developed her own riding techniques using Centered Riding, the Tellington Method, and biomechanics principles. Carol Lang, who worked in the Tellington TTouch Training office for many years, dedicated hours to rehabilitating some macaques rescued from Hunter College research studies, when scientists said it could not be done. (*Six Macaques: A Story of Transformation from Lab Primates to Animal Ambassadors* is a new book detailing this work.) Also in our group was a gentle Austrian woman named Anagrette Ast, who was on the board to test riding teachers and trainers for Austria. She did a sensitive demonstration of grooming your horse in way that enhances your relationship, rather than simply removing dirt and frustrations from your day as you brush quickly without thinking. I was fortunate to be in this group of leaders in the equestrian world, and I thank all of them for inspiring me to develop equine and small animal craniosacral work later in my life.

Next we introduced the horses in the clinic, and Linda asked us to bring them into the group as we learned about them. As each owner described their horse's issues, Linda quietly introduced herself to each horse, exploring their bodies with her fingertips, and then explaining to the group what she saw in each horse's structure, musculature, and, importantly, in their posture. With each horse, she and Robyn began to demonstrate TTouches, the circular bodywork, according to what the horse needed. We saw every horse's eyes soften, head lower, and postural changes in response to the work. It seemed incredible how quickly these changes occurred.

When it was time for me to introduce Burgers, I first talked about his dressage accomplishments and hunter background, and reported what my instructor had said about him being difficult and stubborn. Linda looked sympathetically into Burgers' eyes, knowing that these words were not true of him, or any horse. What so many trainers see as bad behavior, I was to soon learn, is indeed the horse's effort to communicate distress or pain to the rider. I had to explain to the group how Burgers got his name, as Linda believes " ... pay a lot of attention to the names of the horses ... Because what you call a horse is how other people see and treat them." She could see that he liked this name, which was confirmed by an animal communicator in the group, since it was given to him ultimately out of love and appreciation. I had respect for him. Some people in the group pointed out that Burger in German could refer to a government official, or as I knew, is the root of the word harbinger or herald. Burgers would indeed prove to be the herald of many turning points in my life.

Linda explained that of the group, he was the only horse with proper hoof length and angle (his feet were done by the same group who cared for the Budweiser Clydesdale teams, since they were farriers for the championship show Morgans at the big farm where Burgers lived). She found many sore and tight spots along his back. She suggested that he had been ridden in an unnaturally compressed frame, which was indeed true for the time with my old instructor. I quietly realized that it was not reasonable to ask him to perform well under saddle, especially in dressage, when his back was sore. My heart filled with new sympathy for him, and gratitude for Linda Tellington-Jones.

When I led Hawk into the arena, there was a group "ahh" at his shining black coat and beautiful head and neck. Linda gently breathed into his nostrils to introduce herself and told him how handsome he was. As with Moonshine, she looked deeply into Hawk's eyes. She did the body exploration on him, and I told her that his hind legs were quite tight during the circles I had been doing with Alexandra for him. I explained to the group the big improvements we had seen in his lateral work since doing the leg circles. My saddle did not fit Hawk very well, and Linda showed us how placing it farther back changed the fit so that it was more comfortable for him, and showed me how other saddle pads worked better.

From right, me, Linda and a rider happy to ride without a bridle.

Later, we led the clinic horses in the labyrinth, as Linda described what she was seeing with each horse. The labyrinth is a sort of maze we use in this work, with several right angle turns around corners for animals to walk around. Some horses, often the ones with sore hocks and backs, just spun a hoof in the sand to turn, rather than marching 1-2-3-4 lifting the hooves and keeping the cadence of the walk throughout the turn. I had learned to look for this cadence in my lessons with Max Gahwyler. I had already learned from Alexandra how to use the white dressage whip we use in Tellington TTouch Training to tap each leg gently in turn to encourage the horse to pick up each leg throughout the turn. My horses had learned very good walk pirouettes from this technique as well. Even more importantly, when the horses had changed how they walked through the labyrinth, we could see a change in their balance throughout the corners of the arena when they were being led and especially when they were under saddle. Instead of tipping to the side like a motorcycle on a turn, the horses were learning to step under themselves and adjust their weight over all four legs to have better balance. Some horses, Linda showed us, were basically falling onto their inside shoulders in the turns and literally tripping in the corners and having to recover to continue down the long side of the arena.

"When a horse is in physical balance, he is in emotional balance," Linda said to the group, pointing out how some of the horses had spooked at the door near the end of the arena after going through the labyrinth with struggle. The horses who were more balanced in the turns, stepping under their bodies with their hind legs as Burgers did, were much calmer passing the rattling doors of the unfamiliar arena. We saw examples of this more and more over the week, especially under saddle. Linda pointed out that when a horse's head is up, his back is lowered as a matter of mechanics, and he is also in the posture of a horse fleeing in fear. When the head is lower, and the back comes up, the body posture is more in a state of balance. When horses raised their heads, eyes wide, falling onto their inside shoulders, if the riders were able to lower the head and rebalance the horse, the horses avoided shying at something in the arena.

There are two aspects of the autonomic nervous system: the sympathetic, associated with stress, and the parasympathetic, associated with peace. The sympathetic system is engaged during the fight/flight response, and the parasympathetic system is engaged during the rest/digest response. TTouch helps bring these systems into balance. As we looked at trailer loading problems later in the week, this became crucial to understanding how to be successful getting a horse to go into a trailer when he is afraid.

In my past, we just held a bucket of food in front of the horse, hoping to bribe him to enter. However, this will never work if a horse is too fearful and stressed to eat. The first time I took Hawk to a show, unfamiliar with trailers as Hawk was, I sent Jack out to the trailer with the horse and a bucket loaded with grain, and instructed him to politely ask Hawk to walk in as he held the grain out for him. I said I would be in the barn and to call me if he needed anything. I had just disappeared around the corner when I heard Jack's frantic calls, as he had almost no horse experience and did not know how to get out of Hawk's way when he simply walked in, after a moment of assessment and few bites of food. I ran out, talking to Hawk and Jack, telling Jack to duck under the center bar and drop the lead line as I fastened the tail bar. Hawk, munching his hay, quietly turned to look at me, unconcerned about the whole process. I had told Jack that the process could take up to a half-hour, which set him up with minimal if any expectations, and with his limited horse experience, he had no agenda about possible situations when the horse would not go into the trailer—a version of what someone I know called "the gift of non-interference." So Jack's relaxed state and calm mental picture helped Hawk quietly step into the trailer. To this day, Jack will proudly relay his approach to loading a horse onto a trailer and report his success. My sister's six-year-old daughter Gwen earned a similar reputation—she could be handed any lead line and every horse would follow her into a trailer, even with no ramp and a leap up, because she had no expectations for the horse not to follow her.

Linda's approach expanded on this. When a horse is really afraid, food is not enough. The key point Linda added to my understanding of trailering that week was the importance of asking the horse to lower his head, and the use of food to keep the horse from escalating out of the rest/digest parasympathetic response. For horses with many difficult trailering episodes behind them, we also crossed two jump poles to make a V behind the horse, held by at least four people, and gradually and gently brought the poles closer, asking the horse to stop frequently, lower his head, have some food, and then quietly asking him to come forward. After a week of ground exercises working on coming forward, stopping, lowering the head, stepping back, moving just one leg, and so on, all of the horses quietly walked into the trailer. Even the difficult horses all loaded so well that some of us were skeptical of their owner's reports of their prior problems.

"At the heart of the Tellington TTouch philosophy is the concept of acknowledging the personality—the individuality—the very soul of animals. I feel a special connection to all animals, the connection of Oneness—a connection that is essential to the health of my heart and of my soul," Linda said as she began the next morning's discussion. Finally, someone had said to me what I had learned from my mother, and from my own work with my horses and dogs. I was overwhelmed with emotion, looking over at Burgers, who was staring out from his stall into the ring where we had gathered. I felt so much gratitude to him in that moment for bringing me to this clinic, and offered him a silent thank you for tolerating so much treatment that was not respectful of him or his soul.

Connecting with an animal's soul—that is what I wanted with all of the animals in my life, to find that reciprocal connection of love and appreciation.

Linda continued the morning discussion, emphasizing that the Tellington Method is a philosophy, a way of being with animals, as well as a system of training. Our morning discussion focused on a review of the four tenets of the philosophy of Tellington TTouch Training. These are printed in every newsletter that Robyn, Linda's sister, has published since the early '80s. The first is to honor the role of animals as our teachers. Linda emphasizes that we learn from our animals continuously as we try new things with them, and that we learn from each other during the classes. Even if you disagree with someone, you can still learn something from that experience. Being open to learning experiences is an important part of the Tellington Method.

Secondly, respect the individuality of each animal and person. One aspect of this is not to assume that all Arabians, or any breed of horse, are all the same, or that all racetrack horses have the same issues, or that all riders of one discipline of riding share the same ideas. This concept can be challenging in the opinionated horse world. Over the course of the weeks with Linda, we all learned to see each horse and person at the clinic as someone trying to make changes and improvements that were right for them.

Third, celebrate interspecies connections with the Tellington TTouch Method. Linda recounts going for an astrology consultation years before she began doing TTouch when she was told she would develop a form of communication that would be used around the world. Generally, in early TTouch classes, this communication meant connecting to and understanding what our animals were trying to say to us. Now we also know that TTouch enhances communication between the cells in the body. The Tellington Method offers a way to communicate with our animals, and therefore to enhance connections to them. And our connections to our own animals allow us to be connected to all animals, one another, and the planet.

As Lynn McTaggert describes in *The Field*, we know from quantum physics that we indeed are all connected, part of the Oneness described by Larry Dossey in his book, *One Mind: How Our Individual Mind is Part of a Greater Consciousness and Why It Matters*. As the Tellington Method has evolved, we understand now that the TTouches promote intercellular communication, again connecting the whole organism. Linda validated this work with Dr. Fritz Albert Popp at the International Institute of Biophysics in Neuss, Germany. She feels that TTouches "light up the cells" and as Popp states, "We know today that man, essentially, is a being of light." He adds, "In terms of healing, the implications are immense." We now know, for example, that "quanta of light can initiate, or arrest, cascade-like reactions in the cells, and that genetic cellular damage can be virtually repaired, within hours, by faint beams of light." Linda's TTouches can also bring "light" to repair cells and improve function.

The fourth aspect of Tellington philosophy is to encourage trust between humans and animals, and also between humans. When people asked what the TT means in TTouch, Linda explained for a time that TT looks like the I Ching, the gateway to transformation, as TTouch is transformational for us and our horses. For a few years, the TT was understood to represent "Tellington Touch." Currently, the added T represents trust. When we honor our animals, respect them, and therefore improve communication with them, trust develops. This is so important when we ask animals to live in our human world, like when I take my dog on an airplane. Nothing in that environment is known to him, and he only has his trust in me to guide him through strange new experiences. Trust allows for a calmness during the learning process with our animals as we teach them how to be with us in our world. Trust is what brings meaning to our relationships with our animals.

Linda went on to explain that one aspect of her inspiration for TTouch came during her Feldenkrais trainings with Moshe Feldenkrais himself. Moshe had acute observation skills and was able to teach people how to re-educate the central nervous system with very small physical movements. "No part of the body can be moved without all the others being affected," he wrote, and this holistic approach is one unique component of his work. He also wrote "that the unity of mind and body is an objective reality. They are not just parts somehow related to each other, but an indispensable whole while functioning," making him a pioneer in the field of mind body medicine. One thing that struck Linda was the idea of non-habitual movements also being useful to enhance gait, performance, health, and mobility. She suggested the example of TTouch leg circles with the horses as a non-habitual movement. Early in her Feldenkrais trainings, while she was doing an exercise called an ATM, awareness through movement, on the floor, it suddenly came to Linda that she should try this work for horses. Later that day, Linda tried moving horses' legs and tails in new ways, just to see what happened. She noticed horses not dragging their feet, increased spine mobility, and other changes after just a few minutes of the movement exercises. One mare, who was difficult to catch, was waiting by the gate to come in the day after she experienced Linda's TTouches following that Feldenkrais class. So much of the bodywork and ground exercises we do today with TTouch come from this basic idea of non-habitual movement. I raised my hand to report to the group the changes I had seen in Hawk's lateral movements and engagement behind, thanks to the work Alexandra and I had been doing with TTouch leg circles and other TTouches on his hind legs. There was a clear improvement in movement, and in his comfort and enthusiasm, especially in lateral work, since we had been doing the TTouches.

Next, Linda and Robyn led the group as we learned some of the basic circular TTouches and practiced them on ourselves and each other. Linda explained that her grandfather had trained racehorses in Russia, and he massaged them to enhance their performance. She added that he was successful, too, because he would not race a horse unless the horse told him it was ready to run. She said, "We can change a horse's behavior by working on the body. We can give the horse a new self image and a new awareness of the body."

She showed us how some parts of the body can be shut down due to fear, and how the non-habitual movements done without fear or force could allow changes to take place. "If you have a problem with an animal, that gives you a chance to teach them something new, and gives them a new way to cooperate with us," Linda said. Again, I heard that critical point—TTouch is a way to connect with your horse and together become a team, a partner in relationship to your horse, and a way to find that deep understanding.

The bodywork TTouches and the leading positions had animal names, which Linda explained were inspired by specific animals she had worked with. The names also helped to give us more clear pictures of what we were doing, such as leading in the elegant elephant, you might imagine that even if you were leading an elephant, you are in a strong leading position, and able to give tiny signals that your horse would easily understand. Later Alexandra reminded me of the earlier difficulties of trying to remember which was leading position one and two when there were no animal names yet to describe it, and we had joked about this when she first began working with me a few months before this clinic.

I was sitting next to someone who had been to a few clinics already, so I was eager to feel her TTouches on my shoulders and back. Linda said the circles had to be one and a quarter, to visualize a clock and start at the six, going around and coming back to the nine, and then move on to another area. We were to "catch the skin" through the person's shirt, and "move the skin gently in a circle and a quarter." Linda said we could act like horses, snorting, pawing, and moving in response to what the person was doing. My partner seemed to do just the kind of touch I wanted, so I was a calm horse, like my first gray mare, Spooky. Around us, other people were pretending to bite and wiggle, in an effort to tell their partner what they needed to adjust.

When it was time for us to talk to our partners, Linda suggested that we try tensing our toes, or holding our breath, or shift our weight to one leg, as we did the TTouches, and see what differences we noticed. We were amazed—not only did it feel uncomfortable when the person was not breathing or was tense, we could easily identify what the person was doing, or not, with their bodies that was causing the discomfort. We all felt sorry for our horses carrying us when unconsciously we had been holding our breath, or tensing a foot or shoulder or wrist, as we were riding, or even when we were grooming them. We also learned from Linda that if were smiling when we are with our horses or riding, that it is nearly impossible to be stiff, offering us one more way to decrease our tension. Now we also know that smiling releases serotonin, also called the "feel good hormone," and these feelings can be transmitted to our animals, increasing their willingness to work with us.

Linda teaching us about the Cobra leading position.

One woman said she was always late running to the barn, was on a schedule to get home, and barely had time to groom her horse. She said she just tossed up the saddle and jumped on, and her horse, she told us, was generally nervous and jumpy under saddle. Linda pointed out that maybe she was the problem—maybe she should take a moment to breathe, to talk calmly to her horse and come into his world, rather than bringing her world to him, and that perhaps he would be less nervous. Later that day, when we brought the horses into the ring to practice the bodywork on them, Robyn worked with this woman and helped her to keep breathing, and to put on the halter with care and respect, instead of rushing breathlessly. Sure enough, the horse came into the ring calmly, looking around at the other horses to see what we were going to be doing.

What are we doing to our horses and our other animals, I wondered, when we approach so much of our time with them like this person, without any awareness of our own impact on them? When I was nervous about a show or a riding lesson, what message was I sending to my horses? And when a horse is continuously handled by an angry person, what are the long-term effects on the horse's nervous system, and indeed, even the other horses nearby? So many of us long for a calm connection to our animals, and without our even realizing it, many of our own issues make that impossible.

A better way to approach our horses every day is to take a moment to do a TTouch Heart Hug, with your hands one on top of the other over your heart as you do a circle and a quarter, and think about how much you love your horse, or something about him that you are grateful for, before you walk into the barn. This connects you to why you have a horse, slows your breathing, and brings you to a place where you can better find a heart synchrony with your horse. This applies to dogs and other animals too; it only takes a moment to do a Heart Hug when you make the shift from your busy work day to time with your pet.

As Oschman documented in his book *Energy Medicine —The Scientific Basis*, the main source of electricity in the body is the electric field of the heart. He reports, "The biomagnetic field of the heart extends indefinitely into space. While its strength diminishes in distance, there is no point at which we can say the field ends." He later adds that devices can pick up the field of the heart at fifteen feet away. With the much larger heart of horses, it is likely their field extends even farther. When we are connected with our animals, we are connected through Sheldrake's morphic field, and through the electric fields of our hearts. TTouch Heart Hugs bring us into this space gently and with respect.

The next day, we worked on leading the horses over obstacles such as ground poles, cones, plywood and plastic, using the wands to give them small signals and practicing the many leading positions, "elegant elephant" when you are by the horse's head, "dingo" when you are near the shoulder and using the wand to stroke his body, "cobra" when you are in front of the horse asking him to take precise steps forward, "the cheetah" with the soft end of the wand up and the line a bit longer, "the eagle" when the lead line is long and you are far to the side of the horse, and "homing pigeon" when a person is on each side of the horse, which is very useful with nervous horses or when you are helping a person begin to feel comfortable with leading on the off side.

At the end of this time, Linda pointed out that all of this could be done without a lead line, using just one or two wands to give the horse signals. I volunteered to try this with Burgers, since I had done some of this with him at home with Alexandra. Even though he was alone in the ring in this new place, he quietly walked and jogged between the two wands over the obstacles, later to be called the Playground for Higher Learning or the Confidence Course. I was amazed at how easy it was to communicate with him what I'd like him to do, and at how clearly he seemed to understand me. It was as if we really were dance partners, working together through the movements of the ballet we shared that afternoon.

"When you change your mind, you can change your horse," Linda said later that day. This is one of the key concepts of her work with animals. I had viewed Burgers as not very smart and not very talented, because that is what my instructor had told me. And more importantly, without my limited thoughts about him, or my riding, he had endless possibilities of improvement. Lendon Gray had opened doors for us by reminding me that every horse can do third level dressage, regardless of breed or conformation. At this Tellington TTouch Training clinic, I was beginning to see that my horse could do more than third level successfully if I simply opened myself to that possibility for him. Everyone in the class echoed Robyn and Linda's words, telling me that Burgers was a very intelligent horse and that he learned very quickly. As my mind was changing, so was my horse.

One might wonder why I didn't see my horse as talented or intelligent, and ask why I didn't speak up for him when I was working with my old instructor. It was because I felt powerless, not empowered. This came from a system of riding instruction that I had participated in for over twenty years, where the students ride in circles around the instructor doing what they were told—pull here, heels down, sit up, close the outside rein, and on and on, which limited my ability to *feel* when and why these changes were required.

My many lessons with Sally Swift, originator of Centered Riding, and the work at this two week Tellington TTouch Training clinic, would help me learn how to feel my horse under me, and feel my own body—was I straight, was I even, was I still or moving, what was happening under the ball of my foot, what could I see around me when I was riding—and this self-awareness is what led to empowerment in my riding. This made me into the kind of horse owner and rider who would be able to tell an instructor, or a vet or a farrier when something I knew was wrong was happening to my horse. This empowerment allowed me to become engaged in conversations about my horse's welfare, instead of being a victim of other people's opinions. Everyone who has a horse should have the courage to ask why, to stop working with an instructor, to find a different vet or farrier, or even to find a new boarding facility whenever the health and happiness of the horse or rider is compromised.

And most importantly, becoming a self-aware, empowered rider is what allowed me to find what I most wanted from riding—the connection between my horse and me that would allow us to dance together under saddle, doing free work, riding without a bridle, or riding through thick woods without a trail, seeing what we would discover together as I let my horse choose the path we would take, and even more, to choose the path we took in every aspect of our relationship together.

Practitioners Sandy Rakowitz and Marcy Baer using homing pigeon leading position as Linda observes.

Chapter 12

The Dance of Freedom
Riding Free

Burgers and me doing a dressage demonstration riding bridle-less in a wooden neckring at an equine expo.

"Ask me to show you poetry in motion and I will show you a horse."

— Author Unknown

My new connection with Burgers and Hawk was best realized at the clinic when I rode my horses without a bridle. Linda demonstrated the steps to ride without a bridle, first with a lindel (a special type of bitless sidepull bridle), then a rope around the horse's neck with a person still walking next to him with a wand, and finally, riding with a wooden ring around the horse's neck. (A few years later, we began to use lariat rope circles instead that were lighter and easier to hold.) When it was our turn to ride without a bridle, someone took off Burgers' bridle, he shook his head and neck, licked his lips, and stretched his whole top line. We set off at a walk, navigating the turns of the labyrinth and other ground exercises set up in the ring. Next we practiced halts on the rail, and then it was time to trot. On the second long side, Burgers exploded into a brilliant extended trot with more elevation in his hind legs than he'd ever had. He smartly collected in the corner with tiny signals of the ring against his neck and from my seat. I smiled with happiness as he did lovely transitions of collected and extended trot and canter, even a light and rhythmic canter pirouette, all without a bridle. And most of his lead changes were clean without the bridle. Even though for years I had ridden my horses in a halter and lead line, I had never thought it possible to give them such clear and subtle cues without a bridle, nor had I known the joy and freedom bridle-less riding brought to my horses and me.

Throughout the first week of my Tellington TTouch Training classes, we learned about bodywork and ground exercises, and reviewed the philosophy of the Tellington Training Method. During the second week, we were focusing on riding. Linda began the clinic by explaining that riding is the art of communication between horse and rider. I thought back to her earlier question—do we ride to get a horse on the bit, or because we want to dance with our horses? Just as ballroom dancers share subtle communications with one another during a tango, we communicate with our bodies, breath, mind, and spirit when we are riding. Those moments of lightness and connection to the horse that every rider loves—those moments are why we ride.

When Robyn and Linda introduced Burgers and me to rest of the participants, some who had come just for this week, and watched me riding him, they pointed out the gap between what I was trying to tell him and what he was able to understand. I was not sitting evenly, which made my seat aids unclear. My hands were moving and so he could not "hear" clearly the small signals that would have more effectively prepared him for transitions and more collected gaits. As my balance improved and my aids became more subtle, we all witnessed the results of my changes reflected in Burgers' improved balance in extended trot, as well as in the quicker compression of his body going from extended or medium canter to collected canter. Without my unclear aids, he was transformed.

Informed by the military training of her first husband, Linda saw value in having us ride either in pairs or four abreast as we changed gaits and circled across the arena. It was easy to see during these exercises when your signals to your horse were ineffective as he lost pace with the others in the group, or did not halt in line with the others. Burgers, glad to be next to a horse that was not his brother trying to bite him, enjoyed these exercises and excelled at them. I could really feel our partnership improving as we were a pair working together within a bigger group of riders and horses.

Several experiences that helped my riding a great deal didn't even take place on a horse. We sat in pairs facing each other, and Linda and Robyn showed us how to put bridles over our heads; one person held the reins like a rider, and the other person gently held the bit to be the "horse." We used a soft back-and-forth motion to replicate the feeling of a walk while riding a horse. Again we tried tightening our toes or holding our breath, and we noticed what happened to the movement in the bit and the reins. We held the reins many different ways, thumbs up, down, sideways, with tight fingers and loose fingers, and we tried using different kinds of signals to ask for a turn, a half halt, or a halt. It was incredible even sitting in a chair to feel how significantly your balance was compromised when your "rider" did things that many of us commonly did while riding such as holding our breath or gripping with our knees.

Burgers and me jumping with a neck ring at an expo.

We did this for over an hour, changing partners, finding out how different peoples' hands felt, how different bits felt. It became clear that the snaffle bit was no one's favorite, in spite of all of the prior teaching we'd had about it being gentle on the horse. We much preferred a straight bar, as the signals from it were clearer, a smaller signal was needed, and it was easier to stay in balance. Linda also let us try the lindel compared to another type of bitless bridle, and the roller bit (also called the TEAM training bit then). The roller bit—which, although it looks big and heavy, is similar to a western bit with two reins on each side—was nearly everyone's favorite. It moved with your body when you were being the "horse," and it was much easier to stay in balance. A tiny signal, barely the letting out of a breath, was all that was needed to communicate a halt, a turn, or a half halt. Later, when we tried the lindel and the roller bits on our horses when we were riding, everyone could see the greater freedom of movement in the horses, and in my dressage horses there was a marked improvement in the motion in their spines and hips with the roller bit.

The roller bit, also called the Tellington Training bit, has a copper roller in the port and curved shanks that move where they attach to the bit. The bar in the mouth gives that connection we all liked, as opposed to the "bendiness" of the snaffle. The mobility in the shanks translates from the horse's jaw and head, down through the spinal column to release tension in the body and hips. In the *Staying in TTouch* newsletter, Joyce Harman, DVM, MRCVS, "theorizes that the rollerbit is effective due to its release of the tongue, temporomandibular joint (TMJ) and hyoid bone. The high port frees the tongue, and the roller encourages tongue softness and movement." With my background as a physical therapist (including structural mechanics, detailed anatomical knowledge as a craniosacral therapist, and study of biomechanics), I concur with Dr. Harman. Additionally, the movement and freedom in the TMJ and temporal bones—through their connection to the sacrum, sacroiliac joints, and hips via the spinal cord and vertebral column—can improve freedom of movement in the hindquarters. I believe this then allows the horse to better "come through" from behind, improving balance and collection.

As Linda noted, "When one part of the body becomes tight, the tension extends to the rest of the body." The bit encourages a rounder frame in the horse and is therefore good with ewe-necked, hollow, or strung-out horses, as it softens the back and encourages soft flexion at the poll. The bit proved to be very important in helping Burgers to develop clean lead changes behind, as it released tension in his lower back. I am certain it also freed up tension in my own lower back.

In fact, Hilary Clayton, a renowned researcher of equine biomechanics, has taken X-rays of how bits fit in horses' mouths. Linda has used this information to suggest that the roller bit is the best for not interfering with the tongue and is less likely to injure the mouth. "The bit needs to be properly fitted on the horse, which is not the same as with other bits," Linda explained as she adjusted a bridle on Burgers to try the bit. It was quite a different feel for me as a rider, and it would be wise for anyone using a rollerbit to get help from an experienced Tellington TTouch Method practitioner.

We also used long ropes around a person's body and had another person "drive" them around the arena over ground poles, in the labyrinth, and around corners. We did this with our eyes closed, while the person behind us could not use words to tell us where to go. The results of this exercise were unexpected. It was remarkable to experience how lost you felt as the "horse" when the person on the other end of the ropes had little or no contact, letting the ropes droop down. Someone who pulled hard, strangely, felt better. And when you had that ideal contact, all of us were able to confidently trot forward, giggling like children pretending to be a horse in perfect connection with the other half of our pair.

Burgers shown here wearing the roller bit (the Tellington training bit).

In another experience of being a horse, we held halters over our heads and used the Tellington Method lead lines, which are long nylon ribbons with chain or rope at the end that we attached to the halter in various positions to see how it affected our balance. We were amazed to find that when we attached the lead line to the ring in the bottom of the halter, it pulled our heads down, and for some us, it actually hurt the backs of our necks or our lower backs. Attaching the line to the side ring felt incredibly balanced, and all of the signals from the person leading felt clearer. We attached the chain across the noseband on the halter, and it did not feel at all how I expected. It felt light and balanced, and I also realized how terrible it is when someone yanks down sharply with a chain over a horse's nose—it would put him out of balance and make him raise his head, thereby engaging the fight-or-flight posture and response that people who are pulling are trying to discourage in the first place.

With the Tellington Method leading positions, the chain became comfortable and a clear line of communication from the person to the horse was established. I barely had to turn the chain forward half an inch to let a horse know to come forward, or turn it slightly back to ask him to "please halt." Clearly, this points to the fact that knowledge is indeed power—a knowledge of Tellington TTouch Training as a better way to communicate with your horse is all you need to ask a thousand-pound horse to "please halt."

One morning, a person in the clinic was lunging her horse in the indoor ring, since the turnouts were small and muddy and she felt he needed exercise. Linda calmly walked up to her and took the line, asking for the group's attention. We gathered around and she asked, "How many of you lunge your horses regularly?" A few hands went up. Feeling like maybe I should lunge my horses, though they didn't seem to like it, I shrank into the back of the group. Linda asked people to offer reasons why they lunged their horses, with answers ranging from to "get the bucks out," to "exercise him," or to "warm him up." Linda explained that lunging is very hard on the joints in the legs and does not teach the horse about balance. She added that it was far better to long line the horse and walk next to him or behind him, avoiding the small circles so often used when lunging a horse. Lunging in a big oval, with the horse responding to signals rather than blindly bucking and running in circles, can work if you don't have the experience to ground drive. "There are so many more possibilities to teach your horse about balance and how to carry himself when you are ground driving," Linda pointed out.

Linda had told me so clearly what my horses, first Goblin and Richard, and then Burgers, had been saying—that lunging was not good for them, and they did not want to do it. I had instead believed what the local trainers and books suggested, even if it was not what my horses needed. I could have persisted and taught my horses to lunge perfectly, but I was glad that I had soon given up on lunging my horses, and was now relieved that their legs would stay stronger as a result.

That morning, we brought some horses into the ring who were used to being harnessed to pull a carriage, including Burgers. There are many steps to familiarize a horse with ropes around his body, but on this first day Linda wanted people to feel comfortable holding the long reins and the wand, and feel safe moving next to and behind the horse on the ground. Again, we walked over ground poles, through the labyrinth, around cones, and trotted with the horse in a semi-circle around us at the short ends of the ring. I was so impressed at how much Burgers had learned long lining with me and Alexandra Kurland. He was a good teacher, helping people feel safe as they learned this process. It was clear to everyone how much more balanced the horses were in long lines than on a lunge line. No need for side reins, or any of the other equipment I had avoided anyway when we were using long lines. Linda had shown me what Goblin, Richard, and Burgers had been saying to me—lunging is a bad idea, isn't there something else we could be doing?

Long lining was riding from the ground. It was yet another valuable riding experience we had that week without even riding. And everyone's riding was far better at the end of the clinic, more sensitive hands, a better, more balanced seat, better posture in the saddle, and a stirrup length that was ideal for the rider.

I had come to these clinics thinking that Burgers did not listen to me, when all along the problem was that I did not know how to listen to him. I was not hearing so many of the messages he had for me about why my riding was limiting him.

Chapter 13

Precision Dance Steps
Riding With Olympian Lendon Gray

Burgers with me riding as we begin a half pass in a Fourth level dressage test. Photo by Dorothy Barnard.

"Great dancers are not great because of their technique, they are great because of their passion."

— Martha Graham

I returned from my two weeks of Tellington Method training with renewed enthusiasm for this new way I wanted to work with animals, certain that I would pursue becoming a certified Tellington TTouch practitioner. I wanted to bring this work to my riding students and my fellow dressage riders. I continued to work with Alexandra Kurland, training some of the farm's young Morgans, and worked with Burgers on more advanced FEI level dressage, such as the canter pirouette, piaffe and passage, and tempe lead changes. Hawk benefitted especially from my improved riding, advancing quickly through his training. Burgers took more time to develop the correct muscles and strength to progress in dressage because I had made some mistakes along the way before working with Alexandra and Linda Tellington-Jones. Soon after the clinics, I trailered the two horses to New York state for lessons with Olympian Lendon Gray.

As I tacked up Burgers for my first lesson with Lendon, I noticed how quiet everyone was in the barn, nervously doing their jobs cleaning tack, stalls, and horses to the meticulous standards Lendon demanded. Someone whispered to me, "Your first lesson here? You'll being in tears in a few minutes. It happens to everyone. Try not to let it get to you." I nodded in response, and watched a slim young woman lead a bay gelding into the ring, lunge line neatly folded in one hand, the stirrups securely fastened to the saddle. A few moments later as I was adjusting Burgers' girth, I heard a loud screech from the ring, "Are you trying to cripple my horses?!!!"

Giving Burgers a pat, I inched towards the arena door to see what was going on. The woman was lunging the horse, who was bucking and leaping, pulling the line from the woman's hands, nearly getting tangled. Lendon yelled again, "You are crippling my horses!" and marched into the center of the arena, pulling the lunge line from the alarmed student's hands. At the top of her voice she explained that trotting horses in tight circles will damage the ligaments and tendons in their legs and contribute to muscular imbalances that make the straightness required for the horse to do aspects of dressage even more challenging. She added that allowing a horse to leap and buck only added to the myriad reasons why she frowned on lunging. She instructed the woman to get long lines on the horse and to return when she could do something useful. With her face red and shoulders slumped over, the student steadied the gelding and returned to the exit of the ring, walking down the aisle next to us. She mumbled to the other student that she had no idea what she was supposed to do—just get on this rambunctious horse and get hurt? She couldn't just turn him loose in the ring; she had already been scolded for that. The other student shrugged his shoulders and said nothing.

I thought back to Richard, my Arabian, running about with the lunge line streaming behind him, and Burgers, who never did take to the idea of lunging. What had my horses been telling me? They had been saying exactly what Linda Tellington-Jones had shown me, and what Lendon was telling this student. I had not known how to *listen* to my horses until I had worked with Alexandra and Linda Tellington-Jones. I knew my lessons with Lendon would be one more step in understanding how to listen to my horses.

I then heard Lendon's voice booming, "Don't I have an outside lesson here now?" Guessing she meant me, I made the final adjustments on Burgers' bridle, smoothed out the bun in my hair and gave my boots a final wipe with the towel, and led Burgers into the ring. Lendon immediately gave me a compliment, "Well at least you know how to present a well turned-out horse. At the next Olympics, you can be my groom." I led Burgers around the ring, letting him see the big doors to the woods and the outdoor arena, remembering what Janet had told me about Lendon—she can seem mean, but everything she says or does is because she cares so much about the horses and their well-being. She felt that an incorrect rider created a struggling, unbalanced horse. Lendon had demonstrated her brilliance in training with her unexpected success with a Connemara pony named Seldom Seen, and with her Olympic horse, Later On, still sound and competing in young rider classes.

I led Burgers over to the mounting block and got into the saddle. He strode off with his big long gait, and Lendon gave me another compliment, "Well, you haven't ruined the walk yet so you must be doing something right." Burgers had a good four-beat walk, something I had learned from Linda Tellington-Jones and Max Gahwyler. I thought back to Max's lessons teaching me how to feel the horse's hindquarters move under me rhythmically as we did walk pirouettes and walk half pass. He had me close my eyes and tell him which hoof was off the ground, and even where it was in the stride pattern with great precision. Lendon next said, "I think he has a longer stride than his brother," comparing him to Janet's Morgan Action. No tears yet, maybe my lesson would be different.

Burgers always floated in his medium and extended trot gaits. Photo by Dorothy Barnard.

As we moved into the rising trot, Lendon's loud voice boomed, "Stop moving your hands!" I tried to steady my hands, opening and bending my elbow as I had practiced with Alexandra. "Why are your hands still moving?! Keep them still!" Lendon screamed. I recalled what Janet had said—Lendon is a great rider and she has a hard time understanding why once she tells you how to do something better, you can't just do it better. I tried balancing one pinky finger against Burgers' withers to try to steady my hands. It worked enough that Lendon said, "That's more like it." It would take a new saddle, a better seat, and months of riding while holding a crop between my thumbs before my hands would really be anywhere near what one could call "still." But this was a start.

At the end of the lesson, Lendon patted Burgers, telling me how good his lateral work was, saying, "I can have some fun working with you." So far, so good, with no tears.

I quickly changed horses, and led Hawk into the ring. Lendon remarked that he looked like he could be related to Burgers and Action, which he was not. She watched us walk, trot and canter, making corrections to my position. She walked next to us, making adjustments with the reins and tapping Hawk to improve his shoulder movements in half pass at the walk. At the end of the lesson, she stood next to us and told me, "Sally, this is a good horse."

"Yes," I replied. "I'm lucky to have found him. Not many Morgans are this size or move this well."

"You're not understanding me, Sally," she said. "This is a really good horse. I mean for international competition, he is a very good horse. He is one of the best horses I've seen."

I said "Thank you," feeling sudden great responsibility to care for and train such a good horse. I was glad to have the help of the best people in the equestrian world to assist me, Linda Tellington-Jones, Sally Swift, Alexandra Kurland, and Lendon Gray.

Chapter 14

Purpose in the Dance
Applying the Lessons From the Clinics

Thanks to my first weeks of training with Linda Tellington-Jones, my horses dramatically improved their show results.

"Spiritual (riding) is the 'feel,' and the belief in something greater existing between you and your horse. You and your horse will become inspiring and inspired competitors, who move as one being."

— Linda Tellington-Jones, *Dressage with Mind, Body and Soul*

We went to a few practice shows that winter, including one at Millbrook held just after a big snowstorm. There was no ring to warm up in; my horses were doing some fairly difficult tests, and I knew I had to figure out something to prepare them for the show ring. It was too icy to walk in the driveway, so I used my end of one of the barn aisles to do what I could. I used my Tellington Method training to ask my horses to do a few steps of walk, collected walk, back, release, asking with the wand to move one leg, then another, then back. I asked for a few steps of piaffe in hand. When a stall became empty, I led them in and out of the stall, using the entrance as I would an "L" in a labyrinth to ask them to step under themselves. A woman next to me thought I was really silly, leading my horses in and out of a stall a few times. But my work was a success. My horses each went into the ring and did their tests, bright, supple, light in the hand, and quickly responding to gait and tempo changes. They won all of their classes that cold day. And I learned a valuable lesson—that my Tellington TTouch training was indeed what I needed to help my horses to do their best and feel their best.

My success made me more creative at home with my horses that winter. I had been learning from Alexandra how to work Burgers in hand, using my wand to give him signals, and it was a next step to work with him free in the indoor, with two wands or one wand, asking him to come forward, change gaits, trot over poles or jumps, and follow me in the labyrinth as I walked backwards in front of him. I could feel our connection growing, as I really only needed to picture what we would do next and he was there with me. I even worked him around the ring using my arms and hands to give him signals. He loved this new game, big ears straight up every time I took off his halter in the ring with a Confidence Course set up, looking at me to see what was next. I had developed a relationship with him over so many years, and the freedom of playing together without a halter or lead line over the Confidence Course was a demonstration of the deep bond we had formed together.

There are many steps involved in teaching a horse to be comfortable next to and walking over plastic using TTouch.

That winter, I continued to bring the two horses to Lendon Gray for lessons, and my riding progressed. I also continued to work with Alexandra, who helped me feel in my body all that Lendon was pleading with me to correct. As much as Lendon was demanding, I knew that it was because she loved horses so much that she could not bear to see them ridden badly. By the time it was spring, I was able to take some time from my teaching job at the boarding school to go to another Tellington TTouch Training clinic. After that one, I would only need to attend one more to become a practitioner.

During my third Tellington Method clinic, I was discovering more about how Tellington TTouch Training improves a horse's ability to learn. Linda said, "Repetition is not learning." I thought back to the many riders I'd known who would try for twenty minutes to get one correct lead, and then stop for the day, thinking the horse had finally learned. To my mind, the horse had spent twenty minutes not enjoying the canter, likely being out of balance at best and, at worst, struggling with an ill fitting saddle and poor farrier work or lameness, and did not learn anything the rider had wanted. I knew enough Tellington TTouch work at this point to understand that if a horse is not doing what you are asking, then you need to look at why—saddle fit, your balance, the footing, his body pain or imbalances—beyond thinking he is just stubborn.

By taking the slow steps for a horse to navigate our ground-work course, we allowed the horses to learn, to discover that plastic wouldn't hurt them, and that the sound of their hooves on a piece of plywood was nothing to be afraid of. This work translated easily to helping horses walk calmly into a trailer, hearing the sound of their hooves on the floorboards, or to walking calmly next to things very close to them once they had walked between plastic walls. Once a horse had done Tellington TTouch Training, he had learned a different way of being in the world, a place of calm assessment rather than reaction and fear.

Only a month later, I returned again to New Hampshire for the final Tellington Method clinic required for me to become a practitioner. At this clinic, we looked more closely at how to use your body language to communicate with your horse, and how to give them signals that they could understand. This included the concept of changing your approach when you are teaching a horse new things if he does not seem to understand, rather than fighting with him. An aspect of Feldenkrais work that I knew from Alexandra was to "chunk down" the exercise you are trying to do so that the horse can understand it, and you can better help him. For instance, if a horse is afraid to walk over a big sheet of plastic, we learned to fold it and make it thinner, or to make an open space between two pieces of plastic for him to walk through, or to have him follow a calm horse over the plastic. We learned how to look at a situation to find a way to make smaller steps where the horse and rider could be successful.

We also learned the importance of the words we use to describe our horses. Rather than saying, "He is afraid of water," we shifted that to, "In the past, he has been afraid of water," as a way to open up the possibility of change. This tied in the idea of intention, clearly picturing what you want to have the horse do. We especially learned to do this in the earlier clinics with regard to asking the horse to lower his head. At this clinic, it was becoming clear to me that picturing a clear intention when I worked with a horse made a big difference in how the horse responded.

Temple Grandin wrote in her 2005 book *Animals in Translation—Using the Mysteries of Autism to Decode Animal Behavior* that she believes animals think in pictures, based on her experiences as an autistic person who also thinks in pictures. She writes, "I think animals are conscious, too. Do animals see pictures of food when they're hungry the way I do? Do animals see a picture of water when they're thirsty? We know they have constant mental activity of some kind, because their EEGs aren't that different from ours. I expect the content of their consciousness is mostly pictures and probably sounds, too. Animals might even have conscious 'thoughts' of smells, touch, or taste." In 1990, at this clinic, using pictures and clear thoughts to show your horse what you'd like him to do was revolutionary, and the now-popular research and literature on the power of intention was in its early development.

Linda emphasized that we speak to our horses (and dogs, as we were spending time working with some dogs, also) in full sentences, saying "please" and "thank you" when we asked them to do something. The sentences helped us make a clear picture, and it seemed that being polite made a big difference in the animals' willingness to try what we were asking. In 2015, dog trainer Victoria Stillwell wrote about the impact of using open ended statements instead of the short, quick "cues" people have typically used in teaching their dogs. She found that dogs were more likely to do what was asked, and they were more relaxed than if they were constantly "working" for a treat. Linda's suggestion to use statements with polite words emphasized asking in a tone that is similar to what Stilwell describes. Simply speak to our animals the same way we would speak to our close friends.

Linda suggested that we smile as well, which made our instruction to our animals seem like a pleasant request rather than a demand. Current research now describes changes in our body chemistry, such as the release of "feel good" chemicals oxytocin and serotonin when we smile. As Brian Hare writes in *The Genius of Dogs: How Dogs Are Smarter Than You Think,* "One hormone that seems to be particularly affected in our relationship with our dogs is oxytocin. Oxytocin is transmitted from the brain directly into the bloodstream and along nerve fibers to the nervous system. Sometimes called the "hug hormone," oxytocin is what makes you feel good when you are touched by a loved one, get a massage, or enjoy a good meal." Recent research has shown that touching an animal releases oxytocin, also termed the trust hormone, in both the animal and the person. This hormone helps us feel close to our animals. It is the hormone that helps mothers form a bond with their infants. When we look deeply into the eyes of our dogs, or horses, the release of oxytocin is what makes us feel a connection, like we are hugging our animals with our eyes, and they are hugging us. The longer our mutual gaze, the greater the release of oxytocin, and the longer we want to continue our gaze.

I had another experience outside of this clinic that left me perplexed and wary. A participant said that she had a psychic friend who would be visiting her, and that she could do readings for people if they were interested. I thought it would be useful, so I signed up. The woman, French Canadian and Native American in her tradition, used playing cards to answer your questions. She pulled over the seven of clubs when I asked about the horses. She said, "You seem like a person who can hear the truth, so I'm going to tell you. Your black horse is going to die, and there is nothing you can do. It is his destiny. It will be when the leaves come down from the trees."

"What?" I asked, "Can't I do something to help him?" She offered that I could feed him more carrots because they contain the essence of the element gold, but that it really wouldn't help.

"What will Burgers do? Will he be all right,?" I asked.

"He will see him so he will be all right," she replied.

I was shocked, but not completely disturbed by this news. Hawk had struggled with health issues, deficiencies in minerals, tying up, and as a true black horse, he shared a genetic signature that predisposed him to some of the issues some chestnut horses have. I discussed the psychic's news with the friend who had invited her to our group, and she said maybe it is really about transformation, as sometimes that is what death is. This boosted my spirits. Yet somehow, I felt this woman had warned me, and I was grateful that if something would happen to Hawk, I would have had some preparation for it, thanks to her news. I went home from the clinic, and continued my riding and showing as usual, keeping a close eye on Hawk and feeding him bags and bags of carrots.

Practitioners who assisted Linda (far right) at a large Northeast equestrian expo (I am second from the left).

Chapter 15

Bringing Understanding to the Dance
Every Horse and Rider Team Is Unique

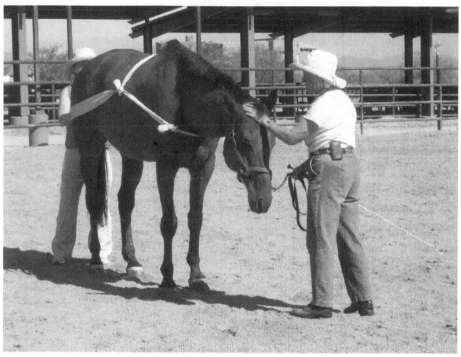

Linda Tellington-Jones demonstrating TTouch at a clinic. The horse is in an ace wrap to bring connection through his body and increase awareness of his hindquarters.

" ... and I whispered to the horse: trust no one in whose eyes you don't see yourself reflected as an equal."

— Don Vincenzo Giobbe

That summer, one of my first Tellington Method clients was a lovely woman with an expensive Dutch horse imported from Europe. She kept the horse beautifully groomed, but he was chronically "off," so she asked me to help her learn to do some bodywork with him. She would ride once or twice around the indoor, maybe not even trot, and dismount, telling me that her horse had "thirty-two" good steps, or some other specific number each day. When I began to teach her how to do the bodywork, I found that she

117

was stiff in her shoulders and had a hard time relaxing enough to do the TTouches, so I did a lot of work on her body, standing in the stall next to her horse. Still, it was hard for her to be less tense when she was working on her horse. I did work on all of his legs, and we found a few areas of tension in his body. She had a very nice saddle that fit the horse well, and she had been riding one of the young Morgans at the farm on the days when her horse was too sore.

After I started to work with her and her horse, he was able to go progressively more soundly, yet she continued to feel more comfortable riding the Morgan, riding her horse even less of the time. She stopped reporting her horse's number of good steps to us, yet she still rode him only a few times around the ring. One night, when she and I were the only ones in the barn, I found her in the stall trying to do TTouches on her horse. I slid open the door and said, "How are you doing?"

I could see tears in her eyes. She said, "I'm having a hard time, such a hard time." Trembling, she told me a long story about a terrible riding accident that she had coming down a hill over a cross country jump when it was getting dark one evening a few years ago. Her life had fallen apart as a result of that, with a long hospital stay, family issues, a divorce, financial issues—and all she really wanted now was to be able to ride. She told me that she took long trips into the city for counseling to help her with her fear of riding, even these many years later. She wanted her horse to be sound, she said, but she was also terrified of riding him.

I realized then that her wonderful horse, whom she spent so much time with, had some deep soul contract with her. He would limp sometimes, and then she could stop riding that day. She would never have to take him to a show, or over jumps, and yet she would still be able to ride him just enough around the indoor arena. The work I had been doing with him was making him sound, and her confidence was growing with her rides on the little Morgan, but neither she nor her horse was ready for anything to change. I am certain her horse could feel the tension mounting in her body as she rode around the ring, and that translated to his limping.

Quietly, I said to her, "Horses come into our lives for many different reasons, and you don't have to go to shows just because you have a show horse, and you don't have to ride for an hour if a few minutes is enough. I think you are very brave to be riding at all, and I admire your courage to do all that you are doing." We hugged, tucked in our horses, and walked together down the long barn aisle. We never discussed this again, and when she would ask me from the arena if her horse looked a little stiff or sore, I'd always say, "I think it's fine to get off of him now."

A few years later, I again saw the importance of being neutral in both my craniosacral and my TTouch work. Neutral is being open to all options, not judging what you see, realizing that you don't see the whole picture—just as I had not seen everything within the relationship between my client and her limping horse until our conversation. I had organized a Tellington TTouch Training clinic at a farm near me. One of Linda's earliest demonstrations was in my area, so many horse caretakers had signed up for the clinic to refresh their knowledge of the work. One horse and rider pair were coming from New Jersey. The horse, named Calvin, was a recent purchase from an auction, a Thoroughbred racehorse who did not make it at the track. The sensitive bay gelding had been difficult to load onto the commercial shipping van to come to the clinic, and it took several experienced TTouch practitioners to help him leave the van calmly. His person, a somewhat experienced horsewoman, was a bit nervous around him, but she really loved him and was committed to doing whatever was required to help him recover from his past and become a nice, quiet horse for her.

During the first morning of the clinic, I arrived at the barn a few hours before the start. Edie Jane Eaton, a TTouch instructor from Canada, was teaching the clinic, as Linda had to re-schedule at the last minute. The barn owner met me when I arrived to let me know that the bay gelding was showing signs of colic, sweating, with an elevated heart and respiration rate. I asked a few of the clinic participants to take turns walking the horse, as he was determined to violently roll, due to pain and discomfort. The barn owner had already called a local vet who did acupuncture as well as Western medicine. Edie Jane and I showed the group how to do TTouch ear work especially ear slides, to access acupuncture points for digestion, respiration, and reproduction, and to reduce the horse's pain. Some of the women walked along next to Calvin working with his ears, which brought him some relief. Edie Jane and I found a big towel to do belly lifts, bringing the towel up against the horse's barrel and then slowly releasing, to help relieve gas and reduce pain. The horse could only stand still for a few moments for this work.

By the time the vet arrived, Calvin was in the main arena, resting, at times lying on his side and pawing, but no longer violently rolling and kicking out. Several people were taking turns with the ear work and his respiration was nearly normal, although he was close to going into shock, with a cold sweat and chills. His new caretaker had come prepared with many blankets and coolers even though it was early summer, so she covered him to keep him warm.

It was very hard for Calvin to stand and tolerate the usual veterinary interventions for colic, the tube up his nose, shots for pain and muscle relaxers, and an exam. While the vet was doing his work, the women doing the TTouch ear work had to stop for a few minutes. The horse's pain level increased, and again, he went down, violently kicking. The vet inserted an acupuncture needle for pain in the horse's nose, and he quieted enough for people to resume the ear work. By this time, the people in the group were feeling the intensity of the situation and loudly pleading with the horse to "try to stay with us" and "hang in there." His new rider was pacing in the aisle, thinking how much she had grown to love this horse in the few weeks since she had brought him to her farm in New Jersey.

I was standing off to the side, away from the group, with a Feldenkrais practitioner and an animal communicator. It was a bit surreal, quiet in our sunlit corner by the big door of the arena, watching the drama surrounded by the loud voices near the horse pleading with him to stay alive. The animal communicator slowly turned to the two of us in the doorway and said, "You know, the horse is really feeling grateful that you two are holding a space for him to make his own decision now. He is really struggling with life and death, deciding which path to take, and he needs to be appreciated for his own choices right now. He knows the new person will take really good care of him, but his life until this time has been so full of pain and misery, both for him and the horses around him at the track, that he does not even know what it is to have good care and be free of pain. He sees that the horses at this farm are relaxed and happy, and he has never been in a place like this."

I was struck by her words. I indeed knew that whatever happened with him, we could take care of him. I also was trying not to be attached to any particular outcome for him, whether he lived or died, as I knew the road to his recovery from being at the track could be challenging. I just wished him freedom from pain, in this moment and in the future.

I walked over to check-in with his rider, and gently told her about what the animal communicator had mentioned. She was relieved, as she too had been unattached to the outcome, if he lived or died, uncertain if she had the skills to help him become a safe horse for her. She was also feeling a little guilty for not wanting to plead with Calvin to live as the others were doing. The words of the animal communicator helped her see that in fact, her mixed feelings about his struggle helped him have a sense of freedom to make his own choices.

Within an hour, the horse made an incredible recovery, surprising even the vet with the improvements he made, passing manure, standing comfortably, munching some hay. Over the week of the clinic, Calvin became a calm and trusting horse with his new person, and with many of the clinic participants. He navigated the labyrinth with confidence, and his rider rode him at the walk without a bridle on the last day of the clinic as I walked next to her. Calvin went on to be a perfect horse for her to ride in hunter shows, with no jumping, and she kept him for the rest of his life, just as she had promised him when she rescued him.

As much as we assume life and soundness is the "right" choice for our animals, it is critical in my work as a craniosacral practitioner and TTouch practitioner to not have attachments to outcomes, or to otherwise impose my will on another person or animal. We all walk our own paths in life, and it's vitally important to respect the choices of others.

The Dance of Interspecies Communication
Hawk's Angel Wings

LHN Night Hawk at one of his last shows at the Millbrook Equestrian Center in 1990.

"The only way to make sense out of change is to plunge into it, move with it, and join the dance."

—Alan W. Watts

In the early summer of 1990, Jack and I decided that we should no longer be married. We tried to be polite about it, but we had a few months of great difficulty before cementing our strong friendship that has lasted nearly thirty years. We had to decide what to do with our animals. Of course, the horses were mine, but my income was not enough to support them and I was facing the choice of selling one of them unless I could find a solution. We had two corgis then, Molly and Winston. Winston came to live with me, and Molly lived happily with Jack, and then Ron and Jack, for the rest of her life. Winston moved with me to an apartment in Connecticut, where he befriended the poodles across the courtyard, and accompanied me giving riding lessons and demonstrations.

Jack and I were scheduled to continue our teaching duties at the school in the fall. I tried to keep up with my summer show schedule, bringing the two horses to New England Morgan and the many dressage shows in the area, while they were boarding at the Morgan farm. By this time, I'd had a banner made advertising Tellington TTouch Training clinics with me, as I wanted to promote to the other riders that my horses' successes were a result of Tellington TTouch Training. During the warm-up time in the crowded rings, my horses, though perfectly braided and advanced in their training, went unnoticed next to the big imported warmbloods. When I came back from the show secretary carrying trophies and blue ribbons to pin on my Tellington TTouch Training banner, people then noticed my horses and came to ask me about the work.

In spite of the stress in my life, our show season was going well, and I was working with private clients teaching Tellington Method work. My parents made the trip from New Jersey to watch me and the horses at the big Millbrook dressage show, where my horses had some of their best rides, winning most of their classes. My parents had never been to a big dressage show, and they were impressed with the formality, the nice luncheon options provided at the show, and how the horses seemed to be dancing in their freestyles.

Yet it was a difficult time for all of us, and in early August, on a rainy day, I brought the two horses to a big show at a friend's farm in New York state, where they had freestyle classes. My horses had been doing fairly well that day, but I was not really connecting with them. Lendon had coached me in the warm-up for my classes, which helped. At the end of day, the freestyle classes began. Burgers was the first of my rides, and he did a beautiful job, ears pricking up when his music began, his legs moving to the rhythm of his music in the ring. I trotted him back to the trailer and tacked up Hawk for his ride. It was warm and gray, and raining in earnest. We did our ride, not with any real mistakes, but Hawk just felt tired. Burgers won the class, and Hawk was third, the only time he did not win a freestyle. I felt like I had let him down.

Eager to get back to our dry barn at the Morgan farm, I loaded the horses in the trailer and Winston climbed into the front of the Suburban to his usual place on the floor. I made one last check on the horses, again hooking Hawk's chest bar closed, since he loved to undo it, and securing the side doors. We set off for the hour ride home. I could feel the Suburban sliding around on the road, and kept reminding myself to drive slower and slower. I got to a winding back and forth road down a big long hill, and as I tried to steer the Suburban on the switch-back in the road, I lost steering and brakes. At that time, cars did not have anti-locking brakes. The Suburban was hydroplaning down the hill. I shifted it to lower gears and hit the emergency brake to try to stop it. I pumped the brake. All I could do was try to steer it towards a big tree behind the guard rail on the opposite side of the road. I could feel the trailer pushing the truck. We hit the tree with a loud bang as glass from the windshield rained down on me. A towel had fallen from the seat, protecting Winston.

I was all right, except for hitting and bending the steering wheel with my nose and getting a deep cut in my chin. I ran to the trailer and opened Burgers' door—he looked out at me. Next to him, Hawk lay on the floor of the trailer, his chin resting on the pile of hay. His chest bar was open and I knew that was not good. I crawled into the trailer under Burgers and held Hawk's neck in my arms; I felt him sink heavily into me as his spirit left his body. I looked back at him, his blue show sheet covered with leaves from a branch that had come through the trailer window on his side of the trailer. The psychic's words echoed in my mind, "When the leaves fall from the trees..." I held Hawk's head, thanking him for his great beauty and all that he had taught me, doing some TTouches on his head and stroking his ears. There was no time to cry, as I had to get Burgers out of the trailer and keep Winston safe.

I crawled back out. Fortunately a man had stopped with a cow trailer. He helped me wedge open the back door of the trailer to get Burgers out. And at that moment, a woman from a nearby farm stopped with her big trailer and offered to take Burgers and Winston back to her farm, along with my precious show tack. By that time, the ambulance had come to bring me to the hospital where I was able to call the owners of the Morgan farm. They brought my trailer home with Hawk in it, and cleaned out my Suburban before it went on a flatbed to a place for wrecked cars. (A few days later, another friend went to get personal things from it and brought me pictures of it; the front end on my side was completely crushed.) My nose was not broken, and the deep cut in my chin was stitched. I went home from the emergency room, missing Winston. The farm owner called to tell me they would pick up Burgers and Winnie the next day, and bury Hawk first thing in the morning. I said I wanted to be there, and they promised to come get me, but they didn't.

I called Jack, telling him that Hawk was gone, and he sprang into action, checking on Burgers and Winnie (who spent the night in a tack room at the strange farm, probably very desolate), calling me with a report, saying he would bring Winnie to me in the morning. It was nearly 10 p.m. at this point, and I lay in my bed with ice on my nose. My neighbor let herself in, hearing about the accident on the police scanner, and offered to lend me her extra car, which I accepted gratefully. I was overwhelmed—so much had happened that day that it was impossible to sleep.

Then I remembered having a phone number for Penelope Smith, an animal communicator who was a pioneer in the field. I'd written down her number somewhere in my notes during a Tellington TTouch Training clinic. I found the number, knowing that she was in California and not really aware of how much earlier it was there, or that it was now after 1 a.m. Eastern Standard time. She answered the phone, and I said, "Hi, um, I need some help with a horse."

She asked if I had a black horse, and I said "Yes." She said he had been keeping her up, telling her she needed to talk to me right away, but she had no idea who I was. I explained briefly what had happened, and she said with the warmth of a hug, "Oh he's just fine. He really didn't want to be a horse and only stayed here long enough to find you because he knew you could let him go."

"What?" I replied, "Not a horse?"

"Yes. He wanted to be a bird, a big black bird. He needed, wanted, to fly. The air is his element." I thought back over his enormous bucks, his leaps nearly out of the dressage rings at shows, his elevation in his passage, and realized what she was saying was absolutely true.

"How will my other horse be without Hawk?" I asked. "He will know Hawk is with him," she said. "And you will too when you see the black birds around you."

"Hawks?" I asked. "No," she said. "Black birds, like crows and ravens, even buzzards."

Her words proved to be so true; ever after when I rode Burgers, I would see crows, and in New Jersey, buzzards. I would silently thank them for reminding me that my lovely black horse was still with me.

Early the next morning, Jack and Winston arrived at my home, and I was overjoyed to see both of them. Winston devoured his breakfast and a bowlful of water, and would not leave my side. Jack told me that the farm people had already buried Hawk by the stream, very early, and I was devastated that I was not able to see him again, although I could still feel the velvet soft hair of his neck in my arms as I had said farewell to him in the trailer.

At the end of that summer, my sister Judy called to tell me that Richard, my Arabian, was in need of a home. In his late twenties, he had been a campus patrol horse with her at Rutgers University, a lesson pony, a pet, and a lawn ornament grazing around a big home. I drove to New Jersey to bring him to fill the stall at Arduns left empty by Hawk. When I introduced him to Burgers, he looked so small and fragile in his senior years. He had navicular disease, taking short steps but not really limping. I wondered over the few weeks that he was stabled next to Burgers if they talked about me, joking about their varied tricks to try to show me that lunging was a bad idea. It was surreal to have two separate times of my life collide like this, and I felt very sad that I had to find a home for Richard, since I could only afford to care for one horse. He went to live with a nearby family with children who just wanted to sit on him and ride around the yard, or so I was told. Unfortunately, the man had been taking people's "free" horses for his kids and then selling them at an auction for quite a long time. I was not aware of this, and sadly, Richard met a terrible end that I did not learn about until nearly a year later. My sister Judy and I both have significant regret over this, as we are people who keep our horses forever, and we just could not take care of Richard at that moment in our lives.

Hawk trotting up the center line in his freestyle test.

I was given a leave of absence from my school job, and went to the final Tellington TTouch Training clinic held at the lovely Equine Inn in New Hampshire. It was an advanced clinic with Linda and Robyn, and I was relieved to be with people who had known Hawk, and to spend more time with Burgers, riding without a bridle, and working without a halter over the ground exercises. It was at this clinic that I first took detailed notes about the work Linda had been doing with Anna Wise (later described in her book *The High Performance Mind.*) In the early '80s, Linda worked with Anna Wise at The Biofeedback Institute of Boulder, Colorado. Anna had worked with biophysicist Maxwell Cade, who had termed the "Awakened Mind State" to be when both hemispheres of the brain showed a consistent pattern of alpha, beta, theta, and delta waves, which occurred in the highest level of mental functioning that he had measured in yogis and skilled meditators. Anna found that both Linda and her students, as well as the people receiving TTouches, all showed this activation in both hemispheres in the Awakened Mind State pattern.

Furthermore, when the headband was attached to a horse, just as in the people receiving TTouches, the same pattern of activation of both hemispheres of the brain was recorded. Later, Anna had a remote headband made, and the same brain wave pattern was seen in the horses going around the corners of the labyrinth. As Linda writes, "The experience was mind-altering. To think that horses could produce brain wave activity mirroring our own gave us a whole new perspective on equine learning, and indeed, gave rise to a new consideration of equine consciousness. And the fact that the human doing the TTouches had the same patterns meant that doing TTouch could be as beneficial for the human as it was for the horse!"

This pattern of activation of the two hemispheres in the brain reflects what is required for optimal learning, so in fact, doing the circular TTouches and working in the labyrinth really was helping horses to learn, and as Linda had said, become able to act instead of react. When I was to take my initial craniosacral class just a few years later, and one of the morning discussions focused on left and right brain strengths, I had my first instinct that TTouch and craniosacral work are closely related. Although as yet, no one has measured brain wave activity with the same type of biofeedback set-up Anna Wise used during TTouch sessions to measure brain wave activity during craniosacral sessions.

Chapter 17

Dancing White Horses
Teaching TTouch, Dancing With White Horses

This is one of my friend Phoebe's wonderful Iberian horses.

"He (the white horse) moved like a dancer, which is not surprising: a horse is a beautiful animal, but it is perhaps most remarkable because it moves as if it always hears music."

— Mark Helprin *Winter's Tale*

After the clinic that fall, I went to Europe to work with horses with TTouch. In Germany, I stayed with a caring woman near Stuttgart, as I wanted to see where the famous Steiff stuffed animals were made. She had a retired dressage horse, a gray mare, and a young white horse who I helped her train to pull a carriage. She also had two goats. I have always had a mixed rapport with goats, and the woman and her husband delighted in playing pranks on me with their goat Liesel. They sent me out to feed the horses, assuring me that she was already in the barn for the night. They did not tell me that Liesel was loose in the barn and could get out through the goat door. Just as I came from the feed room with buckets for the horses, Liesel charged across the barnyard and butted me. Then she scampered around bucking and leaping, very pleased with herself.

One day we went to the local riding school to use the indoor arena. After we worked with the young horse, I rode the retired mare. She was a nicely trained horse, doing piaffe, passage, and two tempe changes for me. When I got off of her, her owner ran into the ring and hugged me. She said it was remarkable that although she and I communicated with difficulty (owing to my poor German and her poor English), clearly her horse and I understood each other perfectly. She was so happy to see the beautiful gaits and movements of her mare. And, she added, she had never before seen her horse perform and did not know that she could dance!

Each evening, we rode the horses bareback down the hill from the grassy pasture where they spent the day, gazing back at the pink and red sunsets at the city below. I will always remember that bucolic place where I learned that the language of horse and rider is universal.

I spent some time with a well-known horse dealer in Holland, where I marveled at how sensitive and light the Dutch horses were. He laughed at me, saying, "We breed our horses to talk to us. It's only in America where you think that is being misbehaving." I thought back to that early client (described in Chapter 15), with her noble horse taking uneven steps to maintain his relationship with his rider, who was afraid to ride, and I remembered that he was a Dutch horse.

That Christmas, with no particular place to spend the holiday, I took a train to Vienna, thinking it would be a romantic and beautiful city at that time of year. I went immediately to the place where the Lipizzaner horses were kept—the Spanish Riding School—to get a ticket to a performance. Shocked, the office person asked how I already knew that there was to be a performance. Unbeknownst to me, the horses do not usually perform in the winter, and this was to be a single special show. As the first to get a ticket, I selected the place I knew so well from the Disney movie about the horses, and from reading Colonel Alois Podhajsky's book *My Horses, My Teachers*—I chose to sit right at the end of the center line past "G" at the edge of the arena. I wore my velvet dress, feeling incredibly honored to see these beautiful white horses in their gorgeous arena for a special holiday performance.

I thought back to the seeming coincidences that led to this moment—first, in 1964, my grandparents taking my sister and me as very small children to see the Lipizzaner show in Philadelphia, the first city of their first American tour, when a Morgan performed with them; and second, riding through the trails on Colonel Reed's property, across from the farm where Goblin lived in Virginia. Colonel Reed had joined forces with General Patton and Colonel Podhajsky to save the Lipizzaner and other precious stallions during World War II. This incredible story has been detailed in a book by Elizabeth Letts, *The Perfect Horse: The Daring U.S. Mission to Rescue the Priceless Stallions Kidnapped by the Nazis*. It was rumored at my barn that two of these white horses were pastured on his land. Although I had seen touring Lipizzaner performances in America several times, I couldn't believe that I was going to see these

Austrian horses perform in their famed arena at the Spanish Riding School.

The gleaming white horses entered the ring in pairs, trotting up the centerline towards me, before splitting into two lines of horses doing ten-meter circles down the long side of the arena. I scarcely breathed, knowing that I was sitting where Presidents, First Ladies, Kings and Queens, and military heroes had sat to watch the famous stallions. As the white horses danced in front of me, in piaffe and passage, demonstrating airs-above-the-ground in long lines and with riders, I knew I was seeing the pinnacle of dressage training, witnessing the life-long connections between these dedicated riders and their splendid horses.

When I returned from Europe, I became a full-time horse trainer. The first place I went to teach a clinic was the farm where Burgers and Winnie had spent the night after our accident. There I met a horse who showed me to always trust my instinct—even if it defied logic—as well as the power of an immediate heart connection with an animal.

At one of my TTouch clinics, my mom is practicing TTouch on her arms as I demonstrate TTouches on my injured ankle.

After my introduction about the day's activities, I asked the owner to bring in a horse for a demonstration. Bubba, a smallish white Thoroughbred stallion, pranced behind his person with a chain over his nose. We could hear his whinnies and the snorts of the horses along the aisle as Bubba pawed and lunged at each one, and we also heard his person shouting at him and pulling heavily on the chain lead. Bubba's shod hooves scrambling on the aisle pavement echoed in the big, metal, indoor arena, where

I waited to do my demonstration. People jostled to get out of his way and the woman leading him used her strength to steer him into a place next to the long side of the ring where people could see him. I carefully stepped up to him to do my body evaluation, holding a wand down at my side, and he reared up, pawing at me, squealing. The person yanked on the lead line again, shouting, "Stop that!"

I stepped back and surveyed the horse. His eyes were wide, his sides heaving. His neck was held high, his head parallel to the ground. His back was arched and his hind legs danced around, unsteady as he tried to move away from everything scaring him. His body told me, "I am terrified. Why are these people staring at me? My legs are aching. The chain on my nose is hurting me. The halter is pressing into the back of my ears and neck, and it is hurting me. Help me. Please, help me."

I reached back and picked up four wands, two in each hand, fanned out at about three feet. I looked deeply into Bubba's brown eyes, and took an audible deep breath in and out. And then, with confidence, I stepped forward and placed the wands on his body, two on his neck and chest, and two on his rump and hind legs. I heard a gasp from the people watching me—what was I thinking? Wasn't he afraid of one whip? And now I was holding four?

As the four wands made contact with Bubba's body, he immediately dropped his head, took a deep breath and continued to breath rhythmically. His eyes softened. I took the lead line from the woman and draped it over his neck. I began to stroke Bubba's body with the wands that had been on his hindquarters. It was clear that speaking to the group at this point would not be respectful of Bubba, and so I spoke only to him, silently and then very quietly. I stroked down all four of his legs with the two wands, down his tail, across his topline and under his belly, down his neck. The entire time, Bubba continued to relax, finally bringing his muzzle to my arm to give me a deep sniff hello.

The four wands worked for two reasons—to give Bubba a sense of where his body was, something that he could feel in front and behind him; and also to ground him, calming him so that he could stop reacting with instinct and habit, and instead think about his situation. My use of the four wands with a deep breath established an immediate connection between us. And, as the second T in TTouch now represents "Trust," Bubba was able to trust me enough to quiet down and become interested in what I had to offer him. I quietly did some TTouches on his body, with the lead line still hanging across his neck, as he stood, relaxed. I could see that doing a body exploration would be wrong in this case because it would further frighten him. What he required was clear from other information, like his coat pattern and the tension in his skin, the scars from pin-firing on his legs, and his shallow breaths which indicated that he had pain in his body.

The other important thing I did with Bubba was to take those deep breaths and connect with him on a heart level, as Linda had done when she met each horse at the clinics. In those few breaths, I put myself into heart coherence with this horse. We know from the HeartMath Institute, where research is done exploring heart-brain communication and its relationship to deepening our connection with self and others, that all beings are energetically interconnected through the heart's magnetic field. That deep connection creates trust, and that is what I gave to Bubba.

He and I embarked on a relationship that lasted nearly a year. I decided to restart him, as if he had never been ridden, beginning with ground driving—of course no lunging! I took him through the steps of teaching him about ropes, and soon enough I was able to walk behind him up and down the dirt roads near the farm, even teaching him piaffe and passage in the long lines. A few weeks into this work, we were far down the road, just around a curve, when a school bus approached us going very fast. Thinking quickly, I directed Bubba off the road, into and out of a big culvert, and into a small clearing in the woods by the road. I asked him to wait as he nervously pawed. I could see his body puff up and his eyes get wide as dirt kicked up from the bus tires hit us when the driver slammed the brakes. I held the reins steady, stroking his rump with the wand as Bubba then began to piaffe nervously. He had so much energy coiled in his body that I knew he would seriously injure me if he kicked out. After the bus had passed us completely, I carefully asked him to move forward into his first passage, trying to use some of that coiled energy. He gracefully trotted out from that, snorting before relaxing back into a walk. "Good boy," I whispered quietly. "You are such a good boy."

For most of that year, I rode him in the lindel on trails and back roads, and someone else at the barn, a talented jumper rider, taught him about jumping big fences. I worked with him on dressage in the ring in a bridle; he was good at collecting his body and learned a lot of basic lateral work. I remember riding to the top of a hill one day with him in the lindel, surveying the russet autumn foliage across the Catskills ahead of us, thinking I was so fortunate that this was my work. And then I laughed to myself that it also included cleaning stalls, lessons for small, sometimes screaming children, and riding in all kinds of bad weather.

Bubba was eventually sold to a young man to whom I had given a lot of lessons that year. He was a good fit for Bubba, and he moved to Vermont, where they competed successfully in eventing. The young man was about sixteen, and after a year, I got a phone call from him asking me if I knew that young riders were not permitted to compete on stallions. Actually, I did know this, I told him. (Stallions are often seen as too unruly to be trusted with inexperienced or younger riders in a busy horse show area.) He informed me that Bubba was still a stallion, and that in his second year of showing, someone at a show finally realized that Bubba was a stallion, and the young man was disqualified from future shows. He said, "Well, it's only a year or so before I am old enough to show him, so I guess I'll wait 'til then." Bubba's good nature and show success were evidence of all he had learned in our time together, during his second-chance training with TTouch.

The farm owner was so impressed with my work with Bubba at the clinic that she hired me to train horses for her and work at her farm, named Sugar Mountain. Burgers soon moved there as well, and Winnie came with me to work there each day. I gave lessons to the children of the weekenders from New York City, taught dressage to amateur owners, took kids to shows, and rode on the hills and trails around the farm. It was here that I found out about Winston's true herding skills, when a rescued sheep came to live there. She generally wandered loose on the property, but at times she would squeeze through the indoor gates and alarm the horses. Winston became adept at not only warning us of the sheep approaching, but also circling around her and herding her back out to the pasture area. Corgis, as herders of cattle, do not typically have the eye contact and skills of border collies to herd sheep, but Winston was not at all intimidated by the big ewe.

When Linda Tellington-Jones came to do a clinic for us at this farm, we spent part of a day working with dogs with TTouch, as the dog work was becoming more established at that time. Janet's dog Lucy (a Lab mix), Winston, and others worked with us through the labyrinth and over ground poles. We used TTouch bodywork and leading positions to help the dogs who pulled on their leashes. By 1996, weeklong companion animal clinics became part of a certification process for people to work with dogs, cats, and companion animals with TTouch.

Later that summer, I accompanied Linda to do workshops at Green Chimneys in New York and in Kent, Conn. At Green Chimneys, a residential school for troubled children, there is a farm environment with a host of endangered livestock species. We taught the students how to do bodywork on each other—particularly mouth work—to help them stay focused in the classroom and to practice de-escalation when confronted with emotional triggers. The mouth has direct neural connections to the limbic system, the emotional center of the brain (see more about this under 'amygdala' in Wikipedia), and we had seen the value of mouth work with sensitive or reactive horses to help calm them and release fear. One practitioner had been teaching prisoners to do TTouch as part of a program to educate them about working with animals. She reported that many of the men had a hard time touching their upper lips, even just gently moving them in a circle, seemingly because of the "emotional baggage" held in their tight upper lips. The expression about "keeping a tight upper lip" has its history in the idea of holding in emotions. The students at Green Chimneys thought working with their mouths was funny. The mouth work lightened the mood and allowed emotional releases to occur gently. Later in the day Linda and I heard a student say to someone, "Hey dude, move your lip. You need to calm down."

A few days later, at Kent School, we demonstrated the bodywork and horse-leading positions, showed bodywork on dogs and other small animals, and it was at this clinic that I met Dr. Allen Schoen, an early pioneer in holistic veterinary medicine. He has authored many books, including texts on veterinary acupuncture. This meeting was especially important to me, because in his presence I immediately felt a connection to someone who values the souls of animals as Linda Tellington-Jones and I do. The three of us hold a great reverence for the life and spirit of animals, listening to animals with a full awareness of the intelligence and soul in all animals.

Riders gathered at one of my TTouch clinics.

Dr. Schoen later came to do some acupuncture treatments with Burgers, who had low liver chi, and when Burgers was older and living with my sister, he received many more acupuncture treatments from her, chiropractic care, as well as Chinese herb supplements that were enormously beneficial in his later years. Perhaps one factor in my sister's decision to pursue a career in holistic veterinary medicine was my enthusiasm after meeting Dr. Schoen and seeing his work at that weekend clinic at Kent. Dr. Schoen has spoken at the Equine Affaire, held in Springfield, Mass., and I am fortunate to have known him for many years.

Chapter 18

To Dance With Confidence
Winter Riding Lessons, Craniosacral Therapy

Winter riding lessons in New England on one of the days it was nice enough to ride outside.

"Think of the body not as a mechanistic machine, but rather as a system of intelligence."

— Dr. John Upledger

"Dancing is the body's song."

— Lynne Sharon Schwartz

Sadly, after Burgers and I were there about a year, Sugar Mountain farm where he was living and where I was working closed, as the owner wanted to move to a warmer climate. Burgers moved to a small farm a friend of a friend had told me about. I was going to work with some horses in exchange for board. It was clear from the start that this was not a good situation. The horses there, Arabians and Morgans, ran in a small herd, with stalls that were more like run-ins, arranged in a row. There was nowhere to tack up a horse, and it was challenging to navigate the electric fence while leading a saddled horse through the group without having any escape.

I had been there only a few days, and I was struggling to lead Burgers through the herd. A small stallion came charging at us and slammed into Burgers' side, and he fell against me, pushing me onto a large boulder. He scrambled up and kicked at the stallion to chase him away, but I was injured. I managed to get up, blood streaming from my arm, and limp, huddled next to Burgers, taking him back to his roped-off stall. I untacked him and drove to the hospital, where I got a few stitches in my arm and an X-ray of my back. Nothing was broken, but I had a massive contusion on the back of my right hip, significant enough that I required physical therapy. Fortunately, a friend who was very handy came to the house made from an old barn where I rented an apartment, and helped me put up an electric fence for Burgers. His paddock surrounded a small pond that never froze, saving me the problem of freezing winter water buckets. My friend also helped me load my equipment at this disorganized farm, and trailer Burgers back to my house, where he lived for a few years.

As terrible as my accident was, it proved to be a life-changing event. The physical therapist I saw for my contusion injury was an early practitioner in the field of Upledger CranioSacral therapy. I had seen him once many years before for headaches and knew that he was a leader in alternative therapy approaches. As I lay on the table in his office, I realized that there was a relationship between his work and TTouch. His presence during a session was similar to how we worked with horses, and I could feel some of the same kinds of changes in my body from his work. For instance, he would be working on my injured arm, but I would feel changes reaching throughout my body. Someone in his office joked to me one day when I was describing the similarities between this work and TTouch, and she said, "Oh sure, you should go to PT school and then you can do what we do."

A few weeks later, I sat in a CranioSacral I course in Vermont, taught through the Upledger Institute (see note). I have thought often of Linda's intuitive insight in her Feldenkrais class to bring the Feldenkrais concepts to the equestrian world, first to horses, and then to riders. I have no doubt that her inspiration was why in my first CranioSacral I class in 1994, I immediately thought this work would be of immense benefit to horses, and to dogs and other small animals. The basis of Feldenkrais' body and movement work was to go *with* the nervous system, not against it. This concept is underlying Tellington Method work as well—meet the animal where it is at, rebalance the central nervous system so the sympathetic fear/stress response is not overriding the parasympathetic peace/rest response. And in Upledger CranioSacral therapy, the work is done in the direction of ease, working *with* the nervous system rather than resisting.

Clearly all of my training and knowledge were in synchrony with Feldenkrais' original concepts, as well as the ideas behind CranioSacral therapy. As Frédéric Pignon of *Cavalia* describes, "When I have a problem with my back I go to my osteopath and he tells me he is 'listening through his hands' to what is going on. I try doing the same with my horses." Linda Tellington-Jones had taught me how to listen with my hands to my horses and dogs as part of TTouch, and CranioSacral therapy was another lesson in listening with my hands for different types of information.

Since my hip injury was making riding so difficult that I felt I could no longer be a trainer, I indeed decided to apply to physical therapy school, which included taking many classes to meet the long list of pre-requisites. Of course, Winnie came with me to the community college where, yet again, I had to endure dissection labs with the same species of animals, this time for classes called Human Anatomy, whereas my undergraduate course work had been called Animal Anatomy. And Winnie came with me to Statistics classes, where I let everyone know about the research that people make fewer math errors with a dog in the room. The teacher was familiar with this work and loved dogs, but the many nursing students in the room did not take the research too seriously.

Winnie and I were commuting to school, teaching riding lessons, and taking care of Burgers in the fenced-in area at my rental house, ironically an old barn made into apartments. Winnie barked at me when it was time for Burgers' dinner, although Burgers never needed a reminder of that. On warm days, I'd let Burgers graze on the lawn under my deck, with my last little gray bunny, Rufus, grazing near him, and Winston keeping a watchful eye over them. One morning, after running inside to answer the phone, I came out to find only Winston and Burgers, and no sign of the rabbit. I searched, saying to Winnie, "Find the bunny, where's the bunny?" and pointing to the ferns and raspberry canes around the lawn. I put Burgers away, and searched for hours with no sign of the rabbit. I knew from past rabbit escapes that they are never more than a few feet from where you last saw them, but his charcoal gray coat and the growing darkness made it impossible to find him. For several days I searched, every morning asking Winnie to "find the bunny" to no avail. But at the end of the week, I saw the rabbit, sitting under Burgers as he ate his grain, munching on the spilled horse feed and hay. At least he was all right, but in the woods as we were, it was not a safe place for a house rabbit.

After a month, it was turning to fall and the nights were growing colder. It was the day of hurricane Andrew, windy and gray, when I let Winnie out to do his business in the morning. He went around the side of the house, and did not come back when I called. It was raining hard, and I grabbed a coat, as I heard Winston's sharp, repeated barks that he made when he was asking me to open the door. But he was not by the door. I went around the corner of the house, and there he was, barking as he held the rabbit pinned to the ground under his chest. He held the bunny as I raced over and scooped him up. Unlike Leo when I brought her in from a week in the wild, this fellow was calm and sweet. I put him back into his pen with a huge bowl of carrots, greens and rabbit food. And Winston was rewarded with treats and grateful pats. The weather was so bad for the next few days that the rabbit may not have made it. Winston, who as a puppy was comforted by my rabbit Leo, and then scampered across the living room doing "binkie" dances with the bunnies when he was a puppy, of course would save a rabbit or two in thanks.

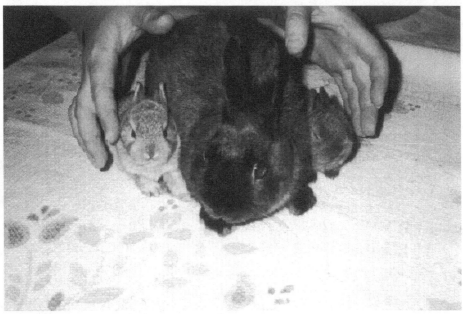

Rufus, rescued by Winston after being lost in the woods for a month, shown here with two of the baby rabbits he sired.

During this time at my house, Burgers lived alone, and though he did not seem to ever have many horse friends, he was apparently lonely. There was a family up the street who had a few horses, one of them a bay mare named Beetsy, who looked like a slightly smaller version of Burgers. More than once, Burgers walked through his electric fence, not bothering to nibble any of the deep grass in the yard, and sprang into a road-trot down the dirt road, jumped the four-rail fence into the field, and grazed happily next to Beetsy. Sometimes the family didn't even notice their extra horse until I came to bring him home. At a small show that summer, I approached Beetsy's rider and we went into the pairs division together. We won the jumping class and got second under saddle, Burgers perfectly slowing his strides to match his look-alike friend.

Burgers and I had a flat hayfield to practice dressage nearby, but with Winnie following, we more often rode through the woods, even where there were no trails. Once, he stopped in the middle of a pine forest, refusing to move. I looked around and did not see a bear or a deer, and then I was aware of the ground moving. We were in a huge flock of turkeys. Winnie sat watching them, and Burgers had turkeys brushing by his legs, as they moved through the ferns into the field ahead. I thought how profound it is that when you are connected with your own animals, as I was to Burgers and Winnie, that you are intimately connected to all animals.

Months later in the early spring, Burgers and I were deep in the woods, not near any trails, and he was wearing just a halter and saddle. Again, he stopped dead, looking off to the left with Winnie beside us. There in a bit of a clearing was a newborn fawn, still wet and blinking in the early spring sunshine. About ten feet behind him, the doe eyed us cautiously. We stepped ahead a ways, and I turned back to watch the deer. The doe calmly returned to washing her fawn, unconcerned about Burgers or me, or the corgi, the legendary mount of the forest fairies. The doe knew we meant no harm.

In October, Winston and I took the Upledger CranioSacral II class outside of Boston. I noticed how he responded when people were on the massage table where I was practicing what I was learning. He seemed to be aware of areas in their bodies where they reported pain, and when I was on the table, he nudged at people's arms, clearly trying to give them some information or directions. He also seemed to spend time sitting or lying by people who were having emotional or physical struggles. People seated near me joked, questioning whether he was taking the course or teaching the course. It was clear to many of us that Winston was intuitive in ways I had not yet understood.

That winter, I was continuing to work as a full time riding instructor, with clients spread throughout Connecticut, New York, and western Massachusetts. Some were riders I had met through the Tellington Method clinics I had given, and remarkably, some had responded to a simple ad I had placed in a few newspapers. I was quite busy, but with snow on the way and few of my clients with indoor arenas, I was worried about how to manage my finances in the winter. I had the idea to ask my clients to sign a sort of contract, to commit to their weekly or biweekly lesson schedule, regardless of the weather. It would be my responsibility to find activities for them and their horses to help their riding. Everyone without exception was eager to make a commitment like this, some even saying they were quite curious what we would do if we had to stay indoors. It turned out to be the worst winter in years, with deep snow covering the entire area and cold temperatures lingering for months.

I used all I had learned, doing TTouch bodywork and craniosacral work on people in their homes, having them balance on a small trampoline or physioball to notice changes in their bodies when I positioned them to perform a shoulder-in, or halt, or renvers. We explored jumping positions as well with them seated on physioballs and standing on the trampoline. My students, sitting on the physioballs and "wearing" their own horse's bridle on their heads, deeply began to understand the effects of their aids, their seats, and their balance, as well as refining the subtlety of the signals they gave with their hands. When it was slightly warmer, I taught them how to do bodywork on their horses, or they made careful observations about their horses as I did TTouch or explored craniosacral work with them. We did ground exercises in the aisle, even using the corners or stall entrances in tiny barns, to help the horses improve their balance. They learned about collection with piaffe in hand in the barn aisle, and, using the dingo leading position, to ask horses to come forward and back, moving one leg at a time. We put ground poles in the aisle and even inverted feed buckets to improve the horse and rider's partnership, balance and coordination going around obstacles.

There is a wonderful booklet called *Riding Through Winter, or Classical Dressage in the Real American World*, by Beth Jenkins, that I also borrowed some exercises from. My students rode or worked their horses in-hand in fresh snow and looked at their hoof prints to improve their understanding of shoulder-in, renvers, travers, leg yield, and half pass. All of this work we did, whether in the barn or in the deep snow, we did at the walk, which allowed the riders and their horses time to organize, rebalance, and become clear about their aids in each movement. And on some days when we rode outside, we would return indoors to the physioball to deepen the riders' understanding of their body positions and aids. They learned when to engage each seat bone, how to position their shoulders, and where to look as they performed shoulder-in or haunches in. I asked them in detail where their horse's legs would be under them as they sat on the ball, shifting their weight or opening their shoulders.

I also used their Breyer horse models, or sometimes a Gumby horse that I carried with me, holding the model in front of the riders, as they sat on the physioball, showing them changes in the horses' bodies as they shifted from one seat bone to the other, or added more inside or outside rein. My clients, competitors and trail riders alike, began to have an in-depth understanding of riding, and of their particular body mechanics when riding, that would not have been possible otherwise.

That spring, at an early April show, one of my students won an open jumper class on her small Morgan, and the fall before she had been racing around 2' 6" courses struggling to make the turns. My other students had similar showing success that spring, owing to the improved balance in both horse and rider, and better seats in the riders. This success with my students solidified my conviction that our answers to improved riding were within our own bodies and our horses' bodies. Horses' seeming stubbornness or apparent unwillingness was clearly a result of the poor communication between horse and rider. It was obvious that improving balance and function allowed maximum performance from our horses. My riders had learned what one friend used to call "the gift of non-interference"—being aware of your own body so that you did not get in the horse's way. I could clearly see how powerful this work was. I knew that learning more about rider and equine anatomy, neurology, and bodywork would tie together all aspects of what I had learned about riding. It would also bring together everything I knew about being with dogs, and walking with them in a way that keeps both people and their dogs in emotional and physical balance.

Chapter 19

The Gift of the Dance
Dancing With Horses Clinic

Burgers and me before our demonstration at the Dancing With Horses Clinic.

"His hooves pound the beat, your heart sings the song."

— Jerry Shulman

"Take 'dancing' for instance. The essence of a brilliant performance by two people is not just that they do the steps perfectly and in time to the music but that they add an emotional quality that lifts the performance into another realm."

— Frédéric Pignon, Cavalia

That summer, I had an extraordinary request for a clinic and celebration demonstration at a farm in Winsted, Conn. One of the boarders there was the artistic director for a regional ballet troupe, and they were putting together a day to celebrate dancing and riding, with a special ballet choreographed to be reminiscent of a dressage ride. I was delighted, quickly telling the organizer that I believed every ride on our horses to be a dance; in fact, every moment we spend with them is a dance. Immediately, she understood what I meant, and we also planned a clinic to work with dancers and riders together to learn Tellington TTouch Training and body awareness exercises, to be held a week after their celebration day.

I arrived with Burgers' coat shining, and his mane neatly done with white bands. He had on his white leg wraps and his show pad with the Morgan insignia on it. I wore my navy blue Shadbelly coat and top hat, with new white gloves. Burgers was bridled in his full bridle, the white padding spotlessly clean. As it was late spring, his rump was sprinkled with bay dapples. When it was time for our demonstration, people gathered at one end of the small indoor arena, where I explained the relationship between dance and riding, pointing out the history of dressage, and the subtlety of the signals one gives the horse when dressage is done well. I did a freestyle ride I had prepared for demonstrations, including elements from many levels of dressage, ending with Burgers' favorite extended trot up the center line, towards the crowd, with a prompt halt, salute.

People broke into applause as I reached forward to take off the bridle and slip on the lariat neck rope we used in Tellington TTouch Training for bridle-less riding. I took off my top hat, undid my bun, and took off my coat. Someone took my things, cued the music, and we did the same ride without a bridle. Burgers was exuberant, with huge strides in the extended gaits and quick collections. As we trotted down the center line for our final halt, I noticed a few people moving to the side for fear he would not stop without a bridle. Of course, he did a perfect square halt, even better than the one he had done in the bridle, shaking his head and snorting before whinnying loudly. The applause was even louder this time, and our demonstration was a huge success.

Later, I watched the ballet troupe present their dressage dance, with young dancers dressed in riding clothes, others acting as the letters in a dressage arena. The lead dancers, performing as a horse and rider together, did a pas de deux, using ballet steps reminiscent of the movements of the horse, leaping cabrioles, tiny steps en pointe like piaffe, lifts, and tour jetes like a canter pirouette. It was beautiful, even more so as the horses from their stalls around the ring reached their heads over their doors to watch. I was holding Burgers, still saddled after our demonstration, as we watched the performance together. At the end of the dance, the lead ballerina did a curtsy bow in front of Burgers, as if to thank him, and all horses for the inspiration.

"This is why I ride," I thought. "This is the culmination of all I know and have learned about horses and riding." Bowing to the ballerina, I clapped, and Burgers again whinnied loudly. There was so much appreciation of the soul and spirit of horses in the arena that day.

I returned the next week inspired to make this a magical clinic. The participants, many of whom were both riders and dancers, had dressed with dancers in riding clothes and riders in dance clothes, not to be silly, but as a way to more fully meld the two arts. I did an overview of TTouch bodywork in the morning, with the people first working on each other and then with the horses at the farm. One student was in tears, saying to me, "I can feel what he feels in his body when I am doing this."

Next, I taught them the leading positions, dingo, elegant elephant, and cobra, where you walk in front of the horse facing him, giving cues with the wand for the horse to step forward and stop. It truly is like a dance, with the horse mirroring your body position and footsteps as you move together. Everyone loved this, and after the lunch break, we did the Feldenkrais pelvic clock exercise on our backs on the fragrant grass outside of the barn. People were interested to see the asymmetry they had not noticed before in their bodies. Later, to surprise me the group did a short "dance" performance for me, using the leading positions, especially "cobra"—everyone was delighted to find a literal way to dance with the horses. We did some riding as well, with people leading the horses at the walk, as riders closed their eyes, shifted their pelvic angles or balance in the saddles, and noticed what their horses did in response. It was a wonderful way to end the day, with both riders and dancers noticing how their bodies affected their dance partners, the horses.

My students at the Dancing With Horses clinic practicing the Feldenkrais pelvic clock. Winston observes us from the lawn.

Chapter 20

Knowledge of the Dance
Physical Therapy School and Riding Lessons

Sneakers, Winston, Vickie & Julia--lucky girl surrounded by corgis.

"If you think dogs can't count, try putting three dog biscuits in your pocket and then give him only two of them."

— Phil Pastoret

After a few years of having Burgers at my house, I moved to the town where I have been for over twenty-five years now, to accept a job teaching English and to attend physical therapy school. I was uncertain where Burgers would live, and of course, Winston would continue to come with me to teach and take classes. Fortunately, Janet, my longtime riding friend who kept Burgers' brother, Action, at her house, stopped me from donating Burgers temporarily to a college riding program, and he became a school master for her daughter Kate. Kate had outgrown her pony, and needed a horse for Pony Club. It was a perfect solution. Kate won first level dressage classes, completed Novice events, and gained confidence riding Burgers. Janet had to keep the two horses separated from each other to avoid terrible fights, but she had enough pastures to keep everyone happy.

Winston and I set off to physical therapy school, where our first class, "Brain and Behavior," was held during the summer. He attended class with me, and I found that my craniosacral courses had given me a thorough background in neurology—I loved the class. I became friends with the instructor, Dr. Robert Wallace, who also loved dogs and said what a good student Winston was. This proved to be fortuitous because when Winston and I sat attentively in our first physical therapy course in the fall, it caused a stir among the staff. At the end of that day, they informed me that Winston could not attend physical therapy school with me. Crestfallen, we were in the hallway when we ran into Dr. Wallace who had an office in the class building. He immediately offered to keep Winston in his office as much as we needed. Thus, Winston had to do his work mostly as an independent study.

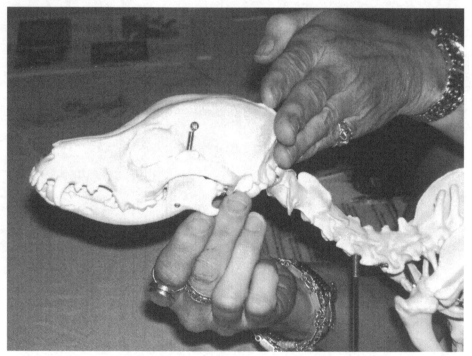

I was fortunate to have private studies in comparative anatomy during physical therapy school.

However, once again, this seeming difficulty led to a wonderful turn of events for me. I became even better friends with Dr. Wallace, and we began to have in-depth conversations about animals and animal anatomy. Even my veterinarian sister did not know animal neurology with the detail of this professor. With more craniosacral classes behind me, I went to him with questions, and his vast knowledge and collections of books and materials taught me much about animal brain anatomy and physiology.

One of the first important things I learned from Dr. Wallace came about when I asked about hand dominance in animals, wondering if horses and dogs are right handed because people handling them are, or if they naturally one sided as we are. He showed me brain anatomy pictures, and some brains in jars, as he explained that the corpus collosum, the central part of the brain that connects the right and left hemispheres, is less well developed in most animal species than it is in humans. We discussed how this works with horses; for instance, in teaching them something in one direction of the ring, you can't assume they will automatically do it perfectly the other way. You have to teach them again in the new direction, as if it is the first time, in order to have the best success. This is also true with dogs. This explained to me why leading horses on the off side in TTouch work was so powerful—they often had no bad habits and experiences on that side, and this new way of leading was truly a new skill for them that would allow them, without being overshadowed by past bad handling, to improve trust and confidence.

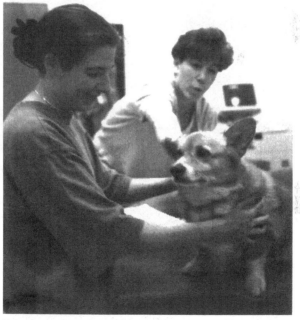

Winston and friends practicing before an exam in physical therapy school.

As I continued learning Upledger CranioSacral therapy, Winston became my practice client as I tried to apply what I was learning to his little twenty-five pound corgi body. Ever patient, he would lie on his back, paws folded and relaxed on his chest like an otter, while I practiced diaphragm releases and dural tube work on him. Dr. Wallace one day suggested that I treat Winston in his normal upright position, a huge shift for me, because I then realized that you would, of course, have to adapt your hand positions to any animal position as they moved through your treatment session, or comfortably slept on one side, just as Upledger instructors were teaching in the pediatrics class. Winston still preferred to be supine, unlike most of the other dogs people were bringing to me for bodywork.

Even during an outdoor lab at physical therapy school Winston, seen in the background, is doing independent study work.

After a year with Kate and Janet, Burgers needed another new place to live, since Kate was getting too tall for him. Janet had given my name to another Pony Club family who needed help braiding their pony at the New England Morgan Show. I found the small chestnut gelding, Epic, in a stall in one of the back barns. It was morning, and he had a scruffy stick-up mane going in every direction. I fed him some carrots and arranged his hay so that he could eat as I braided. He was very good, hardly moving, and I was able to make a neat row of braids on one side of his neck. I also braided his tail, as he was going in the hunter classes. His thick short tail was difficult, and I did a creative braid arrangement to make his tail appear long and slender. When his people stopped by a while later, they were very happy with how professional he looked. I talked to the mother, Esther, as her daughter Katherine, tacked up the pony. We struck up an immediate friendship owing to our similar beliefs in the miracle that animals want to be partners with us, no matter how many mistakes we make along the way. By the end of the day, it was decided that Burgers would go to live at their house, and that I would give Katherine riding lessons on both Burgers and Epic to help her make her way through the levels of Pony Club.

When I arrived at their farm with Burgers, and Winston as well, we were greeted in the driveway by Esther's Cardigan corgi, Sneakers. She and Winston became instant friends, although he did find her habit of eating horse manure well beneath him.

Burgers, who had taught me so much, set out to teach Katherine all that she would need to know. During her many years of weekly lessons, she learned much about TTouch and educated Pony Clubbers across New England about the importance of bodywork with their horses. She explained in detail to club examiners that a riding whip is not the same thing as a Tellington Method wand, and the examiners relented and allowed her to use the white wand when not mounted. She rode Burgers to more victories at the New England Morgan Show, and rode Epic, going along with me and Burgers, to point-to-point meets and mock fox hunts. As I had with my winter riding clients, I gave her many lessons with physioball "horses," taught her about saddle fit and bridles, and coached her up through her "B" rating. She is now a trainer and horse insurance expert in Kentucky, showing at FEI dressage levels with her new horse after successfully eventing with her Connemara.

Esther surprised me one afternoon with a new family member—a Pembroke Welsh corgi named Vicki who was a rescue from people who had to move suddenly. Bigger than Winnie, she was also red and white, a dowdy British girl, who fell in love with Esther's younger daughter, Julia. Julia dressed Vicki in doll clothes and pulled her around the yard in a wagon. In the summer, Esther planted sunflowers in a circle and tied them together at the tops to make a house where Vicki and Julia read stories and daydreamed. Esther cared for Vicki even when she was so elderly that it was hard for her to walk and get outside when she needed to. Vicki lived longer than any corgi I've known, thanks to Esther's care, though we aren't exactly sure of her age when she came to live there.

Katherine, when she was fifteen, gave me one of the best birthday presents I have received. Months before, she was measuring Winston with a tape measure and comparing his size to Sneakers', saying she was working on a project. A few weeks before my birthday, she started to say that I would love my present more than any I'd received. I was curious, supposing she was making a coat for Winston. When I arrived to teach her lesson on the day of my birthday, she came from the house carrying a life-sized papier maché corgi, painted to look like Winston. His head was tilted just as Winston tilted his when he was imploring me to throw a ball or give him a treat. It really was the best present I could have wished for—another corgi! This corgi has come with me to teach Tellington TTouch and craniosacral classes many times. At one massage school where I have taught, the owners have a corgi, and in the doorway to the school their own papier maché corgi greets the students each day. I took a picture of them together to commemorate the meeting of the papier corgis. That corgi Katherine made me is now close to twenty years old!

Several years later, when Katherine's beloved gray cat had passed away, I brought her my last gray rabbit, Rufus, as a birthday present. He was elderly and she needed something small to cuddle. She kept him with her sister's guinea pig and they fell deeply in love. The rabbit and the guinea pig snuggled together, ate delicious salads Esther prepared for them, and basked in the afternoon sun in Esther's delightful kitchen garden planted with herbs. No one told them they were two different species—they found perfection in one another.

Winston and his papier maché replica.

Comet and the papier maché corgi at Bancroft Canine Massage School before our Small Animal Craniosacral Therapy class.

I continued giving riding lessons to many students in the area. My work with Katherine had made me popular with Pony Club members who wanted lessons. Winston accompanied me to all of my lessons. One student we had was about eleven years old, and she had a Quarter horse cross chestnut pony. Her family had rescued the pony and did not know much about her. Initially they called me because the pony clearly needed bodywork, and I did some craniosacral sessions and taught her rider how to do TTouches to release pain and tension from the pony's body. We did ground driving with her in the driveway in the winter, and, after six months, she was ready to work under saddle again. Her people had invested in a well-fitting saddle. However, the pony still had memories of pain in her back in the corners of the arena, and she would stop, sometimes abruptly, as she got to the corners. I also wondered if she had residual pain that surfaced as she tried to compress her body into collection in the corners of the ring. I tried coming behind her with a wand, simply held a bit from my body, and she would buck. Her rider, Mara, was not afraid, but this was not the solution. Winston, who had been mostly in trouble for following and herding horses, finally had a chance to put his skills to good use.

I let him trot behind the pony around the ring, and as she entered the corner, I'd give him a signal and he'd speed up with a soft bark, which was enough to relax and lengthen the pony's topline, sending her forward with no bucking or scooting. Instead of scrunching up her body in the corners, she stretched, perhaps lessening any pain she was experiencing. In two lessons like this, she was trotting and cantering around the ring without stopping, and she continued to be a well-schooled, successful pony for her rider.

Sometimes, I learned, when you need help with a riding lesson, it's nice to have a compact orange and white corgi herding dog handy!

Chapter 21

Trusting the Dance
A Pony Named Smokey, Mrs. Morgan's Bay Thoroughbred

Smokey, with Gwen at the reins, and my sister Judy Morgan, DVM, along for the ride.

"A good rider can hear his horse speak to him. A great rider can hear his horse's whispers."

—Author Unknown

My sister eventually had a new house with five acres of land, where she built a barn and fenced some pastures so that she could have horses and get a pony for her daughter. She had found a perfect horse for herself, a big Quarter horse named Rocky, registered with the name Auto Pilot. Interestingly, we realized years later that he had been briefly ridden and owned by one of the students at the boarding school where I had worked. Judy asked me to help her make the final decision about a pony for her daughter.

We went to a farm in the central part of the state where a woman was selling a few ponies. Judy narrowed her choices to a fancy little bay gelding with fine legs and a pretty head, and a chunky white pony who still had a few dapples on his haunches and had a significant respiratory infection. After working them each in a partial labyrinth I constructed with tree branches, I rode each of the little fellows, mostly at the walk, and found the bay to be easily frustrated with me. Although he had been trained with some care, as he knew the basics of walk, trot, canter, he tended to run forward when confused. The little white pony, who was coughing and snorting, pricked his ears towards me when I asked him for basic lateral work. He stopped when he was confused. He really did not seem to know much about cantering, which at the time made us think that maybe he had been a driving pony, although we later realized he was in need of chiropractic work for his spine. He seemed intelligent to me, quickly learning haunches-in, shoulder-in, and leg yield in walk, though he clearly lacked any of the training the little bay had demonstrated. The white pony, less expensive and terribly sick, was the clear choice for me. Judy trusted me, even though she liked the bay, and after a few weeks in isolation at another barn to recover, the little white pony came home. Gwen, about four or five years old, named the pony Smokey.

From left-- Rocky, Judy, Gwen, Andrew and Smokey soon after he arrived at Judy's first farm.

Since then, my sister has thanked me many times for choosing him, as he proved to be the kindest of ponies. During the pony's first week at the new farm, Judy found Gwen sitting in the straw under Smokey, brushing his belly and the long feathers on his fetlocks. Smokey, so careful, seemed frozen for fear of stepping on the child. Judy was impressed at how sensible he was; never did she fear for her children's safety with him. They dressed Smokey and the other horses in bells and wreaths and sang Christmas carols around the neighborhood, and did trick-or-treating for Halloween on horseback. As Gwen became a better rider, Judy and I taught them to jump, and together we taught Smokey to drive. Gwen enjoyed success with him at driving shows. He was a faithful pony for the rest of his life, teaching many children about horses.

I had seen with Hawk what a foundation in TTouch work can do for animals, and now with Judy's children, Gwen and Andrew, it was clear what the Tellington Method could do to help people develop relationships with animals. Gwen took riding lessons from me and her mom, learned how to use a wand to lead her pony and bring awareness to his body and legs, and like many kids, learned how to do TTouch tail work, as she said, "to wind up my pony so he will stay calm" before she rode him, especially at shows. She became an expert at explaining to other riders the difference between a TTouch wand and a whip, and showing people how to lead a horse "properly" in the Tellington TTouch Training way. Both of Judy's children became top riders (Gwen was very successful at Intercollegiate Shows, earning national recognition), owing largely to their attitudes that horses are individuals trying to do their best, and that clear communication with them on the ground and under saddle is an integral aspect of being a true equestrian.

Smokey, Andrew and Gwen, winners at one of their first horse shows.

Andrew, Judy's son, had a dark gray pony at this farm who showed all of us the power of Tellington TTouches. I arrived at the farm after the drive from Massachusetts to New Jersey, and as I stepped from my truck I saw Andrew walking his pony (BB, for Best in the Business) in circles around the backyard. The pony was obviously distressed, sweating profusely and taking short, shallow breaths. My sister Judy and her husband

Colin, both veterinarians, seemed calm, managing what seemed to be a case of colic. Andrew took some breaks from leading BB, and I showed everyone how to do the ear TTouches and belly lifts for colic. After some hours, BB seemed more comfortable, but Colin's assessments showed he was not improving. So we called in a third vet, who also thought it was colic, and who noticed how BB seemed more comfortable during the TTouch work on his ears and body.

Over the course of the night, we took turns in the barn helping BB by propping him up on bales of hay when he was down, but he was still in a lot of pain despite the medication and TTouches. We added mouth work TTouches to try to decrease the pain coming from his stomach, which helped enough for BB to stand. So we did belly lifts and he passed some manure, which was a good sign. Even still, his condition worsened and we had to take him for a half-hour trailer ride to the University of Pennsylvania. Judy had a wide trailer and several of us slid a blanket under BB as he lay on his side, and then dragged him into the trailer. We had three people in the trailer doing TTouches on his ears to help him make the trip, even though he had already been treated with tranquilizers, muscle relaxers and painkillers. Upon arrival, the University vets determined that BB had botulism poisoning, which horses sometimes get from the soil. Sadly, he could not be saved. However, this tragedy taught all of us, including many veterinarians, the power of TTouches when trying to decrease fear, pain, and anxiety. My sister, her husband, and other local vets have used what they learned of TTouch that day to help manage colic and pain for many horses.

Soon after this, I brought Burgers to live at this small farm so that Judy and her children could ride him. Even my short mother, ever wary of tall horses, enjoyed some rides on Burgers, although she preferred Smokey, who indeed was just the right size for her. I did some demonstrations at local shows about dressage, as this area known for a nationally ranked rodeo, had few people knowledgeable about dressage. I showed the differences between each level in the frame of the horse and the demands of the tests, and I concluded with a performance of a musical freestyle ride in a full bridle, which I then took off, and repeated the performance without a bridle. These demonstrations were very successful and inspired many people who were seeking a deeper connection with their animals to come to the Tellington TTouch Training clinics that I held at Judy's next farm.

It was 2000, and my sister and Colin bought a bigger farm a short distance away in Woodstown, N.J., where we had gone to high school. The farm had previously been owned by another vet who bred Thoroughbreds there, so the pastures were well seeded with nutritious alfalfa and clover; there were hayfields and an eight-stall barn with foaling stalls, as well as several outbuildings and a tack room. It was a perfect place for her two children to learn to ride with others their age, and for me to teach Tellington TTouch Training clinics to these young riders, boarders, and other local equestrians. Judy and my mom ran fun horse shows intended to build confidence and riding skills, including classes like bareback equitation and a command class with the riders holding eggs on a spoon to see who had the most balanced seat. I was often the judge at these shows, and after choosing my winners, I went down the line to give each participant a mini-lesson with advice for improvements and recognition for what they had done well.

Wishing Burgers a safe trip before we set off from Esther's farm to my sister's farm in New Jersey.

At one of the first clinics held at Campbell Farm, we had a kind woman participate with her paint horses, and one of them, Joanie, was nicknamed "One-Up-From-Stuffed" because she was as calm as a stuffed animal. Her rider brought her along to have a safe horse for the beginners to work with. My mom was one of the people participating in the clinic, as well as an instructor my sister was working with, and a few students with their own horses, including a big bay Thoroughbred from the track. We had some of Judy's ponies—Betsy, a tiny white show pony late in her senior years; Smokey, her kids' first pony; her horse, Rocky; as well as Burgers. Everyone except me knew all of these horses.

In our morning circle, I asked people to introduce their horses and tell us what they wanted to get from our work that day, with answers ranging from "have fun" to "feel safer with my horse." After this, we worked in pairs to learn some of the basic TTouches. Then we brought out the horses and paired up with them, some riders working with their own horses, and others not. As we moved through the day, practicing leading exercises over obstacles and in the labyrinth, people struggled with keeping the lead lines neatly folded for safety, holding a wand, and learning to lead ahead of the horses' shoulders, since many of the participants were used to leading by the shoulder for their showmanship classes. At the lunch break, everyone was excited about the changes they were seeing in the horses, how relaxed the horses were, and they remarked on how quickly the TTouch bodywork made changes in the horses' posture and balance. A few people wanted to try riding without a bridle; after all, these were horses ridden Western, many ridden in hackamores regularly, and it would be an easy transition for them. Others, including my mom, wanted to do more work with the leading exercises.

Smokey and Gwen jumping bareback many years after he was her first pony.

So after lunch, I once again paired people with different horses, partnering my short, 4'10" mom with a tall bay Thoroughbred, some timid riders with gentle Joanie, and children with Burgers and Rocky. I had them all follow one another through a Confidence Course of various ground poles, a spiral, pick-up sticks (a random pile of poles), through two labyrinths, a trot section, around cones, and over plastic and plywood, asking them to change leading positions from elegant elephant, to cheetah, to cobra, and others as they progressed around the big ring. Everyone was in perfect synchrony, truly a dance, as each horse seemed to move his legs in time with the ones ahead and behind him, varying pace and collection as the leaders changed to each position. It was beautiful to watch everyone's success, with some of the women becoming tearful at their success, and the kids increasingly excited about their progress. We traded horses, even leading on the off side, and continued, again with great success—no one confused their lines or was pulled around by their horses. It was the harmony of horse and rider we all long to feel, but for a whole group of people and horses.

My mom on Smokey next to me on Burgers at Judy's first farm.

And then a few people saddled and bridled to begin the process of riding without a bridle and to learn Tellington Riding with Awareness skills. Others gathered in their chairs to watch, some holding a pony munching hay. I put neck rings on the riding horses and showed each person how to use them. They walked and halted, easing into the trot, first with the bridle reins tied. Then I took off Joanie's bridle, and she shook her head and turned to look back at her rider, who gave her a pat. She lengthened her topline and walked off calmly, and everyone there would say that Joanie was smiling. Soon Judy and Rocky were riding at the walk and trot without a bridle, Judy grinning and saying what a great horse he was. Gwen, age seven, rode Burgers, and a few others joined in. Gwen even did some small jumps without a bridle, and her mom, not wanting to be outdone, followed with Rocky. Everyone wanted to try riding without a bridle, even my mom, who rode Burgers as I walked next to him.

At the end of the day, during our wrap-up circle, people reported various highlights for them, some asking to go twice as they had gained so much greater awareness that day. The big bay Thoroughbred's owner said, "I never thought I'd see the day when Mrs. Morgan could lead my horse around safely, and quietly do bodywork with him." I asked what she meant, and she explained that until today her horse had been dangerous for even experienced people to handle, and had in fact knocked down her husband when he was leading him into the barn!

"Ohhh," I said, "I thought that you hadn't brought that horse and we were going to work with him alone tomorrow. I had no idea!" The horse had been perfectly calm, even adjusting his height by lowering his head to my mom's level, and calmly standing while she practiced TTouch circles on his shoulders and head. Mom said she didn't know this was the "dangerous" horse either, or she would have worked with another one. The horse was ever after known as the quiet fellow Mrs. Morgan had worked with. The group had a chuckle, and I pointed out the effect that expectations and intentions have on the riding experience. Clearly no one here expected that horse, or any of them, to have any problems that day except his owner, who had been working with one of the ponies for most of the clinic. We had established the shared intention that morning for everyone to have fun and learn some new things, and that's exactly what had happened. No one was hurt or afraid, neither humans nor horses.

Burgers, Winnie and me relaxing after a dressage demonstration in New Jersey.

My mom and Gwen in the background as I demonstrate asking a horse to lower his head as he goes into the labrynth at a clinic at Judy's second farm.

Mrs. Morgan's thoroughbred standing quietly as I explain tension patterns found during my TTouch body evalutaion.

Chapter 22

Dancing With Security
Lucky

Gwen takes the reins as Judy leads Lucky during her training as a driving horse.

"To see a horse is to see an angel on earth."

— Author Unknown

My sister's Campbell Farm was a place for rescued horses to wait for new people to care for them, a place for people to learn kindness and respect for all animals, and it proved to be exactly the sort of place she had wanted for her children. In the spring, when it was time to mow the hayfield, Colin drove the tractor and all of the farm kids spread out through the field around him with big laundry baskets to catch the many baby rabbits and keep them safe during the mowing. There were hundreds of them. After the field was safe, the kids released the rabbits so they could continue their lives. Even at the shows, a baby rabbit or two would sometimes hop out onto the jump course and we'd have to stop the show for a rabbit rescue.

Besides the wildlife around the farm, Judy and Colin cared for barn cats and house cats, several birds, including Esty, a cockatiel who liked to perch in the Christmas tree, and Blink, a large Doberman, who sometimes gave rides to the cockatiel.

The first Christmas at the farm, Judy had planned a big surprise for her daughter. Recalling her own delight when she got a pony for Christmas, she decided to do something special for Gwen, who already had two or three ponies with nice, well-fitting saddles and bridles and blankets. She kept her surprise a secret from everyone, including my mom. On Christmas morning, Gwen opened a card that said her present was in the barn. Thinking it was a saddle, or maybe a cart and harness, Gwen and the rest of us bundled up and put on our shoes to head to the barn. There in the aisle with a big red bow around her neck was Lucky, a dappled gray miniature horse. Gwen squeaked with delight and walked over to greet her new horse. My mom was even more overjoyed than Gwen, as she had always had some level of fear with horses due to their size, and finally, here was one just her size. In the tack room, Gwen found a tiny new halter and a TTouch lead line in pink with a soft rope at the end of the nylon. Gwen put the halter and lead on Lucky, grabbed her wand, and out we went to the driveway.

Lucky Star, the miniature horse with Gwen, Judy's daughter.

I showed Gwen how to lengthen the line and adjust her hands to move Lucky away from her as she walked next to her, around her, and behind her. We showed Lucky neatly folded ropes and did bodywork with the ropes over her shoulders and rump. We did TTouches on her hind legs and tail, some belly lifts with the ropes, and then brought her into the garage for some hay while we ate breakfast. After that, I showed Gwen dingo, a TTouch "dance step" where we were teaching Lucky how to come forward and stop with signals from the wand and the lead line. Everyone else had stayed inside for clean up. Gwen had good success working with Lucky in the garage, and then she innocently asked if we could bring Lucky into the kitchen.

I eyed the six steps leading from the garage to the back door, and thought "Why not?" I said, "OK, but she has to be really good at coming forward and stopping first, because she has to go up some steps." Gwen practiced and Lucky, only two, was very good—calm and patient, quickly learning to follow the signals Gwen was giving her. Unlike me, Gwen had not heard stories that horses could not go up steps, or back down them, and like Jack loading Hawk into the trailer, she simply did what I suggested, asking Lucky to wait at the bottom of the steps giving her a signal with the wand. Gwen went up the steps, opened the kitchen door, and then gave Lucky a signal to come up the stairs.

Lucky carefully went up the first two steps with her front hooves, and when her hind hoof bumped the first stair, she put it down, looked back, looked ahead, and then took a little leap up to the landing where she quietly looked at Gwen, waiting for the next signal. Very calm for a seven-year-old bringing a horse into the kitchen, Gwen signaled for Lucky to go forward as I went up the stairs behind them, and Lucky and Gwen ambled into the kitchen. "Oh my!" my mother gasped. Judy and Colin, at the kitchen sink washing dishes, turned as Judy said, "Honey, don't look now, but there is a horse in the kitchen!" Lucky looked around, taking the carrots offered her from the pile on the counter, giving a cautious glance at Blink, who was taller than she was. Having a horse in the house was almost more fun than getting a new pony at Christmas!

Gwen showing Lucky in-hand at a 4-H show.

Over the next few days, I showed Gwen how to use ropes to teach Lucky to ground drive in her halter, and soon Judy got a harness and cart for a mini horse. Gwen loved driving Lucky around the farm, and she began competing with her in driving shows. Lucky was always calm and trusting. A few years later, Gwen gave Lucky to my mom as her sixty-fifth birthday present, a gesture that she planned entirely on her own, putting her registration papers in an envelop filled out with the changes to make her officially my mom's horse. Mom also went on to show her in-hand at mini shows, and became very skilled at driving her. She even made elaborate costumes for Gwen and Lucky with the cart for some of the fun shows, converting the cart into a school bus, a Noah's arc, a "mini" van, and a bride and groom's carriage.

My mom, Sally Morgan, with her prize-winning driving horse, Lucky.

At one show for the New Jersey Pony Breeder's Association, Mom had harnessed Lucky to her cart and was dressed in her "Alice in Wonderland" costume just as a storm was blowing up in the area. Lucky was to be dressed as the white rabbit. It was getting windy, stall doors banging, people running to put the windows up in their cars, and Lucky stood calmly. Then there was a problem. My sister was in a rush to put on Lucky's big pink rabbit nose, with foam rubber whiskers blowing around in the wind. As soon as Judy had the nose attached and the wind blew the nose up and down on Lucky's muzzle, she reared up, lost her footing, and fell down on her side, tangled in her harness. Fortunately, my sister immediately helped Lucky, who maintained her composure, as hands flew to unharness her and take off the costume so that she could get up. Lucky waited, watching everyone helping her, not moving a leg.

She finally stood up when she was untangled, shook, and looked at everyone around her. My sister carefully checked her to make sure Lucky was uninjured, examining her legs and walking her a bit. She decided it was fine to harness Lucky again, and she took her for a little walk in the rain and wind before putting the costume back together, this time without the nose and whiskers. Lucky went on to win that costume class and was the miniature driving champion that day. Everyone in our family knew that TTouch was the reason that Lucky was so calm and trusting during this situation. She knew how to assess, to look to her people to help her, and how to maintain patience rather than react in fear. She also knew that a horse's muzzle is no place for a rabbit nose on a windy day!

Lucky is a wonderful example of the benefits of working with a horse with TTouch for her entire lifespan. She has visited nursing homes, walking calmly up steps in and out of buildings. She was never afraid of walkers and allowed people to give her treats from their wheelchairs. She has been in buildings while my sister has given lectures and presentations. And she has never "had an accident" inside a building. She seems to know she is in a special place. She has been in parades with fire engines blasting their horns and horses prancing nervously around her, and has handled every situation calmly. She has jumped up into trailers to help other horses load. She is a remarkable horse, and she is less than three feet tall.

Lucky always has been a therapy animal, making indoor visits to nursing homes.

She is now approaching twenty years old, and on a recent visit I decided to take her for a short drive along with Trystan, my newest corgi riding in the cart with me. She had not been on a drive in nearly a year, but it was a beautiful day. Friends at the farm where Lucky lived helped me assemble the harness, liberate the cart from it's dusty place in the shed, fill the tires with air, and we three set out for our drive. Lucky walked along smartly, knowing her job so well, and Trystan sat close to me on the seat, his first time going for a cart ride. Lucky calmly walked along as cars and trucks occasionally passed us.

Judy successfully showed Lucky in many driving classes.

We came to a fairly steep hill, and because of Lucky's lack of exercise lately, I decided to turn around. As we completed the turn, I heard a slight mushing sound, and as the cart straightened out, I realized we had a flat tire. Hopping out of the cart, I coiled up the lines, ready to drive back to the farm walking next to Lucky. She, as ever, stood patiently as I sorted things out, and we proceeded. The sun was shining and the sky a cloudless blue, lovely for driving, or walking. Little Trystan gradually got more nervous in the cart alone, as he heard gunshots from nearby hunters. I urged Lucky into a slow trot to hasten our return, but saw that Trystan was losing his footing on the cart floor. As Lucky slowed to a walk, Trystan slipped out, tangled in the long whip, and lay on the ground inches from the one inflated tire. Lucky stopped immediately, and stood quietly as I rescued Trystan, did a few TTouches on his ears, and safely returned him to the cart. He was shivering from the gunshots around us, so I urged Lucky into a strong walk and we made it back just fine. I thanked her again for being such a sensible girl, and rewarded her with lots of carrots and some grazing time.

With her blinkers on, could Lucky see Trystan leave the cart behind her? Could she feel the shift in the harness weight as his twenty pounds slipped out? Did Trystan somehow communicate to Lucky that he needed her to stop? She stopped immediately, even before I could ask her, and I am grateful that her response was so intelligent and appropriate. Lucky's years of TTouch training had taught her to think and respond, rather than react with fear when something went awry.

Today, my parents and my sister and her new husband share a house filled with many rescued Cavalier King Charles spaniels, other spaniels and mixes, some cats, my mom's schnauzer, and in the back yard, two miniature horses. Mom visits Lucky and her pasture pal Lightning many times throughout the day, brushing her, freshening her water bucket, feeding her, moving her from the pasture to the small barn paddock. The horse paddock shares a gate with the dog area, and Lucky often wanders through the dog pen and up a few steps to the back patio. My mom reports that many times when the family is eating a meal at the kitchen table, Lucky is standing right outside the window, awaiting the carrots that Mom will bring to her after dinner. Judy even has brought Lucky into the kitchen a few times. It seems that Lucky remains polite and comfortable inside of the house to this day.

Gwen taking a jump with Lucky many years later after Lucky was a present to my mother.

Chapter 23

The Dance of Love
Comet Arrives

Winston and baby Comet, age 3.5 months.

"We give dogs our home, our time, and our lives. In return, they give us everything—it's the humans that get the best deal."

— Joel Evans

Winston was fourteen years old, and I started to look for a new corgi puppy so that Winston would have plenty of time to teach him to be as wonderful as he himself was. I had seen many horses learn from observing others in our TTouch classes, and I knew it would take a few years for Winston to impart all of his knowledge to the new corgi. I had kept prize lists from the Mayflower Corgi shows and had called a few breeders, but no one had any puppies at that time. Someone at work told me they had seen an ad in the local paper for corgis, and sure enough, when I looked, there it was. It was a cold February day when a voice at the end of the phone said yes, she had one red male puppy who was about three months old. I had wanted a younger pup, but I didn't really see a problem getting one this age. She mentioned that she had sold lots of puppies over the years and ran a corgi Yahoo group—this was in the early years of the Internet. I thought it was worth a drive to see her puppy, so my girlfriend and I, along with Winston (who, after all, had to approve of the new kid), took the hour-long drive to the far northwestern corner of Massachusetts.

We arrived at a tiny mobile home, not really what I would have imagined as the ideal "corgi farm." Once inside, we saw that the owner had removed the kitchen cupboards and filled the spaces with dog crates and cages that were clearly too small for the corgis inside of them. My girlfriend and I exchanged troubled looks and waited as the woman pulled the puppy from a crate so small that it did not seem like he could even turn around in it. He was a very big guy, with ears still floppy and huge white paws. He looked nothing like Winnie did when he was a puppy. I asked if we could bring him outside for a while so we could see if Winston liked him.

The woman placed the puppy in the snow, and my girlfriend knelt down to make sure he did not escape. He sat blinking in the bright sunlight, slowly surveying the area as if he had never left his crate before. I kept Winnie on a leash and he paused a minute and looked over at the puppy. Did he know that this puppy was going to come to live in his house? He approached the puppy slowly, gave him a quick sniff, and then walked off. It looked to me that Winston was unimpressed with this puppy. The puppy still sat in the snow, examining the yard, the sky, my truck, and the people around him. He certainly did not appear to be lively. I whispered to my girlfriend, "I don't know about this puppy, but we can't leave him here in this terrible place." She agreed that we could not leave him there.

I offered the woman a little less money than she asked for, but she refused, so I wrote out a check for ten times the amount Winston had cost. I figured she needed the money to take better care of the dogs she had. My girlfriend stayed in the yard with Winnie and the puppy as I went inside to write the check. The woman said she did have his papers, and in fact, I never got the papers from her after many attempts. The woman also showed me my little guy's brother, who she had called Tiny Tim because he was small, had some deformities, and did not walk normally. I asked if she would sell him to me also, knowing my sister and I could really help the puppy, but she said she had to keep him herself because only she could provide the care he needed. She said that my puppy had a third litter mate who had been born dead. I sighed, realizing that my puppy had survived under very difficult circumstances.

My girlfriend held him in her lap on the drive back, with Winston in the back seat, not very interested in the new puppy. He seemed to be sulking. I told Winnie, "You have a big job now. You have to teach this puppy everything you know. It's going to be a lot of work." Winston gave me a long look.

Once home, the puppy went straight into the claw-foot tub for a badly needed bath. Winston watched, remembering his many visits to the bathtub. I set up a puppy pen in the apartment kitchen, deciding that this dog should not be in a crate again for a very long time. He was completely fascinated by everything—the kitchen chairs, the squeaky toys I gave him, his food and water bowl, and most of all Winnie. I knew it would be very hard to teach him to do his business outside, since he had been trapped in his crate with his food and poo mashed together. He had lost his innate sense of tidiness.

Soon he settled into the apartment, and Winston seemed to enjoy chasing the puppy around the rooms, playing tug with his sock toy, and snuggling up with him for a nap. The puppy's large size meant that Winston had a lot of work to socialize this kid before he was bigger than him and he could no longer have an advantage over the pup. I would be busy in the kitchen and hear Winston barking from the living room, the short, quick barks he used to tell me, "Come quick; you have to come!" Each time I'd respond to Winston's call, the puppy would be "up to no good," tearing up the rug, chewing a table leg, or his favorite, pulling things out of the laundry basket and tossing them about the house. These were things Winston had never done, and I was impressed that he understood the puppy should not do these things either.

It took weeks to name the puppy. I tried the names of other British Prime Ministers, but none of them fit. And the puppy was rambunctious, needing a lot of supervision and frequent trips up and down the steep steps to the outside world for his potty breaks, which was quickly trying my patience. I had to find a name that he liked so that maybe we could develop a better rapport about the dog behavior requirements of our household. One night, at two in the morning, having been awakened by Winston's barks about puppy naughtiness, I stood in the snow-filled yard in my PJs and slippers, staring up at the stars as the puppy scampered around, thinking I might name him "Star", but he had a long stripe up his nose, which didn't fit. And then I saw a clear, bright streak shooting across the sky—a comet! I brightly called "Comet!" The puppy looked up and trotted right over to me. "You are Comet the corgi," I said to him. "Comet."

Once inside, I reported the news to Winnie, "Your little brother's name is Comet." He looked at me, at the puppy, and back at me. I could tell he was still going to call him by the short quick barks he used to let me know there was trouble afoot.

That weekend there was a party at my friend's house, and I did not want to leave the puppy home alone any more than I had to. So I tucked him inside of my coat and brought him along. Winston loved to play with my friend's corgi, Duffy, and I knew he would want to meet Comet. Duffy and Winnie made the rounds asking for snacks, and little Comet had snuggles and a nap on Jack's lap. He agreed that Comet was a good name, seeing that no Prime Minister name matched this pup. Comet was a big hit, of course, being an adorable puppy, and his presence allowed Winnie and Duffy to go unnoticed as they devoured all sorts of party foods they were offered.

One of Winnie's first lessons for Comet was retrieving. Winston, famous for his endless retrieving of tennis balls, was also fond of bringing me sticks to throw for him. One Saturday, we went to a sunny field with patches of grass appearing through the snow, and I found a good stick for Winnie. I tossed it and he ran for it, as Comet sat thoughtfully watching. We repeated this a few times, and then Comet rose and ran after Winston and the stick, his big ears flopping and his big paws sliding on the snow. He caught up to Winnie just as he turned to bring the stick back to me. Then Winston paused, holding the end of the stick out to Comet, short muffled barks erupting around the stick in his mouth. Comet finally grabbed the end of the stick and together they brought it back to me. They continued to do this for half an hour, and ever after whenever I threw a stick. At the beach, if one dog picked up a seashell to carry, the other would trot close by, trying to share the job of bringing the shell to me, even though there was barely enough room on the shell for both corgi noses. A decade later, Comet showed Trystan how to bring sticks to me in the same way.

Winston's first fetch lesson with Comet, who quickly learned to share bringing sticks to me with Winston at the other end of the stick.

When Comet was two years old, the corgis came with me to Provincetown, Mass. for a vacation. Winnie was using a cart to walk and was struggling through the deep sand as I carried our umbrella, blankets, and water to the beach while Comet bounced ahead of us. A man came up behind me, telling me that he also had several corgis; in fact, at his home in Philadelphia, he had a miniature-sized garden with short plants and a wading pool especially for his corgis. He carried Winnie and his cart to the beach for me, and we became friends. When he heard the story of Comet's early life, he demanded details about the breeder's location. He simply said, "I think I want to get another corgi." When next I heard from him, he told me that he had gone to Comet's breeder and purchased every corgi she would sell him (Tiny Tim was not among them), and he had Comet's mother, father, and others safely enjoying the Eden he had built for his corgis. I was so relieved to hear his news, glad that an irresponsible breeder was out of business.

I took the lessons of Linda Tellington-Jones's work and my innate sense of how animals are in the world with us into my journey with Comet. Comet later became my work partner, support system, teacher, and companion with a depth I could never have foreseen.

Winston took his job of training Comet very seriously. He informed me of every one of Comet's mishaps, and like all of my corgis who were reluctant on the leash, Winston pulled on Comet's leash to show him how to keep up. They would stride down the street side by side, in perfect synchrony, like a pair of the golden fairy steeds corgis are known to be.

Winston's fetching lessons were so effective that Comet even shared sea shell retrieving with him.

Chapter 24

Dancing With Intuition
Corgis Share My Job

Winston visited many nursing homes in his career as a therapy dog and worked in animal assisted physical therapy treatments.

"I think dogs are the most amazing creatures; they give unconditional love. For me, they are the role model for being alive."

— Gilda Radner

Although Winston had been dismissed from physical therapy school, he did go to work with me several days a week at my first physical therapy job. After all, he had attended every CranioSacral course with me and had been my first practice client, and he'd had lots of TTouch over the years as well. At the time, I was treating many children with seizure disorders, and they loved to have Winston share the big table in the room, petting him and snuggling him while they had their sessions. I very quickly realized that Winston was tuning in to my young patients and was responding right in the moment when a potential seizure could occur, often as I was adjusting the temporal bones. My instructors had cautioned us that sometimes, in working with kids who had seizures, they could have a seizure on the table as we worked with the temporal bones, and that sometimes this would need explanation for the parents.

Winston, I noticed, would look up at me, give a slight woof, and then place his chest against the child's, resting his head over the child's left shoulder, breathing deeply and rhythmically. He seemed to me to be grounding the child, or somehow connecting their two heart rates to decrease the child's level of anxiety, and this seemed to stop every patient from having any seizures during my work. It is entirely possible that Winston was finding heart coherence with the child, and indeed using his calm heart rate and breathing to calm the child's nervous system.

He also was an expert at a technique called arcing, where a therapist can tune into the energetic waves coming from a person's body and find areas where the movement is interrupted, like seeing a stick in a pond interrupting the circles emanating from a stone tossed into the pond. Winston would walk under my massage table at our home office or at our job, or lie on the table next to the person, and then push his nose or paw at a particular area. This was nearly always the same area where I had arced. To test Winston's skills, sometimes I asked another craniosacral therapist to "arc" the person on the table, and write down his findings. Then I did the same thing, writing my own notes about findings. Finally, a third person with no training in craniosacral therapy would write where she felt Winston was pointing. Winston, the other craniosacral therapist, and I nearly always had one-hundred percent agreement.

Comet was a young puppy, and the house training was a challenge for him. Since it was early spring, I just brought him to work with Winston and me, and they stayed in my truck under a big shady tree until my lunch break when we all had a long walk. It was not yet too warm or too cold for the corgis to spend the mornings in the truck outside. In the afternoons, they both came inside to work with me. For two years, clients had been joking with the desk person, "I'm here to see my therapist, Winston, for my appointment." Many of them felt certain that he was helping them as much as I was.

Soon Comet was also allowed to work with clients, and Winston taught him the two important skills of how to work with children who have seizures and how to arc. I observed Winston using his nose to direct Comet to the places on a client where

Winston thought he should work, and gradually Winston allowed Comet to arc first. Then he would give an approving look and find another area on the person to focus his treatment. Some of my clients were fortunate enough to have a "multi-paws" session with the two corgis and me. Comet's arcing skills became highly developed, and in one case he later saved a dog's life by pinpointing something that might have otherwise gone unseen.

Winston was a very high-powered healer, working on the physical, emotional, and spiritual levels with people, and his presence opened hearts and moved energy. He participated in conventional animal assisted therapy sessions as well, playing catch with shoulder rehab patients, calming nervous patients and children, and he was very skilled at helping elderly people improve their balance abilities. He would walk on his leash and pull just the right amount to challenge peoples' balance, but not enough to put them in danger of falling. Once, when I was with a man learning to use a hemi-walker to get around in the community after a stroke, Winton came to a dead stop and refused to cross the street. He blocked the man from moving his legs and barked at me. I tried to move Winnie out of the way and proceed, as we had a "walk" light to cross the street. At that moment, a car raced by, breaking the speed limit and running the light. If Winston had not kept us from going, we would have not been able to move the man quickly enough to get across and the car would have struck us.

Winston told many animal communicators that he worked in many ways, and often he was doing healing work that I was not even aware of. He did not just focus on problems, but connected with people in other ways. I always had a strong sense that Winston did this work, as he did everything else with me, because he wanted to help me, just as his herding ancestors had helped their people.

Winston participating in a Craniosacral Therapy session with me in an outpatient setting.

Chapter 25

Letting Go of the Dance
Kitty Saffron Sugarspot

Saffron Sugarspot, 2002, before she went to her forever home.

"Cats seem to go on the principle that it never does any harm to ask for what you want."

— Joseph Wood Kruth

On a warm, starlit, early summer night, I emerged from a crowded bar near Albany, N.Y., where I had gone to see a concert by my favorite singer-songwriter. I walked a few blocks on deserted city streets to my truck, where my corgis were waiting for me, having had several walks and a visit to the venue earlier that evening. As I rounded the corner to the parking lot of the bank where my truck waited, I saw what at first looked like a small corgi walking under my truck. As I approached, I realized the orange fur belonged to a young cat, meowing back at me.

I called her over, saying, "Hey kitty, why are you out so late this evening?" She walked right up to me, circling between my legs and purring. She had no collar and was rather thin. I talked to her for a few minutes, trying to decide if she was lost. There were no residential buildings in the area, and she seemed very hungry, eating a bite of my leftover sandwich from the front seat of the truck. I didn't want to leave such a sweet cat, and it was becoming more and more clear that she had no home. I opened the door to the truck, where Comet was sitting on the back seat observing the cat. Winnie was curled up on the floor under the seat; it was long past his bedtime. I said to the cat, "Well if you need a home, jump in. There are two corgis in there, so make sure you think carefully about this."

The cat immediately jumped into my car as handily as any of my dogs, and sat up tall in the passenger's seat as if to say, "Home, please, driver."

Off I went. Comet was very much afraid of cats, having met some grumpy barn cats in his life who did not like him barking at them. Winston liked cats, though he had not known too many in his lifetime except for those he met on visits to my sister's house. Comet cowered next to Winnie under the back seat, while "Kitty" began to explore the truck, carefully tiptoeing her way over and under the front seat, and then jumping from the headrest to the back seat.

I had about a two-hour drive home, and Kitty did not settle down once on the trip. She sat on my head, much as Leo bunny used to do when I was driving. She jumped from the front to the back, and she put her face against the cracked passenger window, feeling the wind as a dog would. I could hear Comet's woofs of distress as Kitty came too close to him, and I tried to reach back to reassure him. It was fairly chaotic, and my driving was less than perfect. I was pulled over by a policeman not once, but twice before I'd even gotten to the Massachusetts border.

Each time, I explained to the policeman that I had just rescued this cat, and we were trying to get home with my dog who is afraid of cats, but with everyone calm and safe nonetheless. Each time, they drove behind me with flashers on to warn other cars of my possible unpredictable driving. Finally, we got back to my house.

The dogs trotted inside behind me, and I was thinking I would go back and carry Kitty inside so that she would not get lost. Instead she squeezed out of the car and followed the dogs through the front door as if she'd been doing it for years. I set out a bowl of water for Kitty and gave her some lunchmeat, sharing with the corgis. The dogs followed me upstairs and the three of us took our places in my bed. Kitty, amused by the fountain in my living room, was happily seated on a nearby armchair, watching the water bounce over the edges into the bowl of the fountain—until about 3:30 a.m. or so.

I awoke with a start, hearing Comet barking as Kitty jumped onto the bed. I tried to keep my orange bedfellows calm, but Comet jumped down, hiding under the bed. Winston moved in close to me, but made no effort to leave. Kitty settled in next to him and finally slept for a few hours.

I awoke early to the sound of meows coming from the kitchen. I knew Kitty needed a box and proper food, so I embarked immediately to get cat provisions. When

I returned, I found the three of them sitting in a row in the kitchen, waiting for me. I noticed the beautiful patch of white fur on Kitty's chest, and orange tiger markings clearly etched into her golden fur. A rare female orange marmalade—she was a stunning cat. She looked less than a year old.

She and the dogs were intrigued by the smells from the can of cat food, but everyone kept to their assigned bowls. I set up the litter box in the corner of the kitchen, as my small house had no ideal spot, and it did not seem right to put the box in the dark basement. Besides, I was leaving for the beach that afternoon and had to pack up the car and the dogs.

Kitty found a comfortable spot on the window sill on her first night with me, Comet, and Winston.

I called the shelters in Albany to see if anyone was missing a cat. At both places, the receptionists told me that they had rarely received a call from someone looking for a lost cat. This seemed incredible to me. One person took a description of Kitty, and said that someone had reported a lost cat about a week ago, and that she would call them to see if their missing cat matched the description of my cat. I urged the woman to have the people call me personally if they thought I had their cat.

I also called my neighbors to see if anyone could take care of Kitty for four days while I was gone, but they too were going away for the holiday weekend. I decided I would just have to take Kitty with me, this time in a carrier so I would not be a distracted driver. I loaded the litter box, litter and cat food into the truck along with the dogs and their food and beds and my own suitcases. Last in was Kitty, in Winnie's old carrier. At the final moment, I ran back into the house, rummaged around to find my old rabbit harness and leashes—which was in fact a cat harness anyway—and threw them into passenger seat.

We arrived at the tip of Cape Cod at Provincetown and it was warm and sunny. I headed to the beach with the dogs to take a nap after my long night, leaving Kitty in the room. When I woke up an hour later, I thought I should take the dogs for a walk on the beach. As I was putting my beach gear back in the room, Kitty jumped onto one of the beds, straining to look over the cars and catch a glimpse of the beach. She had not used her litter box since the morning, and I thought maybe I could take her for a walk with the dogs on the beach. After all, for years, my cat-loving neighbor had come home from work each day and taken her three cats for evening walks, circling around her house to do their business. They just trotted behind her, sniffing, batting at leaves with their paws and playing under her porch. They never were more than ten feet from her.

I dressed Kitty in the red harness and attached one of the extra dog leashes. I got the corgis dressed in their collars and leashes for the trip across the street to the beach where they could then run free. I was not at all sure how I was going to handle the three of them. I opened the door, gathered up the two dogs' leashes in my left hand and Kitty's leash in my right, and off we went. Comet led the way, trying to stay as far from the cat as possible, and the rest of us followed along. Kitty walked perfectly beside me.

Comet loved Kitty's catnip mouse toys.

When we got to the beach, the dogs rolled in the sand and then raced up and down the beach. Kitty continued to follow me on her leash down the beach, even stopping to do her business along the way, covering it thoroughly, and then giving me a strange look when I unearthed it to pick it up with a poo bag. A woman came running to catch up to me to meet Kitty.

She explained that she had two cats, asking how long it had taken me to teach her to walk on a leash. She looked shocked when I explained I'd had her less than twenty-four hours, and she had gone about a thousand feet on the leash so far. Kitty drew a crowd of admirers as we strolled along. She swatted her paws at the incoming waves, investigated the seashells, and sat regally inhaling the scents of surf and seafood restaurants along the beach. She didn't appear to have any regrets about jumping into my car last night.

As Comet loved fish, I ordered some takeout for him and Kitty to share. Winston preferred his usual food. The dogs slept in their own beds and Kitty, ever nocturnal, slept with me sometimes and wandered around the tiny hotel room much of the night. Her daily walks were popular with other people at my hotel, and she had quite a fan club by the end of our time there. The litter box was unused the whole weekend.

When I arrived home, the phone message light was blinking. I heard the voice of a woman in Albany, Linda M., describing her lost orange marmalade cat. I called her, asking if her cat had a white chest like Kitty's. She said, "No, our cat is entirely orange." I was relieved, but also concerned enough to email her a picture of Kitty to be sure, and I also called an animal communicator to see if I could learn anything that could help me find out if Kitty had another home perhaps. She was gaining weight and already returning to health, and I had a visit to a vet planned to check her for feline leukemia, a virus that affects the immune system.

The animal communicator suggested that Kitty had lived with an elderly woman who had passed away unexpectedly. She had wandered the apartment, hungry and confused for a few days before jumping out of a window. She found me a few days later. This seemed plausible, but I also called the concert venue and asked the person I knew there to put up some flyers about a found cat in the neighborhood.

Meanwhile, Kitty's nocturnal behavior was creating havoc in my life. She delighted in flinging the seashells around my fountain across the living room floor in the middle of the night. She walked across shelves and tables, toppling books and plants to the floor. Her midnight litter box visits were so aromatic that I had to jump out of bed and clean the box immediately when she was done. When I had another trip out of town and I could not bring her, she expressed her disapproval with the neighbor's care by making some kitty art on the wall of the kitchen with materials gathered from her litter box. Kitty was overtaking the realm of the dogs on my bed for those early morning hours when she did sleep. She was also enjoying the habit of sleeping near my head on my pillow.

My sister had a bit of an allergy to cats, which she learned about shortly after vet school when she brought some cats into her home. She gave them showers periodically to cut down on the dander allergens and took medication so that she could adjust to having cats in close proximity. I was developing a chronic runny nose and cough, which was getting worse, as Kitty enjoyed sleeping closer and closer to my face each night. I was not sure what to do next after Kitty had had a shower and a bath, and my allergy was getting no better.

About three weeks after our beach trip, I got another call from Linda M. from Albany, who had lost her cat. She confirmed that the cat in the email picture I had sent them was not theirs, as they had found their missing cat under a leaf pile in their backyard. In the meantime, one of their senior females had died, and they were looking for another cat. She asked if I was still looking for a home for Kitty. "I'm not sure," I mumbled into the phone.

Linda M. told me that she and her husband, Marty, were near retirement and had no children. Their many cats filled their lives with love and enjoyment. The whole bottom level of their house was set up for cats, with ramps and shelves along the walls for them to walk on, scratching posts and houses for them, and a screened area on a porch where they could safely interact with the outside world and watch the bird feeders. It was clear that Linda and Marty loved cats very much. I watched Kitty tiptoeing across my china closet near some antique plates and said, "You know what? I think this cat would love it at your house. It's a miracle that she has found you after meeting me."

Kitty had to get some tests at the vet, and then wait a few weeks with me until we could arrange a meeting with her new family. I met her new "dad," who had brought a pink cat carrier for her, and I gave him her box and her toys. Marty immediately gave her a kiss and told her how beautiful she was. When Kitty drove off with him to Albany, I was sad to see her go, but I knew she would have a perfect home with her new family.

They sent me pictures of her, with a note about her walking past their dinner plates loaded with scallops and without breaking stride, pawing one for herself off the plate, with the comment, "We think it's really cute." They gave her a proper name—Saffron Sugarspot, as she was the color of saffron, with a little spot of sweetness on her chest. She was a peacemaker among their cat family and delighted all of the other cats, choosing another younger one as her special friend.

Linda M. sent me a Christmas note the next year:

> *Sugarspot flourishes, enjoying her toys, her friends, and views of our four bird feeders. She has become a lap cat, a joy she never believed she would experience. We made a set of "lapsit" pillows called lumpy-gumpys (egg crate foam in pillowcases, colored to accent her yellow satin coat) for her. Wouldn't you like to be a cat in our home? When not sitting on a lap, Saffy kneads herself to sleep on her special kitty*

fleeces strategically located throughout the house. She is a wonderful companion for all of us. Love, Linda, Marty, Saffy, Cookie, and Chrissy."

I soon recovered from my runny nose, though to this day I am fairly allergic to cats. Saffron Sugarspot lived happily in her new home thanks to Linda's cat, who had squeezed out the door to get lost in a leaf pile, and thanks to her courage to take a ride home in my truck with two corgis. Sometimes it's true—when you love someone, you have to let her go.

Chapter 26

The Dance of Renewal
Winnie Runs Free

Jack's Winsome Winston, an incredible friend, partner, and colleague.

"If there are no dogs in Heaven, then when I die I want to go where they went."

— Will Rogers

Winston was growing older and starting to lose the use of one of his hind legs. Judy and I, closely observing his gait for tiny asymmetries in the hind end, had become aware that he was likely to be stricken by a neurological condition in dogs called degenerative myelopathy, which is similar to ALS—or Lou Gehrig's Disease—in humans. Winston had led a very athletic and active life, with dramatic slides and leaps to retrieve balls and toys, and it was owing to his relatively shorter body length that he avoided any spine or disc problems. But this disease, later found to be genetic, was inescapable for him. Winston gradually began to skip on one hind leg, dragging it later, until finally he could not hold himself completely upright. Months later, his other hind leg became weak as well, and Judy said it was time to find him a cart. Providentially, Eddie's Wheels, a leader in producing dog "wheelchairs," is located nearby my house, so Winston and I took a ride up there to get a cart.

Not even his wheels kept Winston from swimming and running at top speed to retrieve tennis balls.

We walked into the shop, Winston limping on one hind leg with me, and Eddie shook my hand and showed us around. Then he said, "You know, we haven't had too much luck with corgis with carts." Since Winston was so willing to do anything I had ever asked of him, I found this unbelievable, and I said, "OK, let's find a cart that will fit him and I'll show you that he will be fine." I ran to the car, getting a bunch of my long TTouch dog leashes and ropes, and Eddie pulled out a cart he was making for a small cocker spaniel. Using the ropes and leashes, I hooked Winnie into the cart and called him to follow me around the shop. After a moment to assess the contraption behind him, Winnie strutted behind me with no problems. I wrote the check to Eddie to make Winston's custom cart.

We returned about two weeks later, and Winston's short dog special cart was ready. It had all terrain tires, perfect for an active dog like Winnie. I attached the harness and strapped the front piece around him. Eddie made a few adjustments to get the cart at the proper height. Winston was standing at the large garage door opening at the end of the building, looking out over a grassy lawn. I tossed a tennis ball and it rolled across the street and into the next field. "Go get it Winnie," I said enthusiastically. He trotted off, gaining speed on the hills, running across the street and through a wide, deep stream, barking happily when he reached his tennis ball. He galloped back brightly to give me the ball. "I've never seen anything like this," Eddie said.

"Well, there aren't any dogs like Winnie," I said smiling.

Winston loved his new wheels, following Comet and me on short walks, wearing a variety of booties to protect his hind paws. His "bike," as we called it, became an inspiration to some of the people in wheelchairs who we worked with as well. Comet was terrified of the cart until Winston was in it. He learned to run in circles around and around Winnie, barking and nipping at him as he raced past, with Winnie nipping back at him, playing their own special game of tag. Even when Winnie was immobile, Comet still played tag with him this way. Although Winston needed his wheels, his life with Comet and me was as it had always been, until the DM progressed and Winston started to lose the ability to control his bladder.

Jack, a careful corgi dad, watching Winnie and Molly wading together.

Comet was still coming to work with me some days, and I hired people to take Winston out while I was at work. Gradually this became too difficult, as he was growing weaker. I had towels to soak up urine from his bladder problems, a vinyl covered bed with blankets on top for him to sleep on, but Winston was increasingly frustrated with the mess he was accidentally making. He began to try to eat the towels where they were wet to clean up his mess, and I'd find pieces of them in his poo. Eventually he developed an obstruction that became apparent when he refused food. Jack came with me and we rushed him to a new state-of-the-art veterinary hospital nearby. Winnie was well beyond fourteen years old, but we elected to do the surgery, as I recalled Susan telling me about her corgi Arnold's major surgeries for many years. "Corgis are very tough dogs," she had said. I knew, just as I had known Winston would thrive with his "bike," that he would survive the surgery.

When they called me in after his surgery, they showed me a considerable wad of towel that had been obstructing his bowel. It was incredible. He was, of course, feeling much better, eating and drinking happily. He stayed almost two weeks at the hospital, and many of my friends went to do TTouch on him during the day and in the evenings. I did craniosacral therapy with him, and played with his squeaky carrot with him. The doctors at the hospital could not believe how well he was doing. He made a remarkable recovery and came home.

Winnie still had a lingering bladder infection, one of the biggest complications with DM, as the dogs cannot fully empty their bladders on their own, which is something that is hard to notice in your dog until there is an infection. The vet gave me a prescription for enormous green pills for him that I had to pick up at the compounding center and handle with gloves. I should have known from this that they were not the right thing for him. I would not want to give something seemingly so strong to my recovering senior corgi.

Winston was home for only a few weeks before he passed away. I came downstairs, having awoken extra early one morning, and he seemed to be only faintly breathing. As I had done with Hawk, I held his little head on my lap and felt the life slip out of him. His eyes stared ahead for a few final moments, and then Winston was gone.

I cried out, and Comet—big, fluffy, wonderful Comet—came right to me and I cried into his fur. But I still had to go to work at my physical therapy job, as someone had to open the building that day. I called Jack and he made arrangements to meet me at the big vet hospital with Molly, his own corgi and Winnie's childhood friend, and I would bring Comet and Winston.

I don't know how I made it through that terrible hour at work, where I had to see two clients with my deceased dog in the car outside. I had Comet with me, and once other therapists came in, I left to meet Jack at the hospital. I sang corgi songs to Winston in the car, and told him it would be all right, that I would not leave him. Somehow I made it safely to the hospital through the heavy morning traffic.

Inside, carrying Winston in his blanket with Comet trotting next to us, I met Jack and Molly, and the vet who had worked with Winnie led us into a room to ask about our "arrangements." There was nothing left to do, but to leave. And yet we could not leave. Jack and I, with our two corgis, sat with Winston for many, many hours—all day, in fact. We told each other corgi stories about Winston, and I stroked his fur and snipped a bit from his ruff. I was calm, but overwhelmed by grief. Winston had been with me for fifteen years. Finally, when our vet came to see how we were doing, he happened to mention that another corgi had come in last night. This is what I needed to hear—knowing that Winston would be near another corgi helped me to feel that he was safe.

Jack followed me home to help me take care of Comet and put away Winnie's things, including his bike. I knew I would not be able to sleep that night, or for the next few nights. I knew that I would not have been able to get through any of it without Comet.

Winston's ashes came back to us in a small tin box, and I put it in my lovely wooden green bridle box painted with a picture of Winnie, along with his toys, leashes, and bowls. I placed it next to where I sat on the sofa so that he would always be near me. Comet sniffed the box of Winnie's things from time to time before planting himself at the other end of the sofa each evening for the rest of the time we lived in that house.

A short time later, I received a phone call from a woman I knew from craniosacral therapy classes, who was also a shaman. I told her about Winston crossing the rainbow bridge, and she told me that she had known many corgis who had passed away in the last few months. She told me she'd heard about a Celtic legend that when the corgis go to heaven, it is because the children there need to play because there is too much grief here. It was just after 9/11. My mind filled with green fields and boisterous children throwing balls for corgis jumping through the meadows beneath a brilliant blue sky, and I knew this could be true.

The Rainbow Bridge

There is a bridge connecting Heaven and Earth.
It is called the Rainbow Bridge because of its many
colors. Just this side of the Rainbow Bridge there is a
land of meadows, hills and valleys with lush green grass.

When a beloved pet dies, the pet goes to this place.
There is always food and water and warm spring weather.
The old and frail animals are made whole again.
Those who are maimed are made whole again.
They play all day with each other.

There is only one thing missing. They are not with
their special person who loved them on Earth.
So, each day they run and play until the day comes
when one suddenly stops playing and looks up! The
nose twitches! The ears are up! The eyes are staring!
And this one suddenly runs from the group!

You have been seen, and when you and your
special friend meet, you take him or her in your
arms and embrace. Your face is kissed again and
again and again, and you look once more into the
eyes of your trusting pet.

Then you cross over the Rainbow Bridge together,
never again to be separated.

—*Anonymous*

Winston, an amazing animal spirit I am so fortunate to have known.

Healing With the Dance
Comet the Therapist

Comet working as a therapy dog and PT assistant with me at a long term care facility.

"Why does watching a dog be a dog fill one with happiness?"

— Jonathan Safran Foe

On the day of 9/11, I was at my physical therapy job. The entire staff was glued to a television in the reception area. I was trying, as so many were, to telephone my friends and relatives in the city. One of my clients was doing the same, so we paused halfway through the session to make our calls. He was seeing me for back pain, and had only just started his treatment series. Once again, what seemed difficult at the time, working while others were not, turned out to be a lucky turn of events for me.

Tad Wanveer, a lead therapist from the Upledger Institute, organized a group of CranioSacral therapists to go to New York a few months after 9/11 to offer free sessions for anyone who wanted to come. We had a group of therapists from across the country, and Comet, the craniosacral corgi. We would be working at the Swedish Massage Institute in a very large treatment room, and would be in New York City for over a week.

Fortunately, the client I'd been treating on 9/11 connected me with some friends in the city with an extra apartment where I could stay with Comet during our time working in New York. I will always be grateful to this man, as his thoughtfulness helped many people during a time of great need.

After my first day doing CranioSacral sessions with Comet assisting, Tad pulled me aside to tell me that the people with the Swedish Massage Institute did not want us to bring Comet there. Even though he was a licensed service and therapy dog, they had a strict policy. Tad understood that it was essentially illegal to dismiss a service dog, but asked me to please understand and to make some other arrangements, as people were on edge already with the situation in New York. Again, distressing news proved to be the best possible outcome.

The owners of the apartment I was staying in were two psychotherapists who loved animals. They had been working at the site and with grieving families for weeks. When I set off to work the second day, I left them a note to thank them for the apartment, explaining why Comet was there if they stopped by, and added that they could take him for a walk if they wanted, or even bring him to work, as he was used to working with people. When I returned that day, I had a letter back from them informing me that Comet had gone to the site and their offices with them and had comforted grieving families. The note also said that he was a huge help, and would I mind if he went with them every day to their offices? I was amazed—here was my wonderful dog working with strangers in a very stressful situation, and all he wanted in return was a walk and some chicken for dinner.

I called the psychotherapists and got the full report, explaining how to tell if Comet was becoming stressed, and asking them to do some TTouch ear work with him from time to time. They were kind and compassionate people, and they told me how much better Comet seemed to be coping than some of the other dogs. I knew they would take good care of him.

Comet went to the site and also spent some time in the therapists' offices with people struggling with grief and turmoil for over a week. And when I returned each night he greeted me, eager to play and go to our favorite deli to pick up his chicken dinner. He seemed to have a deeper understanding of the situation. He seemed to know that this sadness around him was not really about his own life or his personal people, and that he could help just by being with those who needed his compassion. He earned a certificate from a group working there for his dedication and good spirit. He was one of the last three surviving dogs who had worked in New York after 9/11, and he was just over a year old when we'd gone to help.

Comet accompanied me to every craniosacral class that I attended or taught.

For many years, Comet accompanied me to every craniosacral class I taught, assisted, or attended. He came with me to assist at an advanced class in Connecticut a few years after 9/11. Our group was staying at religious retreat site, Wisdom House, so we worked, ate, and slept in close quarters. During this week, Comet was with me in the room where two groups were working doing CranioSacral sessions. He had a choice of where and how to work, or not to work. One evening a man was on the massage table in a place of very deep distress, but he was not quite tapping into his emotions. The lead therapist was very skilled, using the man's verbal cues to help him unlock emotional and physical restrictions in his body.

Comet was drawn to this group. He paced around the table, jumping up onto it with his front paws. The lead therapist gave Comet a hopeful look, and finally Comet leapt onto the man on the table, laying his heavy corgi body on the man's chest, licking him gently on the cheek. Comet had never before done anything like this, and I would have said there was no way he could make such a jump. Tears slipped out from the man's eyes, his face red with emotion, as he whispered to the lead therapist. His words grew louder as he told the story of his own beloved dog, who was hit by a car when he was a small child. He had seen it from the window of his house, but his mother had lied to him about it, and she continued to lie to him about many things in his life. He explained the complications and heartbreak this had caused him, all the while hugging Comet close. It was a turning point in his life.

Comet assisted me in craniosacral therapy sessions with animal and human clients for many years.

The next morning, the man asked to take Comet with him on his run, and so they set off for an hour together. When we had our morning circle, Comet sat with his rump on the man's feet, and the man, in his turn, reported his incredible experience with Comet to the group. Years later, when Comet accompanied me when I spoke at the International CranioSacral conference, Comet recognized this man from across the room and ran over to sit near him.

At the same advanced class with this man, there was a woman who did not especially like dogs. Every day Comet sat in front of her and stared up at her during our morning circles. The lead instructor knew there was more to this, so he did not remove

Comet from the group, though I did try to keep him at a distance from the woman. On the last day, we took turns around the circle making comments about Comet, as I was working on a presentation about how animals participate in craniosacral sessions. During this time, Comet sat directly in front of the woman, staring at her. When it was her turn, she fumbled over her words, not knowing what to say after ten others had explained what a powerful and interesting experience it had been to have Comet in their sessions. Comet then leapt up into her lap and kissed her. She reacted like Lucy in the Charlie Brown comics—"Ew!! Dog germs, ew!" The lead instructor simply said, "What's this really about?"

The woman said, tears starting to flow, "I don't know. This dog just wants to love me, and I don't like it. I don't know what's wrong with me."

"Who else won't you let love you?" the instructor asked. The woman broke down, and told us about the difficult relationships in her life. Then she hugged Comet, kissed his nose, and said, "Oh all right, thank you, Comet. You are a great therapist after all. I'm glad you were here."

Chapter 28

Life Dance
Stillpoint—The Intersection of CST and TTouch

Linda Tellington-Jones doing TTouches during my assessments of the craniosacral rhythm with a dog participating in the session.

"Allow nature to teach you stillness."

— Eckhart Tolle

In February 2002, Linda Tellington-Jones invited me to present a one-day introduction to craniosacral therapy for horses at the advanced Tellington TTouch Training in Florida, which included a demonstration on some horses at the end of the day. I taught the group about the craniosacral stillpoint, wherein the practitioner gently asks the rhythm of the fluid in the brain and spinal cord to slow to a point of stillness. The students were fascinated by the stop in the craniosacral rhythm, as they appreciated the quietness of this moment of self-correction. Some reported having sensed a deep stillness in themselves and their animal partners during TTouch sessions. They asked if this was perhaps an experience of a stillpoint. It seemed entirely likely, and I decided to set up some experiences to test the craniosacral rhythm during TTouch sessions.

From this one-day class, I decided to investigate this phenomenon further at an Advanced TTouch training to be held in Sante Fe in June 2002. I taught a one-day craniosacral class to the group of experienced TTouch practitioners. As I introduced the work, I noted that Tad Wanveer had mentioned during our work after 9/11 that he knew of no other work where you came to a session from a neutral place, with no expectations for the outcome. I felt that TTouch sessions also started like this. At the break later, a woman approached me—Pam Wanveer. She had been briefly married to Tad's brother many years before, and was among the first groups of certified companion animal TTouch practitioners in the United States. We have been friends for many years since then, and much of what I know about difficult dogs I learned from Pam. She has taken and assists with the classes I teach for equine and small animal craniosacral therapy, and she continues to host and teach companion animal TTouch classes in the Washington, D.C. area.

I taught an introduction to craniosacral therapy to advanced TTouch practitioners from around the world.

The next day, I asked several craniosacral therapists in the area to join me in testing the craniosacral rhythm in both the practitioner and the person or animal receiving the TTouch work. We had many dogs, each paired with a TTouch practitioner. Some dogs were working with two people, and some people were working on other people. Groups were asked to do various TTouches of their own choosing, and they were scattered around on a lawn area with about eight feet between each group.

We had three people testing the craniosacral rhythm of all participants in each group in a random order. Testers made note of what they felt, and also recorded which TTouches the practitioners had reported doing at the time. Testers had also practiced and reviewed of the idea of "neutral" so as not to disrupt a group when they approached. As the participants did TTouches, the testers quietly monitored the craniosacral rhythms of the people doing the TTouches, as well as those of the dogs and the people being touched. Testers used physical palpation to minimize bias. Testers also spent only a few seconds in each group, and were aware of the possibility that their presence in the group might create stillpoints.

Advanced TTouch practitioners feeling their craniosacral rhythms during my class.

It very soon became obvious to the testers which participants in a group were experiencing stops in the craniosacral rhythm, and when. Some testers reported that it was so obvious that they wouldn't have even needed formal palpation to detect the stillpoints. At several moments it seemed that everyone on the lawn was in a stillpoint simultaneously, or experiencing stops in the craniosacral rhythm, which would imply that states of deep healing had been occurring within both dogs and people—those giving TTouches and those receiving. And the stillpoints were occurring without the purposeful induction that is sometimes part of a craniosacral session.

I repeated a similar trial a few weeks later in Vermont, with people doing TTouches on horses, all in an indoor arena, about twenty-five feet apart. The results were compelling. In both trials, every person and animal experienced stillpoints, which most often occurred during the circular TTouches, as well as during ear strokes, tail work, and python lifts on the legs. We also found that talking between the people working together with a dog or horse interrupted the craniosacral rhythm stops, and very long Noah's march strokes did as well.

Furthermore, we found that the circular TTouches produced a deeper sort of work than the other touches; even if only one person in a group did circular TTouches, it resulted in simultaneous stillpoints in everyone in the group. In these cases, testers also commented that the stillpoints had a quality like those purposefully induced in a craniosacral therapy session like those used, for instance, to decrease a fever. Even with the less experienced TTouch group in the second trial, the same results prevailed.

So what did the results of my study mean? First, if the stillpoint is a moment of deep self-correction and deep healing, then it is remarkable that the people doing the work are also making changes in themselves at the same time they are working on another being. This underscores the idea of the connection between people and animals, and between therapists and clients. The connection established by experiencing simultaneous stillpoints likely facilitates a deeper interspecies bond, as well as a fostering a deeper interspecies understanding. The incidences of the simultaneous craniosacral rhythm stops also point to the depth of both TTouch and craniosacral work. Given the results of the brain wave work Linda Tellington-Jones did with Anna Wise, it is likely that both the practitioner and the client in a craniosacral session are also in Cade's "awakened mind state."

Robyn, Linda's sister, doing TTouches during my craniosacral stillpoint research.

It is indeed likely that human and animal craniosacral rhythms adjust to each other and smooth out restrictions when they are connected (even though different species have differing rates in their craniosacral rhythms). Perhaps this is a part of the connection people report experiencing when they swim with dolphins, ride a horse, or sit with a dog or a cat.

Kirsten Henry, a long time TTouch practitioner, participating in the test assessing the craniosacral rhythm during a TTouch session, while Sumati does circular TTouches on a dog.

Researchers have previously found that being in the presence of a dog lowers a person's blood pressure. We also know that you can lower blood pressure for both you and the animal you work with using slow TTouches. So it is likely that craniosacral rhythms could also make adjustments in the amplitude, symmetry, quality, and overall vitality during TTouch sessions. In Tellington TTouch Training work, I have seen how changing the rate of my breathing can help calm an anxious horse or dog, as our breathing rates naturally fall into a synchrony.

More recently, we have learned from work at the HeartMath Institute that there is more at play in the connection between a person and an animal than breath rates and synchronous craniosacral rhythms, which researchers at the institute describe as Heart Coherence. As explained on the website:

> Coherence, in any system, from the human body to social affairs, refers to a logical, orderly and harmonious connectedness between parts of a system or between people. When we speak of heart-rhythm coherence or physiological coherence, we are referring to a specific assessment of the heart's rhythms that appears as smooth, ordered and sine-wavelike patterns. From a physics perspective, when we are in a coherent state, virtually no energy is wasted

because our systems are performing optimally and there is synchronization between heart rhythms, the respiratory system, blood-pressure rhythms, etc. Among the many benefits of personal coherence are increased composure, more energy, clear thinking, enhanced immune-system function and hormonal balance. ... One of the simplest and quickest paths to personal heart coherence is through the intentional self-generation of positive feelings such as compassion, care, love and other renewing types of emotions.

Heart coherence is what allows Linda Tellington-Jones to make an immediate connection with any animal she works with, just as I did in my work with Bubba the white horse. When you approach an animal from a place of understanding and appreciation, that deep connection allows for healing to take place.

Chapter 29

The Dance of Magic
Sharing CST, TTouch and Dancing Horses

Dr. John Upledger meets Comet at the international Beyond the Dura conference in 2003.

"Except for the oint, the still point,
There would be no dance, and there is only the
dance."

— TS Eliot, *Four Quartets Burnt Norton II*

In 2003, I presented the results of my study about stillpoints and TTouches at the Beyond the Dura International CranioSacral Therapy Conference. In doing TTouch work with some of my horse and dog clients, I also had begun noticing craniosacral stillpoints occurring in people and animals walking in the corners of the TTouch labyrinth. This reminded me of the "awakened mind state" pattern of deeper theta and delta brain waves, which also occurred in the corners of the labyrinth. My talk included this observation and information about how some TTouches impact areas of the brain and spinal cord in similar ways to some of the craniosacral techniques. Remarkably, a woman in the group, now a craniosacral therapist and healer, had attended some of the Tellington TTouch Training equine clinics I had taught, and she was at the conference with her dog, who volunteered to be the demonstration client by stepping up to the stage at the right moment. Of course, as I showed the hand positions of many of the techniques, Comet stood patiently on the front table as the perfect model, barking appropriately when people asked questions.

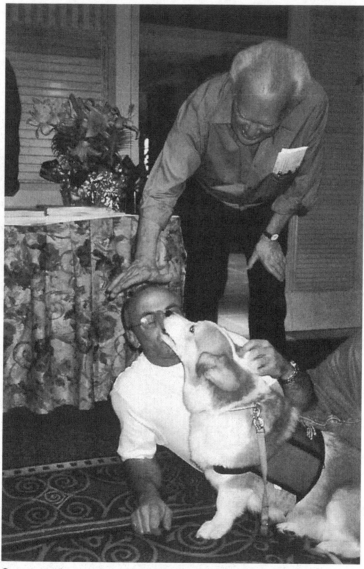

Comet and Dr. Upledger befriending a doctor at the conference who was the keynote speaker at the next Beyond the Dura Conference.

Additionally, there was a man in the audience who is a doctor, and who has horses. He had become a particular favorite of Comet's, who sought him out each morning before the lectures. His enthusiasm for CranioSacral therapy was ignited after hearing my lecture inspired by the Tellington Method equine work he was familiar with. Over the next year, he took all of the Upledger CranioSacral courses he could and adapted those techniques to his medical practice with labor and delivery. Two years later, at the next conference, he presented amazing findings of smoothing the delivery process with decreased infant and mom stress, detailing a program he had developed. His lecture included measurable improvements in heart rate, blood pressure, etc., with the use of CranioSacral treatments during the birthing process for both moms, dads, and babies. This doctor, inspired by his love of animals and his connections with them and as a result of my presentation, changed how he practiced medicine to bring an integrated knowledge of manual therapy and Western medicine into the delivery room.

After my talk, practitioners at the Beyond the Dura Conference shared with me many stories of inspiring animals in their lives. Dr. Upledger himself was excited about the new work he was doing having dolphins participate in therapy sessions, and over the next year, as I continued to work with Comet and record what he was doing in our own sessions with clients, I learned from many people that animals were participating in craniosacral therapy sessions with them. As more craniosacral therapy practitioners were contacting me about their animals assisting them during sessions, I decided to compile peoples' stories and do some further investigating of my own.

That summer, 2003, my sister moved with her horses to another farm, Just Dandy Equestrian Center. It had an indoor ring, lots of parking, and a outdoor riding ring with lights, which made it a perfect place to hold small horse shows. One of the things we recalled from our childhood shows was a farm that had a "trophy" room, where you could go and select whatever prize you wanted when you won a class. Judy recreated this at her farm, and we had so much fun stocking it with silver, picture frames, and even pony toys for the youngest riders. Her farm continued to be a place of learning, with her shows still emphasizing comments from the judges, and instructors being allowed in the ring when the smaller or inexperienced riders got lost on their jump course, or could not get their ponies trotting.

Burgers moved to this farm, too, and Gwen was now about twelve years old. She was beginning to understand more about dressage, as well as riding gaited horses. It was a cold winter day when I was visiting, and Gwen jumped on Burgers without a bridle or even a lead line on his halter. Burgers always gave a few little hops when you first got on him bareback to remind you that something was missing, or maybe to get you positioned in a place that was comfortable for him. Gwen asked me to help her try some dressage, which, given her riding equipment, I thought was just for fun.

I walked next to Burgers and tapped him on the shoulder and he collected, and as

I tapped his croup, he did a piaffe for the delighted Gwen. She quickly followed my directions for seat aids and position for shoulder-in and haunches-in at the trot, as well as half pass. She wanted to try some lead changes, so she turned the corner of the arena and came across the middle of the ring, asking Burgers for changes, sitting with her hands resting on either side of his neck at the withers. Before I could even offer suggestions, Burgers did beautiful clean two tempe changes across the ring! This had always been rather difficult for him, and I could see that day that it was possible that the saddle and bridle had been in the way all along. But Gwen's perfectly balanced seat and lack of complicated thoughts of cues and weight shifts allowed her to naturally follow the motion of the horse, and just by changing her gaze, she and Burgers were doing some of the best work he had ever done. I gave Gwen a standing ovation, and she said, "That was so much fun! It's magic! I didn't do anything and Burgers was dancing!"

Anything, indeed—another lesson to show me that doing less as a rider allows the horse to do so much more.

Chapter 30

Sharing the Dance With Compassion
Animals Healing People

Comet and Willie the pony assisting in a Craniosacral session with Willie's rider, Gwen.

"There is something about the outside of a horse that is good for the inside of a man."

— Winston S. Churchill

"Most dancers I know, especially the talented and successful ones, seem to possess [my dog's] knack for living moment to moment. You see, their idea of time is related to those infinitely short moments when they are being their super selves."

— Paul Taylor, *Privat Doman: An Autobiography*

In August of 2004, I was fortunate to be invited by Dr. Upledger to work with dolphins during CranioSacral therapy sessions, and was accompanied by Mary Getten, an animal communicator known for her book *Communicating with Orcas*. Dr. John loved dolphins and felt very connected to them. Having worked with Winston and Comet during sessions for years, and having shared a few sessions with horses at this point, I was interested to see what the dolphins would offer us. While many people marvel at the energy of the dolphins and have life changing experiences with them, I was intrigued about experiencing a connection with them to see what they shared with the other animal therapists I had worked with, Winston and Comet.

We were in groups of five. The "client" was supported in the water by the other four people in the group doing a CranioSacral therapy session. We stood on a platform in about four feet of water while the dolphins swam in deeper water in an area surrounding us. These dolphins were not born in the wild, though they did get to swim in the ocean each day, following a boat and then returning to their home. It was remarkable to feel their bodies swim by us, and they often placed their rostrums, or noses, on the heads or bodies of the people being treated during a session. When the dolphin touched anyone in the group, the entire group could feel the increased energy as it radiated through everyone. It was as if the dolphin's energy amped up the electrical circuit created by our joined hands and bodies.

Dolphins participating in Craniosacral sessions; I am floating on the left and Dr. Upledger is on the right with his wife, Lisa.

We had the benefit of Mary Getten's insight to tell us something about what the dolphins were thinking in this process. She told us they knew that people needed healing and did a quick scan of a body, noticing where there were disturbances in energy frequencies, seeing disharmonies and not specific causes. Dolphins work with frequencies, so it did not matter how long a disharmony had existed—whether a genetic issue or recent injury—they simply put the body into a space of "correct harmony." The dolphins relayed to Mary that they send all frequencies at one time, but some dolphins focus more intently on a particular problem, or they might send more of one frequency than another. The energy sent by the dolphins corrects the abnormal frequency and disharmony in the energy system of the body.

The dolphins said they do hold an intention and understand what they are doing. They don't simply beam energy in a random way, but hold the intention to create a whole body, to leave a body in its perfect form. As Mary reported this, I was struck by the similarity in the words Linda Tellington-Jones uses to describe her intention during TTouches—to remind the cells and the body of their potential for perfection.

The dolphins said that the speed of healing is increased if many dolphins participate in the same session, as one dolphin can only send so much energy. As we were doing in our groups of four "multi-hands sessions," the dolphins were doing "multi-rostrum/ beak sessions" to accelerate healing. The dolphins do not use their echolocation energy to do healing, as that comes from the forehead, not the beak, and is not healing energy.

Participants noticed that the dolphins varied the quality and depth of their touch for different people, generally using a lighter approach with children or very badly injured people. I did not notice them doing arcing the way Comet did, though sometimes they positioned themselves at different places on the client. The dolphins explained that "bonking" someone harder was a way to loosen up something on a cellular level, a stuck energy where something needs to be broken up.

The dolphins told Mary that they generally enjoyed this work because it gave them a focus, and they sensed that the craniosacral therapists had an understanding of them. One dolphin, Coral, told Mary, "There are loving and highly spiritual beings who come through this program, and we dolphins want to meet them at the heart level." This dolphin's words reminded me of the heart coherence we experience in TTouch and craniosacral sessions, and it was fascinating to see that Coral felt the heart connection as well.

After this profound experience, I partnered with Mary to provide insight from many other animals participating in craniosacral sessions. I returned to Judy's farm to explore more deeply how horses worked with me. I had once heard someone say that horses are dolphins on land. My own thought was that dolphins are dolphins, and horses are horses; they each have unique gifts to offer.

Horses are highly sensitive and seem to often work at a "gut level." Candace Pert's work has shown that neuropeptides—molecules carrying emotional information— are found throughout the body, especially in the heart and the gut. With such long intestinal tracts, fifteen to twenty-one feet of small intestine in a horse, there is a large surface area to give and respond to emotional information. The equine heart is many times bigger than a human's, surrounded by a much larger electromagnetic field. Horses are brilliant at sensing the emotions of others. A horse's neocortex is not as well developed as a human's, so horses function more in their limbic systems, the emotional centers of their brains. I have often seen a so-called problem horse simply mirroring the feelings and intentions of their owners, even when the owners were unaware they were projecting these feelings.

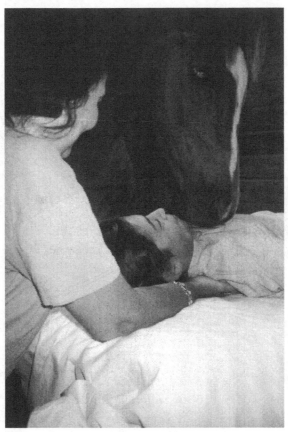

Willie is doing a thoracic inlet release with me, meeting the energy of my hands underneath Gwen with his muzzle on her clavicles.

Linda Tellington-Jones has told me that she believes one reason horses are in our lives is to open our hearts. They willingly cooperate with us because they are socio-sensual beings in the extreme—they feel good when their riders feel good. Horses can sense intention and energy very clearly, as anyone who has worked closely with them could attest. With riders positioned over the horses' spinal cords, and with bridles surrounding the skull and brain, we are connected with the horse's central nervous system when we ride.

I wondered if horses would show an interest when I was working with the dural tube (the spinal cord) in particular during a craniosacral session, because that was the interface they shared with their riders.

I set up a massage table in the indoor arena, with Burgers and Judy's horse Rocky free to roam where they wanted. We removed their blankets and halters, giving them complete freedom. Comet positioned himself under the table, as he sometimes did for a session, and I asked him to let the horses know what we were doing. Judy volunteered to be on the table but had to leave, so her son Andrew, who had also ridden Rocky, acted as the client. I proceeded with a session, wondering if the horses would participate, but allowed them freedom not to. Since we were their people, they were curious, and they wandered about the arena for a while.

For the first half of the session, the horses played with each other, chewed on the jumps in the corner of the ring, and then began a session of mutual grooming. Did they suppose that is what we were doing on the massage table? Then Burgers approached us and placed his muzzle on Andrew's head, resting it over Andrew's frontal bone. As a soccer player, Andrew had had several concussions. Then Rocky approached and worked at Andrew's right ankle and knee, areas he had injured skate boarding. Rocky picked up Andrew's leg, biting his pants, and held the leg above the table for several minutes before placing it back on the table with his mouth resting on Andrew's ankle. Burgers moved his muzzle down to Andrew's upper chest, in a thoracic inlet release, and then stood with his head and neck over Andrew's chakras, seeming to integrate the other work he and Rocky had done. Andrew, then a teenager, said that he could feel the horses' energy in the session, and that his neck and ankle felt much better.

Burgers told Mary Getten that he thinks most people have a lot of tense spots and need help. He appeared to understand what we were doing, and when he did work with my sister in another session, he stood over my sister's foot that she'd injured in a fall. Judy said she could feel "energy or something" from him in her foot, which she described as "tingling," asking me, "What is he doing? It feels weird." Then she complimented him, saying he knew more about riding than she would ever know. Burgers said that he focuses energy out of his muzzle and head over areas he perceived as blocked in a person. He said he would be happy to work with me often doing energy work, like Comet.

A month before, I had set up a table in the outdoor riding arena with my mom on the table, giving her miniature horse Lucky an opportunity to join us. Lucky is calm and very oriented to relate to people. Lucky had visited nursing homes where seniors brushed her and sang to her from their wheelchairs, and had gone to schools where children read stories to her. Interestingly, she only came up to the table near the end of the session when I was working on my mom's sacrum, dural tube, and occiput. Since Lucky was never ridden (though she did wear harnesses and bridles), her choice intrigued me.

A child from the farm had asked to try a craniosacral treatment with Lucky. Once the child was on the table, Lucky went immediately to her right knee and rested her muzzle there. A few minutes later, she picked up the child's arm by the T-shirt sleeve and gave it a shake. When I inquired about past injuries, the child reported having pain in her right knee from a fall, and recently in her arm after a tetanus shot. Once again, Comet helped in the session from under the table. When Mary Getten connected with Lucky, Lucky said healing work was not for her, adding, "I really just want to play and go on trips!"

Similarly, Smokey, Gwen's pony, told Mary, "I'm just not that interested in healing work. I want to play with people and make them laugh. I can't get serious about healing work—that's just not fun to do." And Smokey did wander around the ring, nibbling grass and enjoying himself rather than participating in the craniosacral sessions.

Another newer pony for Gwen named Pepper, had received many craniosacral sessions from me to address her health issues, so I was curious how she would interact with a session for her rider. Pepper rested her head on my shoulder for a few moments and then stood by the gate asking to leave. She told Mary it was not her place to do healing work with humans. She explained that she did energy work on her riders, and that she had an ability to make her riders feel calm, and that other healing was not for her.

Two of the horses most interested in doing healing work were unexpected. Willie, Gwen's show pony, was eight, and she had had some falls from him. As soon as I asked Comet to explain to him what we were doing, the four people observing could sense a big shift in his energy. He looked at Comet closely, as if listening to him in a silent language. First, Willie checked in with me, nosing my arms, and went right to Gwen's knee, the one she had injured in a fall from him. He rested his muzzle on the knee, and then as I was working on Gwen's cranial base and neck, he moved his muzzle to her collarbone. Gwen and I could feel the shift of a deeper release in her upper back and neck.

Then he picked up her right leg by her boot and shook it lightly, holding her leg in the air as Rocky had done with Andrew's leg. Earlier, when I had done a regional release on her other leg, lifting it off the table, he had shown no interest. Still holding Gwen's leg with her boot in his mouth, Willie gently moved her leg right and left, up and down, doing a regional release very much like any craniosacral therapist. As I worked on Gwen's pelvic diaphragm next, my hand resting on her stomach, Willie placed his muzzle on my hand. Finally, he walked around the table to Gwen's left iliac crest, and pressed his muzzle heavily over the bone, actually using his teeth as if he were about to bite. Gwen said it did not hurt at all, but she could feel changes in her back, "like I was getting flatter, and more relaxed and even," she reported.

During this session, a barn cat came and rested on Gwen's chest as well, and another cat sat on the gate next to us, watching the entire session. Clearly, the five observers, as well as Gwen and me, could feel the connection between all of the people and animals in this session. Judy noticed so many changes in Gwen that she asked if Willie could maybe help with her headache. Gwen stood up and Judy got onto the table.

I was really not sure if Willie would do another session right away, but as I began to work, he placed his muzzle on my top hand as I worked over different areas of Judy's body. When I worked on her cranial base, Willie placed his muzzle over her forehead and then made contact there gently, moving his muzzle and lips and blowing air over her face. As she sat up, Judy said she felt relief. Willie told Mary that he really liked doing healing work and that he breaks up restrictions physically with his teeth. He said he scanned the body and focused on an area of tension, similar to Comet's arcing. He said he really cared about this work, knew he had a lot of ability, and wanted to do a good job. He really loved this work and wanted to do more!

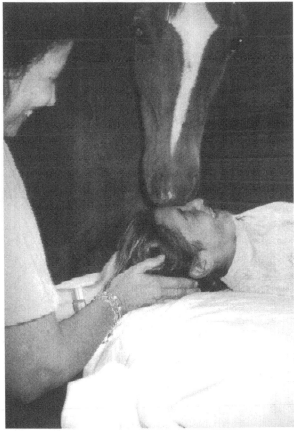

Willie, Judy and I laugh as tension is released from her neck.

While we were doing this work over a week, a two-year-old Paso Fino stallion in a nearby stall was snorting and pawing at the wall. We could see Donnie peering at what we were doing through a space between the boards. At times he stood up on his hind legs to look over the top of the stall. In the pasture he was a bit of a pest, trying to play with you and any horse you were leading away from the group. People were afraid of him, as he had a reputation for biting and kicking people, but it was clear he wanted to participate, so Judy volunteered to be on the table with Donnie, since she felt compassion for him.

We opened his stall door and he raced around the corner at top speed to where we were with the massage table. As soon as he was near the table, he contained himself and assessed everyone. One cat was with us, and Comet was watching Donnie from under the table. Very carefully and gently, Donnie touched his nose on Judy's still sore ankle. Donnie had a calm, meditative expression, with his ears pricked forward in seeming concentration. Judy was somewhat wary, but as the session progressed, she closed her eyes and trusted Donnie as he moved his muzzle carefully over her body, blowing air in some areas, as I have seen shamans do in their work. When he was done, he surveyed Judy's body, quietly backed away, and then ran at top speed around the paddock.

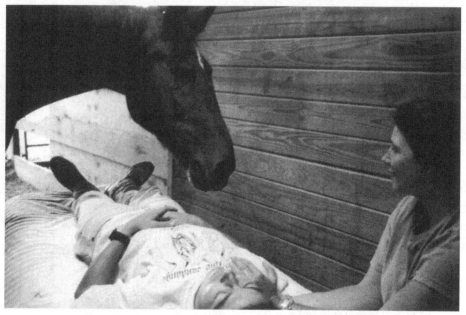

Burgers is working over my sister's pelvic diaphragm as I am releasing her right shoulder.

Donnie told Mary that he would really like to do healing work. It was very important to him that people see he could be gentle, and that he really is a good horse. He was grateful for the opportunity to prove himself with something he knew he could do well. He told us he would love to have a chance to do more of this work.

After his work with the horses, Comet had a chance to talk to Mary as well about his work. He told her that he could see energy and blockages, and that sometimes he just sent energy to blockages, and other times he used his paws or nose to break them up. He said he sometimes does work from a distance, as he was often on the sofa next to my clients, and that he also tried to be further away so as not to scare the cat clients. Comet explained that he saw white light, with dark spots where restrictions are located. He added that when he really likes a client, he works very hard and makes an extra effort to help. He said it was sometimes hard for him to work at the office in our home because he had to make a bigger shift than when we went out to an office, and that it's hardest for him to work with dogs because he would rather just play with them.

Comet reported that he really loved working with me, and that he did not need help from other animals, or from spirit animals like Winston. Comet had a lot of confidence in his abilities and knew that he was very good at doing healing work, adding that when I was on the table, he especially felt responsible to make sure people were "doing it right." And, he told Mary, "I could work with chickens," something he had mentioned to other animal communicators over the years as well. Comet was gentle and patient, and he worked with many small animals such as rabbits and guinea pigs. Though he met many chickens, he never had a chance to do craniosacral work with them.

I interviewed my friend Sue S., who had noticed that her cat Artemis was also participating in craniosacral sessions with her. Sue had participated in the work with dolphins, and when she returned home, Artemis, as usual, jumped onto the treatment table. Sue was able to see with new eyes what her cat was doing. Artemis, with her delicate cat steps, would walk over and around the person on the table and choose a place to work, giving Sue second choice, as the cat did not want to share an area. If Sue tried to put a hand near or under the cat, Artemis would push her away.

Sue reported that Artemis liked to do what she called "kitty massage" on a person's abdomen, and Sue recognized this as specific, visceral work, freeing up organs in the gut, especially sphincters. Artemis, in fact, seemed to know when a person with bowel problems needed her help and preferred to work with those clients. Sometimes she sat near a person's feet or lay across a person's heart and draped one paw on a person's arm. Sue told me that she silently talked to Artemis in pictures during a session, and in this way discussed the progress of a session with her. At times, Artemis treated from a distance across the room; at other times, she chose not to participate at all, especially in the mornings when she liked to have her naps. I could see many similarities between the ways I had noticed Winston and Comet working, and the way Sue's cat worked with her.

My friend Martine also had a dog who worked with her, a golden retriever named Spirit. She told me that he was a special soulmate for her. She felt that people who do healing work draw animals to them who want to do that work as well. Spirit had a natural ability, and he did steer clear of certain types of tough energy. Like Comet, he chose to lay under a table in a particular way, and Martine believed he was often working on chakras, noting that he was good at "holding a space." People would say, "Your dog is really touching my heart," or "Your dog has a green energy," while others just commented on his physical beauty. Sometimes Spirit would jump up and put his paws on the table, and once he jumped entirely onto the table, which Martine felt was relevant to the session at the time. She said that he was very clear, and gave unconditionally when he was working with her.

It was obvious to me from these and other interviews with friends working with their animals in craniosacral sessions that animals instinctively knew the right actions to take. As Diane Guerrero reminds us, "One of the biggest obstacles in human relationships with animals is ignorance about animals' intelligence, capacity to learn, and memory. [...] Being open-minded is important. Changing your viewpoint from seeing animals as 'lesser' creatures to seeing them as divine creations is important in connecting with animals." It was apparent to me that allowing a space for animals to work with us is to come from a truly neutral place with no ego, not trying to send energy and not getting emotionally charged during a session. Over several months, I read many books about animals and healing, and I prepared a presentation for the next Beyond the Dura Conference.

Chapter 31

The Dance of Honesty

Small Animal Craniosacral Therapy, TTouch Cell-abration

Comet is doing temporal release work on this rabbit who was born with a type of torticollis.

"But learn we might, if not too proud to stoop
To quadruped instructors, many a good
And useful quality, and virtue too—"

— William Cooper

Judy's new farm provided a setting not only to explore how animals wanted to participate in craniosacral sessions, but it was also a perfect place to hold my first small animal craniosacral therapy class. The animals at her farm included a few rescued parrots, a cockatiel, a cockatoo, some other small birds, a variety of indoor and outdoor cats, and a large Doberman, as well as the horses, including Lucky the miniature horse,

221

joined by another mini, Lightning. She also had vet techs at her office with ferrets, guinea pigs, hamsters, and rats, so we had many species of animals to work with.

When I was preparing the course book for my small animal craniosacral therapy class, it was of course fitting that Comet serve as the model in many of the pictures. My friend Tammy's cat was also a model, and Tammy did an evening photo shoot at one of our classes together, with Comet posing for all of the hand positions. We both noticed how he positioned his body and ears for each picture—he seemed to be posing in a way to emphasize what the picture was about. Many students who refer to this book have also recognized Comet's posing so well to illustrate the techniques. He received many notes thanking him for his help during the classes we taught together. Later, in the weeks before his passing, he would comment to the animal communicator that he was a critical part in developing this work, and that he hoped we would all remember him.

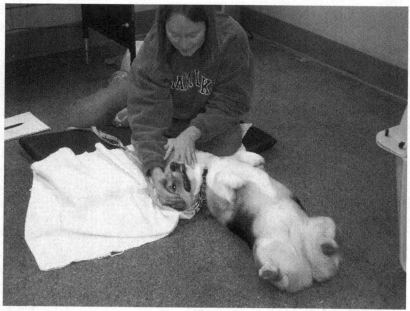

Veterinarian, Dr. Gretchen Ham, doing a sphenoid release with Watson the corgi at our Small Animal Craniosacral class held at Bancroft.

Comet demonstrated his arcing skills with many types of other animals at the class, including birds and a ferret. My friend Tracy Vroom, who now teaches animal craniosacral classes, especially with horses, sat with Comet between her legs as she did a thoughtful session with a ferret who had fallen down a set of stairs. Ferrets are generally squirmy, but this little one did a very clear demonstration of whole body unwinding, with moments of deep stillness as he integrated the changes in his body. He scampered off with no lameness after his session.

We also had a big Rottweiler, a client of my sister's, who had been getting chiropractic treatment and acupuncture recently. This dog was happy to be a demonstration client for my colleague. Then he worked with some of the students, overseen by Comet, to release every spinal vertebral segment in his painful back. After the session, we saw many improvements in the dog's gait and spinal mobility, as he was then walking squarely with equal weight on all four paws. The intensive work he received over the four days of the class helped him improve so much that his gait appeared completely normal, and he was strong for many years with maintenance chiropractic and acupuncture visits every six weeks.

Comet was also the model for hand positions during the lectures, especially for work on the skull, with my colleague holding a coyote skull next to him where she showed bony landmarks to match Comet's furry ones. At the conference center where we did classroom work, we allowed the dogs in the class to be off leash and go where they wanted in the room. I was interested to see that many of them wanted to assist in the practice work on the people in the group. I observed small dogs resting on people, eyes closed and paws outstretched, while we practiced diaphragm releases on the person's body, and bigger dogs positioning themselves quite particularly under tables during the practice sessions on the people. My mom brought her big schnauzer to the class, and my sister attended the class also. When the group gathered in Judy's great room to go through a sample protocol session on the last day, students were working with cats, dogs, guinea pigs, and a parrot, each quietly resting peacefully next to one another. It was a successful class with many animals benefitting from the work, and with excellent group discussions about honoring and respecting the spirits of animals with this work.

Comet, shown here during a temporal circumferencial technique, poses for the Small Animal Craniosacral Therapy manual.

Soon after this, Comet was with me at a massage conference where a colleague and I were offering demonstration craniosacral sessions, assisted by Comet. A few participants invited Comet onto the table, but he mostly worked underneath, at times jumping up and pawing at an area, or pushing his nose towards a place on the person's body. My colleague and I began to see where Comet arced and treated that area first, asking the person on the table simple questions like, "Do you have something to say about your left knee?" In every case, the person had a story of injury to match Comet's sense of restrictions in that area of the body. When Comet thought a session was complete, he'd walk around the table looking up, and then go sit under one of our chairs beside the table to indicate he thought everything was in order at the moment. People at this conference, primarily massage therapists, all remarked upon noticing that Comet was doing "something" during their sessions, and that they were happy for his presence.

When Comet was arcing, what was he really doing? We are all aware of dogs who are trained to smell cancer in a body, and if a person lies on the floor, a cancer sniffing dog will pace around them and paw at an area if he smells cancer. But Comet was sensing many kinds of problems in people's bodies. Was he sensing an area of increased or decreased heat? Perhaps. Many times his findings were validated with tests such as X-rays or MRIs. His skills were not limited to humans.

When he came with me to do craniosacral and TTouch sessions with clients at my sister's holistic veterinary office, Comet did some incredible things. I had a client with several dogs who brought them to me whenever I was in the area. This time she had a different dog, who seemed somewhat healthy, but "off." She was older, with no particular symptoms. I did my session with her, noticing issues at the thoraco-lumbar junction, and I began working there and on the dog's neck. Comet kept pushing under my arm and licking an area on the dog's side. I felt a bit of heat there and did some work, but did not feel more drawn to that area than to the issues in the low back. My sister came in and I told her that it was unusual for Comet to act like this, and that I was not sure what was going on. She took the dog back for an X-ray and discovered a significant case of pancreatitis that we all could have missed if not for Comet. The dog's calm demeanor had not in any way indicated the severity of her condition. The dog's owner was very grateful, bringing Comet a special bag of treats as a thank you.

In another instance at Judy's office, Comet and I were working with a big dog, who came in with significant issues in the lower back. The dog had been getting some chiropractic and acupuncture treatments, but his back issues were not resolving. Judy was not sure where the dog's problem was coming from, so she suggested Comet and I give our opinions.

After working with the dog for over thirty minutes, I concluded that the primary lesion was at the lumbar 3-4 level, and Comet was pointing with his nose at lumbar 4-5. Judy had looked at X-rays, and felt the problem was at the lumbar 5-6 level. The dog went to the University of Pennsylvania for an MRI, which simply stated that the dog had multiple disc disruptions in the lumbar spine. We all joked that even Comet was more specific than a university. After the dog had orthopedic surgery to correct the ruptured disc, the surgeon mentioned to my sister that it was quite significant at the lumbar 4-5 level, the same area that Comet insisted was the primary area of restriction. Of course, a disc problem at one level does create issues at the levels above and below it sometimes, but clearly Comet was able to show us something that the surgeon was also noticing.

Comet worked with me in my private practice for many years, always greeting people at the door and then letting me know where I needed to work. After a few minutes, he would retire to rest upstairs for most of the session. He had an uncanny ability to know when a session was concluding, and would trot down the stairs to check the person to make sure we had not left something undone. My patients even commented on this, saying that their session could not be over until Comet had said it was so.

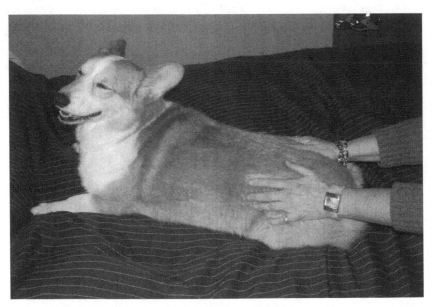

Comet is very relaxed during stillpoints induced on his hips.

By the time of the first Tellington TTouch Training Cell-abration in November 2005, the power of intention was well rooted in both the craniosacral work I was teaching, as well as in the TTouch classes I was participating in. The groundbreaking work of Masaru Emoto was available in English in 2004 in the book *The Hidden Messages In Water*, showing the changes in water crystals in response to different words, music, thoughts and feelings. This work was to become a part of both TTouch and craniosacral work as an illustration of the power of the words we use with our animals and with each other. I was also familiar with the work of Esther and Jerry Hicks from their 2004 book *Ask and It Is Given*. Also in 2004, Wayne Dyer's book *The Power of Intention* became available. There was a growing awareness and nationwide attention on the power of intention. At that first Cell-abration, we had several showings of the film *The Secret*, which had been recently released. We were finding increasing validation that having clear intentions during bodywork was not only a crucial part of improving the health and well being of animals, but an integral aspect of clearly communicating and connecting with our animals.

At that first international TTouch conference, I presented my observations of the similarities of TTouch and craniosacral therapy. I showed how the four ideas in craniosacral work—ego subordination, impartiality, nonjudgment, and unconditional presence—relate to TTouch, and in fact, could apply to any TTouch session as well. I made suggestions on how to integrate the two, as I had been giving "homework" of TTouches for my human and animal craniosacral clients for many years. With Comet's help as a model, I demonstrated how some TTouch and craniosacral techniques relate to one another, such as hair slides and the parietal lift, ear work and temporal techniques, the tail pull and dural tube work, and TTouch mouth work and the mouth work and TMJ release in craniosacral. People were particularly interested in pictures of the deeper structures impacted with TTouch techniques and their influence on the central nervous system and behavior. Some shelter dogs that helped with demonstrations showed great improvements in gait and posture after the demonstrations with short craniosacral sessions. The room was packed, especially during the demonstration. Many people wanted to learn more about craniosacral therapy. A friend, Sue, who, like me, loved rabbits and used TTouch with them, even adopted one of the shelter dogs following the demonstration.

Here I am with Linda Tellington-Jones at the first Cell-abration in 2006.

After this, Linda asked me to write a chapter for her book for healthcare practitioners about the relationships between TTouch and craniosacral work, and how to integrate them in a healthcare setting. I did an additional chapter about the power of TTouch to help people take more responsibility for their health care. Also, in my small animal and equine craniosacral courses, I added a section about TTouch techniques to help my students find safe and respectful ways to interact with animals. For several years, I was fortunate to teach small animal craniosacral classes outside of Boston where other craniosacral classes were being taught. The wonderful people at the MSPCA at Nevins Farm, a well-known rescue, along with many of my clients with several pets, brought us animals to help teach the classes. Once again, we had that remarkable experience of a room full of many species of animals and people working together with TTouch and craniosacral therapy during our protocol on the final day—cats purring next to dogs known to chase cats, dogs fearful of other dogs safely resting near others, and rabbits unconcerned that under other circumstances many of these animals would have wanted to chase them. Sadly, the venue was torn down, so that special setting was lost.

Chapter 32

Harmonious Dancing
Seeing Eye Horses, Guiding Burgers Home

Burgers was a 'seeing eye' horse for Snowden, an elderly Appaloosa shown here at one of Judy's farms.

"But the Phantom was not running a race. She was enjoying herself. She was a piece of thistledown borne by the wind, moving through space in wild abandon. She was coming up, not to pass Firefly and Black Comet, but for the joy of flying. Her legs went like music."

— Marguerite Henry, *Misty of Chincoteague*

Burgers was in his twenties by this time, and Judy was selling the farm where he had lived with her. It was time for me to bring him home to New England again. He was developing some health problems, including laryngeal paralysis, which, along with his missing teeth, made him require a special diet to prevent choking. At Judy's, he was in a pasture with some other, older horses—a chestnut Quarter horse named Frizzle and a white Appaloosa with brown ears, who was also covered with chestnut spots, named Snowden. He suffered from uveitis, which was common in his breed, and as he aged he became increasingly blind. Burgers had not had many equine friends in his lifetime—the horse in the stall next to him where I had bought him, Skybird, had played with him for hours with chasing and mutual grooming games; my horse Hawk had a cordial but not really friendly relationship with him; with Judy's horse Rocky, he had an uneven rapport. And then he became friends with this aging blind horse, Snowden, at Judy's farm.

Carly, his owner, called Burgers a seeing eye guide horse for Snowden, and they grazed close to each other for the three years Burgers lived at that farm. When it was time for Burgers to move back to Massachusetts with me, I was not aware of his close relationship with Snowden. I was in New Jersey for a week, and Carly, who had also attended some of my Tellington TTouch Training clinics, wondered how Snowden would get along without Burgers. I spent hours watching them grazing together, noticing that when it was time to go up to the barn for dinner, Snowden walked close behind Burgers to avoid the posts around the barn and find his way to his stall for his dinner. I heard them nickering to each other through the boards dividing their stalls. It was clear to me that these two horses had a special relationship, and separating them was going to be heart wrenching.

Burgers and I share a quiet moment together before leaving New Jersey to return to Massachusetts.

I decided to spend some time in the pasture with both of them, visualizing Burgers leaving and Snowden understanding that he would find a new way in the world without Burgers. Carly told Snowden that he would be all right, and that she, too, was sorry that his friend had to leave. On the morning of the move, we brought both horses into the barn and let Snowden smell the leg wraps and sheet before we put them on Burgers. We led Snowden around the trailer, let him smell the tailgate, and Carly held him as we loaded Burgers. We let them sniff noses through the trailer door, and Snowden had a nibble of Burgers' hay bag. Carly led Snowden around the trailer and back to the barnyard so he could hear the trailer leaving. Burgers and Snowden called to each other a few times as I drove slowly down the long driveway, but it seemed to be more of a "So long, old friend," than a desperate "What's happening? Oh no!"

Linda Tellington-Jones, Burgers and me at one of his last clinics with Linda. He is 28 here.

That night, Snowden made his way carefully to the barn on his own, and when he nickered in his stall, it was Frizzle who answered—Frizzle even more elderly, but still going on trail rides with his owner. Frizzle became Snowden's new eyes, and when they moved together a few weeks later to a new barn, Frizzle's sight helped Snowden settle in. When Snowden crossed the rainbow bridge about a year later, it was not much longer before his friend Frizzle followed. It is so clear to all of the people who knew these horses that indeed they had formed close friendships, and that Frizzle and Burgers understood that Snowden needed their help.

Burgers arrived in Massachusetts after a long ride in his old show trailer. It was a cold and wet spring, and he was thin. We had discovered that his New Jersey pasture was filled with tansy, which is toxic to horses over time, and he was in need of the deep, lush grass in the new pastures. Jack came to visit him, bringing a special blue wool blanket to help keep him warm on the cool nights, since even his winter blankets were not enough. Within a month, the shine came back to his coat and we were going on trail rides together on the miles of wooded trails around the farm. We began his old routine of walk work in renvers and travers, collected and extended work, pirouettes, and piaffe to help him restore his muscles and balance under saddle. He seemed so happy to see me when I came each day, as usual, not trotting up to me in the field, but instead waiting until I walked to him. Then I just tapped him on the neck and asked him to come in with me for a ride, and he would follow me in from the field.

We practiced our free work in the indoor ring, with him moving between my extended arms at the walk, trot and canter, backing up and moving forward. After a bit, he'd squeal and trot off around the ring on his own, starting to feel strong and happy again. I brought him a carrot cake on his birthday, which, after his time with Judy's daughter Gwen, who had introduced him to peppermints, Skittles, and other treats, he devoured happily, getting cream cheese frosting all over his whiskers. At the end of June, I surprised him with the news that we were having a Tellington TTouch Training clinic with Linda Tellington-Jones right here at his new farm, and he would be the wise teacher horse for the whole clinic.

He was a gentle teacher, but was certainly no pushover. When beginner students fumbled with the lines and the wand on his off side for leading exercises, he would just walk in the other direction until they sorted it out. If he did not like the bodywork, he would move away, and conversely, when he enjoyed it, he would smile and look back at the people working with him, his lips quivering as will happen when horses are happy. He and I demonstrated riding without a bridle, even with some steps of piaffe and a levade, and then he patiently taught some of the other students about riding without a bridle. It seemed fitting that at his age, and after all of our years apart, we re-strengthened our bond at a Tellington TTouch Training clinic with Linda.

A few weeks later, I decided he was ready to return one final time to the New England Morgan show for the trail class. On the way to the show, only about ten miles from the farm, the trailer got a flat tire, which delayed our arrival. During the process of AAA fixing the tire, Burgers remained in the trailer, calmly watching the traffic go by. He was in his show halter and wraps—I am sure he understood where he was going. When we arrived and he looked around at the old fairgrounds he knew so well, he snorted and shook before diving into the deep grass by the trailer.

I tacked him up, wondering if anyone here had seen him at this show over twenty-five years before, when he got his first ribbon with me. And in the many years since then, he had been Hunter Champion several times, Combined Training Champion, Training, First, Second, and Upper Level Dressage Champion, and of course he and his brother Action, and later with Hawk, had done dressage demonstrations together. Now definitely a senior horse, he was here to walk over a bridge, stand quietly for mounting and dismounting, back through an "L," and open and close a rope gate for the trail class. We walked over to the ring and warmed up as people admired his neatly taped dressage braids and shiny coat. In only two months, he had fully recovered from his time in the bad pasture in New Jersey, and he looked young and strong.

Burgers and I are navigating the 'bridge' during one of our Trail classes back at the New England Morgan show.

He won the class. We walked back to the trailer, his blue ribbon streaming from his bridle, knowing that New England Morgan would be his last show, just as it had been his first. As we pulled out of the driveway, Burgers gave a long whinny, as if to say he would remember this place and all of his victories in the show ring.

As luck would have it, Janet, having retired Burgers' brother Action, purchased an older Lipizzaner and boarded him at the same barn where Burgers lived. This meant that we could ride together on the weekends, over miles and miles of trails, crossing streams with our horses, getting lost on back roads that appeared at the ends of trails, galloping up old dirt roads. We giggled like kids, always planning to bring a lunch and ride all day, but instead going without even a bottle of water. Shama and Burgers were friends and seemed to enjoy the game of who would cross the many streams first, and then splashing at each other midstream once they stepped into the water. Janet's dog, Jake, inevitably found a porcupine, and we would hear his far off high, sharp barks, knowing we had to head back to the barn. He always found porcupines irresistible and could not stop himself from irritating them until he was quilled. Once, to surprise Janet, I dressed a patient Shama in black crepe paper stripes so that he looked like a zebra. She did not even recognize him at first, and Shama enjoyed a big shake as the streamers fell away, having been secured only with tape. Janet thought costumes to be undignified, and maybe Shama agreed with her.

Burgers wins the Trail class! My riding student, Katherine Short, holds the trophy.

Burgers and I, however, loved wearing the horse necklaces my sister made—long beaded circles with charms and bells and feathers—as we rode through the woods. He often stopped on trails when I was out with him to show me a turkey feather, and I would put them in the brow band of his bridle. At Christmas time, he wore red-ribboned jingle bells I attached to an old stirrup leather, and of course, he had saddle pads in many colors to match his other accessories and glitter painted hooves, courtesy of our farrier, Jack M.

One evening, riding up the trail in the deepest part of the pinewoods, Burgers stopped with his head up, eyes fixed straight ahead. I did not see anything at first, worried that we were near a cow pasture and even at his advanced years, he could turn and charge mindlessly from any cow. Instead I saw a very tall rump slipping away among the pines. It was a moose. It was the only time that I have seen a wild moose, and they can be dangerous. Burgers and I stayed motionless until he disappeared into the woods.

It was a hot summer day when we made our way up one of my favorite trails to the top of a hill where you could see the nearby university buildings across the Connecticut River. Again, Burgers stopped mid-stride. I looked ahead on the trail to see a lynx, which, like moose, are seen in our area, but rarely. The lynx, as tall as a boxer dog and shaped like one as well, looked back at us. We were all transfixed in one another's gazes until the lynx walked off on those cat-soft paws, silently into the forest.

Burgers and I sometimes saw black bears shuffling up the leaves in search of acorns or scratching on a tree, and we just walked by. Another Arabian crossbred mare that I rode for someone went into complete panic when a bear crossed the road ahead of us, turning quickly and racing for the barn. Burgers seemed to nod a cordial hello and we continued down the trail, thankfully never crossing between a mother and her cubs.

One of our favorite trails was reputed to have been the original "highway" to the bigger town fifteen miles south of the farm during the 1800's. It was a wide, clearly well used trail. Along the sides were the remains of old farm houses, tumbled down rock basements surrounded by stonewalls meant to corral livestock. I sometimes thought back to Linda Tellington-Jones' stories of riding through the night for endurance rides with a new awareness of how challenging that would be in unfamiliar rugged terrain. Riding in the moonlight on that trail in the early winter, it was easy to imagine coming home from a secret meeting with my beloved, or returning from an urgent errand in the town. Burgers' Morgan ancestors very likely were among the horses to have frequented the trail two hundred years before his hooves rhythmically trotted across the packed earth and stony grades of the trail.

Comet came to the barn sometimes, usually when I was doing craniosacral sessions and not planning to ride. He demonstrated his healing powers with horses especially well with a chestnut Thoroughbred named Hatchet, who lived in the stall next to Burgers. Hatchet was somewhat dangerous and in his first sessions, he sometimes kicked violently and unexpectedly, releasing trauma from his time at the track a few years before. Over time he became more predictable, and Comet would often choose to stand between his front legs, looking up at Hatchet's head as I worked on his poll and jaw. Hatchet never endangered Comet, and instead his head would drop and their noses would lightly touch.

Later, when it was safe to treat Hatchet in his stall, he sometimes chose to lie down during his sessions as Comet sat in the corner of the stall watching him. Hatchet attended the Tellington TTouch Trainings at the farm, and I remember his person leading him into the ring set up with poles on the ground, chairs for the people, and bags and books piled by the chairs. He snorted and balked, eyes wide. His person just stood at the end of his rope, watching him. He took hesitant steps forward, carefully looking around at everything before walking up to the nearest chair with a coat tossed over it, and he sniffed. He took another deep breath and relaxed completely as Bubba had done when I stroked him with four wands. I was so impressed with his person for not making an issue with him, and with Hatchet's ability to maintain his calm and not react.

Only a handful of times did Comet try to follow us on a trail ride as Winston had often done. Comet was simply not an adventurous sort of dog in the way that Winnie had been. One weekend evening, I set out on a short ride for maybe twenty minutes with Comet trotting beside us. When we got to the main road, we turned to head back to the farm, and when I looked down, I could not find Comet anywhere. I called and called, trotted up and down the road, but there was no sign of Comet. I galloped back to the barn to see if he was there, but he was not, and no one had seen him. Some other people leaving for a trail ride promised to look for him, but it was getting colder, and dark. I called Jack, knowing that Comet would surely come if he heard Jack's voice, as it would be unexpected, so he headed up from town.

Comet had rarely left my side all of his life, and I was so upset with myself for trying to bring him even on a short ride. I decided to get in my car and drive to each of the neighbors' houses to ask them to look out for my corgi. The people at the first house had cats, and had not seen him but said they would take a walk later and look for him, and even would leave a light on, with cat food outside in case he found their house.

I drove down the long drive of the next neighbor and stepped out of my car. I made my way to the door, next to a window box with an overhead porch light, thinking it looked similar to my own house. I knocked and heard a bark from inside that sounded like a corgi. A man came to the door and beside him was Comet! He explained that the dog had been standing outside his door for nearly forty-five minutes, emitting one loud bark every thirty seconds until the man had decided to let him inside. He had checked the dog's collar and had been calling my home phone number. I was so relieved, thanking the man for keeping him safe, and silently thanking Winston for so thoroughly teaching Comet the "let me inside, please" bark. As I made my way up the driveway towards my truck with Comet beside me, Jack slowed his car on the road and called to Comet. He jumped out of the car and his legs were lost in a blur of golden corgi fur greetings. "Comet, you silly dog, scaring your mom like that!" Jack said. Comet never went for another trail ride, preferring to stay home in the warm house until I returned.

In the winters at this lovely farm, the trails were still worthy of exploration, even on the coldest or snowiest of days. Burgers and I often set out at sunset, alone, with his blue wool quarter sheet and red jingle bells around his neck, leaving a trail of snowy hoof prints in the road behind us. I know Burgers enjoyed these rides, and I'd let him choose which way to go, dropping the reins on his neck once we topped the hill up the road from the barn. The blanket of snow brought a heavy stillness to the woods, such that I could only hear Burgers' breath and the faint jingle of the bells as we made our way to the hilltop to see the lights coming on across the river at the University. A friend gave me her long Barbour coat, thinking I needed better weather gear. Yet I was so at peace with Burgers in the woods, so connected to the trees and animals around us that I was unaware of my cold hands until we were back in the barn.

Chapter 33

Dancing With Grace
Burgers Travels Over The Rainbow Bridge

Burgers' face shows the wisdom of his lifetime with me. Photo by Helena Sullivan.

"The hoofs of the horses!—Oh! welcome and sweet
Is the music earth steels from the iron-shod feet;
No whisper of lover, no trilling of bird
Can stir me as hoofs of the horses have stirred ...

"When you lay me to slumber no sport can you choose
But will ring to the rhythm of galloping shoes,
And under the daisies no grave be so deep
But the hoofs of the horses shall sound in my sleep."

— Will H. Ogilvie, *The Hoofs of Horses, Racing Rhymes*

Our time at this farm was idyllic, and as one friend who kept her retired Morgan mare there said, it was heaven on earth for horses, with large, lush pastures, big stalls in a warm, insulated barn, a heated tack room, enormous hay loft, very roomy indoor arena, and an outdoor arena for dressage and jumping. It was a perfect place for Tellington Training clinics, and Linda returned again in 2007 and 2008 to do week-long clinics at this beautiful farm.

In July of 2008, just a few weeks after the Tellington TTouch Training clinic, Burgers started to show signs of his age. We were going on short trail rides, mostly walking with a bit of trotting, and spending more time just being together while he grazed, sometimes not even coming in from the pasture. One Sunday, we went for a ride with Burgers' friend Sebastian, another Lipizzaner, past the remains of the old homestead farms in the woods and back to the barn. It was not a very warm day for early July, and it was early in the morning. Burgers seemed rather tired, so after I untacked him, I gave him a warm shower and did some TTouches on his long ears— lick of the cow's tongue, a favorite of his—and some craniosacral work with him. I tucked him in, and when I returned to the farm the next day, he seemed listless, not finishing his breakfast. He had a slight temperature, so concerned that he might have colic, I called the veterinarian. I did belly lifts and ear work while we waited, and craniosacral stillpoints to lower his temperature. The vet arrived and gave him some IV fluids, as he seemed dehydrated. He asked me, "Do you have a trailer?"

"Of course," I said. He suggested that I take Burgers for a short ride on the bumpy road by the farm to improve his digestive movements. He also said that his heart seemed weak.

So I took Burgers for a drive around the long block of bumpy gravel roads, and when we returned to the farm, Burgers had done some manure and seemed much brighter. I did some more bodywork with him and tucked him into his stall for the evening, with extra carrots. The next day, the barn staff called to tell me that Burgers still did not look well, and that the vet was on the way. I raced to the farm and began doing belly lifts and ear work, thinking that perhaps it was still colic. Again, the vet gave him IV fluids and suggested another ride in the trailer. This time he did only a bit of manure and did not look any better after the trip around the block. I returned him to his stall, very concerned about what was happening to him. Now the third day of Burgers' illness, the vet gave him IV fluids throughout the day, and I did bodywork with him, coaxing him to eat some soupy hay cube mix with treats and molasses in it. He was too weak for another trip in the trailer.

The following day, the barn manager called, saying that Burgers did not look good at all. He was still on fluids, and he was not eating or drinking. He was in his wool blanket, even though it was early July. I got there in the evening and stayed with him, doing TTouches on his ears, stroking him and playing with his mane, weaving in some dandelions as I had done with him years before. I offered him peppermints, which he weakly nibbled, dropping pieces on the stall floor. I told him what a wonderful horse he had been, how much I appreciated all he had done with me, how beautiful he was, and how much I loved his very large ears and spring dapples each year. He rested his head against my chest, breathing heavily, his eyes half closed. I had no way to offer all of the gratitude in my soul to him other than to hug him, listening to our hearts beating together. It was the last time I saw him alive.

He was twenty-nine years old when he died, and we had been together for over twenty-seven years. He had simply collapsed suddenly in his stall the next day. After I got the message, I called his friends, Esther, Samantha (who had given lessons with him), my friend Sarah, and Jack, his unofficial "dad," who said he really could not come to see Burgers now that he was gone. Another Jack, his farrier, kindly came to take off Burgers' last set of shoes. We met at the barn, where Burgers was on his side in the aisle. I gently brushed his coat, clipped his mane and tail, saying, "I know you don't need these anymore, but I really do, Burgers. Thank you so much." I trimmed some of the mahogany hair from his chest. Jack pulled his shoes and said, "You were a good boy, Burgers, a really good boy," as he painted his front hooves with the sparkles he usually gave Burgers after a trim.

The care of a horse in death is at best grim, and often terrible. We had an understanding man come with a backhoe to dig a place for Burgers in the back of the field near his chestnut friend Hatchet, who had died unexpectedly the year before. And then Samantha and I followed Burgers in the bucket loader across the huge field, talking about what a wonderful horse he was. The man let us pull the IV lead from Burgers' neck and give him a last kiss, a last time to feel the soft length of his long ears, and then we two stood there watching the earth cover his body. It was difficult, but we talked quietly about the other horses buried in this corner of the field, and it seemed better. We imagined them running together up and down the heavenly green hills of this farm, splashing in the stream no one was afraid of anymore, running in a place where there were no fences. We walked back to the barn in silence.

Losing a horse is the end of a lifestyle, my friend had once said after her horse Hatchet had died. Unless you have another horse, you take home your saddles, bridles, blankets, and trailer, and this place where you spent four hours a day is gone from your life. It was years before I could unfold the towel holding Burgers' mane and tail, smell the horse-ness of him, and touch the soft hairs from his chest. I knew that I was not going to get another horse, and that no horse would ever be as close to me as he had been.

This picture of me, Comet and Burgers was taken a month before Burgers crossed the rainbow bridge. Photo by Helena Sullivan.

Chapter 34

Dancing Creates Wellness
Comet, Cancer and Bernie Siegel

Bernie Siegel and me, in my purple wig, looking together at his wonderful book, 'Buddy's Candle.'

"Having a loving relationship with an animal is one of the most powerful factors in healing and maintaining well-being."

— Dr. Bernie Siegel, *Love, Animals & Miracles*

Five days later I was diagnosed with cancer. Two days after that, the house I had been interested in buying was hit with a lightening bolt that divided in half the large apple tree that was the centerpiece of the back yard, where I had considered bringing Burgers to live. And the next day, Jack was getting married to his beloved Ron, and family and friends were coming to the area. I was so looking forward to seeing Jack's mother because, as a life-long equestrian, I knew she would deeply understand the loss of a horse. It was a gorgeous wedding on a hilltop with a double rainbow over the grooms. The symbol of the two rainbows was fitting for Jack's political work to change the laws so that he could marry Ron, and additionally for me as a symbol of the bridge our animals cross to another place. I held Jack's mother's hand, both of us quite emotional, as a cheer rose from the crowd in celebration.

After the wedding weekend, I began a series of doctors' appointments and tests, all accompanied by Comet, who became my support, my comfort, and my humor through the adventure that is a cancer diagnosis. I knew I needed to read about this, and I was staring at my bookcase of wellness and holistic healing books when a very old book, possibly from my undergraduate classes, fell from the top shelf and hit me in the shoulder. Comet, lying on the floor next to me, jumped up and woofed. I picked up the book—it was Bernie Siegel's *Love, Medicine and Miracles*. As I read the cover, I saw that it was about cancer, and I snuggled next to Comet and began to read. I found my answers in the first story about a person diagnosed with pancreatic cancer who did not die, who indeed thrived under Bernie's care. If there was a way for someone to be all right with that grave diagnosis, then I knew the truth in my doctor's words: "This will be all-consuming for a time, but it will be ultimately just a blip in your life, and you'll be just fine."

I was able to find Bernie Siegel, who is anything but low profile. He was a renowned cancer surgeon at Yale and a pioneer in the field of mind body medicine. He began groups called ECap, or Exceptional Cancer Patients, that meet worldwide. He runs support groups for people with cancer and other significant diseases. I was able to attend his monthly support group, a forty-minute drive from my house, with Comet. I walked into the first meeting quite late, thanks to my round-about bad directions, wearing my long purple wig to cover my bald head, a twenty-five dollar wig so like my real hair that friends thought I had just dyed it. Bernie stopped mid-sentence to quiz me. "Why is your hair purple?"

Not ready with a prepared answer, I spontaneously said, "Because that's the color of the crown chakra?" Bernie added, "Oh good, so you are a spiritual person?"

"Yes, very much so," I answered.

Bernie went on to explain the importance of colors, and that purple is a color associated with a very spiritual person or favored by someone near the time of her death. His first book contained artwork by cancer patients, which, thanks to his work with Elizabeth Kubler Ross, he became skilled at interpreting. Bernie is able to predict the outcomes of people's cancer diagnoses based on what he sees in their artwork. Part of this interpretation includes understanding what the colors in the pictures denote. It is remarkable how many people leave out body parts or simply can't create any pictures at all. In order to attend the meeting, I was asked to bring a crayon picture of myself, myself and my cancer, and myself and my cure. My pictures were full of green leaves and plants and I looked like Eve in the Garden of Eden as I tried to convey that alternative medicine and work with a naturopath was my answer. Bernie later told me that green is a healing color, indicating that I would be just fine.

He explained that his shaved head was not just because he worked with bald kids who had cancer, but like monks, it kept him closer to God, connected to his spiritual self. "Yes, that's exactly what my wig is about," I told him and the group. "I just did not have the words yet." This is why my hair is still purple ten years later; it connects me to the spiritual divine, a constant reminder to see the higher meaning in events in my life.

Comet was sitting behind me, still in the doorway, when I saw Bernie's two dogs next to him. I told him that I had a dog with me, and Comet was already being gently stroked by a lovely blond woman in a glittering pink baseball hat. Bernie said that his dogs were not so friendly with other dogs, so it would be better for Comet to wait in the car. Yet later we sometimes walked, the three dogs together in the little field beside the building, and talked about the wonder of animals in our lives. Bernie advised me to absolutely bring my dog to every test and doctor visit, because it would help keep everyone relaxed, bring a sense of humor to the doctor, and a sense of comfort to me. I told him that I had actually "fired" my first oncologist because she had no sense of humor. When I frantically asked her what I should eat, deadpan she said, "Whatever you want." I shot back, "Oh, so all of those lab mice that died eating saccharine were fine eating anything?" She stared blankly at me, and I said, "Thanks for your help." When I went to see my next doctor with Comet, a buoyant, mini Aussie bounded down the hall to greet us. "Well, Comet, I think we are in the right place here," I said. Bernie, of course, heartily approved of any doctor with a dog in her office.

Comet even came with me for my surgery to remove the breast lump, though of course he did not go into the operating room. For the second follow-up surgery, he was there with Jack before and after. Jack, I'm sure, was a bit uncomfortable sitting in the waiting room with a dog, but he would be the first to appreciate Comet's calming presence for everyone there. Comet came to my four chemotherapy appointments and once again proved to be a bright furry healer for everyone in the room. When I went for radiation treatments, Comet was invited to wait in a safe area, just as he was in the MRI booth at other times while I was being treated. Comet was a service dog, having passed many tests, which is one reason the hospital and staff were so welcoming to him. Cancer treatment is stressful for the doctors and staff as well, and I think many of them would say that calm, clean pets should be welcomed into treatments for everyone's benefit.

Bernie taught me to have positive ideas about the treatments I was undergoing. So I did not see the chemotherapy as poison that could kill me, and taking a cue from *The Secret*, I stuck a red paper heart with the words "love and gratitude" on the bag of chemicals. When I was in the radiation room, I held a cheerful, blue, small stuffed duck I've had for a few years and imagined him dancing to the song we often repeat at TTouch classes: "Every little cell in my body is happy, every little cell in my body is well." I also stuck a red paper heart on the radiation machine when I was there. The nurses loved it, and I left one there on my last day of treatment. Bernie suggests that you must give your body messages to be alive and in good health every day, and so that is what I did.

Bernie's brand of helping people with cancer goes a long way beyond positive thoughts and the old idea of "fighting" the disease. He learned from one Quaker patient, who did not believe in violence, that there are images to remove the cancer cells from your body that do not involve armies or poison, each one meaningful to the individual. At one meeting, we went around the room and all but one of the twenty-five people there reported no regrets for having had cancer. They all were able to see how that "wake up call" forced them to make changes in their lives to make them healthier and happier, and to find purpose and meaning in their lives. I was among that number, agreeing that cancer had made me see clearly my life's priorities. I had a busy private practice incorporating physical therapy, Tellington TTouch, and craniosacral therapy for people and all animals, and I was teaching classes in Tellington TTouch and craniosacral therapy. I was training to become a certified Phoenix Rising yoga instructor and learning how to navigate life without a horse to share my days. Everything seemed fine, but in many ways I was adrift, looking for that deeper spiritual connection between my life and my work.

Bernie's teaching emphasizes finding meaning in the events in your life, being able to step back and look at the "bigger picture," to see how "troubles can turn into blessings." He suggests that you take yourself out of the victim role of "why did this happen *to* me" and into the empowered role of "why is this happening *for* me?" He would point out that having cancer was indeed a challenge, but then ask, "What are you learning from this experience? What do you know about yourself that you did not know before? What is the meaning of these events in your life?" He explained that once you knew the answers to these questions you would gain an understanding of your situation, and no matter what course your treatment took, you would adjust.

His words reminded me of Hamlet's line, "There is nothing good or bad, but thinking makes it so." Things happen to us in our lives, and we have the ability to choose how to respond. Like the other people in the room that night, I knew that having cancer was not exactly a good thing. But there was no denying that it was meaningful and would make positive changes in me.

At one of Bernie's meetings, he shared that he had had some near-death experiences. I waited to talk to him afterwards, as I wanted to tell him about my own near-death experience a few years before. I was curious about what his reaction to my story would be, and whether there would be any similarities between our experiences. I told Bernie my story.

Trystan and me, with my 'naturally purple' hair, with Bernie Siegel and Rags at one of his support group meetings in 2016.

I had a client who had two Icelandic horses and lived about a forty-five minute drive from my house. One of the horses had been working with me for many years, and when he had lived closer to me for a summer, I had taken him on scenic trail rides on the small mountain by the farm. I had worked with Icelandics for many years; in spite of my dressage riding, the Icelandic instructors would say I was skilled at improving the horses' balance for better freedom in their gaits. I grew to love this little black horse, and I thought that his sensitivity and tendency to bolt were not well suited to his beginner rider. She'd had many falls from him, and so had some of her friends. I had not worked with him for over a year when the owner asked me to see him. A vet she had consulted said that he was ready to be ridden after recovering from Lyme disease.

The horse was living in a small pasture in the middle of a town that was really a crossroads, with a strip of green dividing the main road. Houses were lining the streets and the grassy space between the roads was where I had enough room to ride the horse. His person held him as I did some bodywork with him and he seemed to be feeling well, even taking into account the seemingly stoic demeanor Icelandics sometimes have. We saddled him and he began to move around the owner, and she thought he was excited to go riding. I was not so sure.

She led him out to the green strip and held him as I mounted. The horse pulled away from her and he simply bolted quickly, tolting (an Icelandic gait) as fast as he could, while I was still halfway into the saddle. I tried to organize my reins and position myself, but the horse lost his balance as he skittered onto the pavement. We fell and I landed hard on my helmet—owing to his small size I could not reach out my arm to break my fall, and maybe break my arm, but protect my head and body from worse injury—I was dragged a short way, and once my foot was free, the horse's hoof kicked it on the bottom with his hind hoof, and shattered the talus bone in my foot. I was knocked unconscious for maybe fifteen minutes.

There are near-death experiences when a person codes on an operating table, and then there are those such as I experienced, where my heart continued to beat on through each moment that I might leave the earth. I saw the white light and felt warmth and brightness surrounding me. I saw the branches of the old oak tree above me, the last image I'd seen as I fell. And then I became aware of the feeling of branches instead of arms, of the flow of sap within the tree, within me. I imagined my mother getting a phone call that I was seriously injured or even killed. I felt the grief flood her body as if it were my own grief. I floated above my mother and felt a connection with all things—beyond that even, I *was* all things, and all things were part of me. Many people have felt this profound interconnectedness between all things when they have nearly died.

And then I saw people that I did not know, very clearly telling me to come back, as I was important to them and they needed me to stay on earth. I woke up just as the medevac helicopter took off. I was looking out into the cold autumn night, stars shining in the clear sky surrounding us. I knew that I was alive, and that I would be fine. I was overwhelmed with the experience of the interconnectedness of all living things. I knew I had to tell other people about this experience.

Bernie listened to my story, nodding in agreement as I described what I had experienced. "Everything is part of God's plan," he said. "Us, the animals, the plants, we are all the same." I told him that I thought dying wasn't scary, and he agreed. He told me that once he had asked people at a support group what scared them the most, and a woman replied, "Driving on the freeway at night." Bernie and I laughed, knowing this woman had a very good point. Bernie told me then that I would be fine, especially since I was not afraid of cancer, or of dying.

Thanks to alternative medicine, including craniosacral treatments and a good naturopath, I was not really sick during the entire process, but very tired after the injections following chemo to improve white cell production. Comet stayed close to me for the entire six months, barely trotting three feet outside to relieve himself. I could see in his eyes that he knew I would be all right.

Comet and I continued to attend Bernie's many lectures in New England at health expos, and to attend his monthly support group meetings for many years. Bernie did not bring his dogs to the lectures, but he welcomed Comet's presence, and later, little Trystan's, as Comet always barked when Bernie got to the section in his talks about the importance of animals in our lives. Bernie would remark on how when Comet was off his leash, he would choose one person in a room of a hundred and lie next to that person who needed him most. In craniosacral terms, was he arcing the room? Or did he have some other special dog sense to help him find that person?

Chapter 35

Wisdom From the Dance
Comet's Teamwork Skills, Lessons From The Rainbow Bridge

Comet and Trystan running out to greet the pack of corgis at the beach in Provincetown, MA.

"Humankind has not woven the web of life. We are but one thread within it. Whatever we do to the web, we do to ourselves. All things are bound together. All things connect."

— Chief Seattle

Comet had other skills, which became apparent to me when we met a group of corgis at the beach in Provincetown. My corgis always seemed to recognize and like other corgis. There was an incident at a corgi show when Jack was holding Molly on a leash, and a nearby corgi jumped up barking and lunging at his exercise-pen, very upset. The owner quickly scolded Jack very abruptly—"What are you doing? Get that dog away from there. Don't you know corgis don't like other corgis?" Jack looked at me in surprise because we had always found the opposite to be true. A few other people at the show who had observed the incident did apologize to Jack later that day, saying that often corgis do like other corgis.

Comet and I had just walked onto the beach. I took off Comet's leash and he rolled and rolled in the sand, delighted by the sun and the cool beach. When he stood up and shook, his ears pricked toward some dogs on a sand bar far out in the low tide. He began a smart trot in their direction, with me trying to keep up behind him. As we got closer, we saw a group of corgis barking and playing ball with their people. They all looked much smaller than Comet, and as we got closer, he loped ahead of me. Soon there was a carpet of corgis surrounding the woman holding up the ball on a chuck-it scoop, and Comet—not an obsessive retriever—was waiting with the others to see where the ball went. Observing her dogs closely, the woman, Sherri, tossed the ball into the shallow water and her corgis ran and swam after it, Comet barking happily behind, preferring just to wade in the shallows.

Trystan, Comet and I enjoy a sail around the harbor in Provincetown.

The woman she was with, her wife Linda, remarked to me that Comet must be a confident dog, as her group does not usually like outsiders. I said that, indeed, he seemed to always get along with every other dog he had met. Especially when he was young and strong, he was a good, neutral dog, meaning that he had good self-confidence and was not easily rattled by dogs barking or jumping at him. Often he just turned slowly and walked back to me if another dog was barking at him. The pack of six corgis romped on the beach a few times on that vacation, Comet looking like a mother hen with his group of shorter corgis circling around him.

Comet's skill with other dogs helped especially with a dog client I had when Comet was getting older. The dog, a Doberman mix named Max, came to us because he had problems on walks, fearfully jumping up on his people when something scared him, such as another dog or person across the street. He had a dog friend he lived with named Rosie, but he was really fearful with all other dogs. Also, he was a rescue with a terrible trauma in his past. Traditional dog training had not helped him because no one had managed to help him process the deep emotions linked to his trauma. I started with some craniosacral sessions to help him process the past trauma and feel more comfortable in his body. We did maybe six of these sessions, all without Comet in the room. Eventually, Comet could be behind a gate in the kitchen so that Max could see him, but know Comet could not get to him.

Max, who benefitted from TTouch, Craniosacral Therapy and Comet's expert help.

Then I began to work with TTouch ground exercises with Max, first in the house and then outside. Once his person felt comfortable doing TTouches with him in the labyrinth outside, I brought Comet out on a leash, talking to Max and reassuring him. Then Comet waited under a tree with some snacks, where he lounged as we worked Max through a Confidence Course. Finally we could walk Max in the labyrinth, while I walked ten feet away with Comet on his leash. Comet, of course, paid no attention to Max. Gradually, over a few sessions, Max learned to relax enough so that I could walk Comet closely past him, and they could both go through the labyrinth, Max following Comet.

Finally, Max was completely comfortable with Comet, and we had a walk in the neighborhood with them next to each other, discussing the squirrels and cats that we passed. It was a huge victory for Max, and he was able to resume training with other dogs at a dog school near his home. In order to help Max, I had needed to use all I knew of craniosacral therapy and TTouch, and Comet's expert help was also essential. Comet and I were a team.

Every animal in our lives has something to teach us, as Ted Andrews demonstrated so well in his books *Animal Wise* and *Animal Speak*. His books include photographs of animals and details about the meanings and wisdom associated with many species of animals so that, for instance, when you hear an owl, you can refer to his books and see if anything written in the owl section resonates with you. So often with our own animals, these lessons go more deeply and touch our souls in ways that become part of our being, and bring us closer to the spiritual and natural worlds. One horse with whom I had worked for many years would need all of the lessons I had learned from living with my own animals to assist him in his time of crisis.

Yeshe ("Yeshe" is the Tibetan word for wisdom) was an elderly shorter bay gelding who had been raced at small tracks in his youth before being rescued by his caretaker, who had cared for him most of his life. I had been seeing him for a few years for craniosacral and TTouch work to keep him and his palomino pasture friend, Bodhi, comfortable in their senior years. Sadly, his beloved pasture friend, a gentle and sweet half Arabian with a golden palomino coat, had died a few years before. Yeshe then shared his life with a miniature horse and an Icelandic, a golden buckskin who was so like his old friend. Yeshe's feisty attitude belied his age, which was over thirty. We had resolved his chronic digestive challenges, and he had been doing well.

This horse had very flat soles in his front hooves from racing too hard and too young, and he was prone to abscesses. He developed an abscess in his front hoof on his stronger side, where he carried more weight, and it became so painful that he had bouts of colic as well. He was deteriorating, and eventually he lay down in the shavings in his run-in stall, and he did not have the strength to get up. His owner called on the services of a veterinarian who did acupuncture, and who stopped by frequently to assess the horse's pain level, progress, and provide medications as needed. I worked with this vet frequently, and I knew that his skills in Eastern and Western medicine were providing a high quality of care for the horse.

I went to see the horse nearly daily for a week, using TTouch on his ears and mouth to decrease pain and big, abalone TTouches to improve his circulation, as he was having a harder time shifting positions as the week progressed. I did techniques to decrease the inflammation in his abscessed hoof and joints, and he was visibly more comfortable for several hours after our sessions. I monitored his chakras as well, noticing after a few days that they were beginning to rotate counter-clockwise, especially his lower chakras, a sign that an animal is getting ready to cross the rainbow bridge.

I had seen from Linda Tellington-Jones the importance of not getting attached to an outcome when working with an animal. We had a pinto Paso Fino with badly damaged hooves and forelegs come to an advanced Tellington TTouch Training clinic in Florida, and he was crawling on his knees to not bear weight on his hooves and legs. We could see terrible pain in his pinned ears and grimacing facial muscles. People were shocked to see him and cried, or felt anger at the horse's past owners. Only a few us could remain neutral, keeping our emotions in check to allow whatever needed to happen for this pinto to unfold. My partner to work with him for the week was a grandmother, who sang songs to him about her grandchildren loving a pinto pony. I tried to hold a picture of health for him, standing to look out of the stall window at the grassy pastures beyond the ring. We noticed small improvements in his pain level over the week, doing two sessions with him each day. Linda was very strict about no one discussing pity or sadness over his lameness, especially near his stall, and that instead the group should hold an intention for health and peace for all beings. By the end of the week, after bits of daily progress, the pinto was able to stand in very deep shavings in his stall and whinny out the window to the mares in the distance. He remained under the care of the veterinarian who owned that farm and continued to improve.

Yeshe meeting his beloved pasture friend Bodhi for the first time.

With Yeshe, I knew the importance of not making choices for him that he needed to make, knowing that every being knows the time of their own passing. His owners, devout Buddhists, held strong beliefs about not putting him down if he was not suffering, and the skillful veterinarian was able to keep the horse comfortable. The woman who so loved this horse was able to adjust her schedule to spend days with him and hold his head during the frosty early spring nights. She did TTouch ear work as well. At the end of the week she would have to be gone overnight, and she was very concerned about leaving Yeshe.

Further complicating the situation, the caretaker who did the daily feeding for the horses was very upset and thought that he should be put down. She continued to arrive to change the IV bag or give him shots of pain medication, but she was very angry, expressing these feelings to the horse's owner. I assured the owner that only she, who had known Yeshe nearly his entire life, could sense what he needed. I used a pendulum to ask him yes and no questions. Yeshe showed his owner and me that he did not want to be put down, and that it was not yet his time.

His owner made a beautiful altar for him with pictures of his pasture friend and him at their first meeting, windhorse Tibetan peace flags, flowers, and LED candles to light his way. I asked people in my network of energy workers, craniosacral and TTouch practitioners, and others to hold a space for his journey and his passing.

On the day of her overnight trip we met in the morning, and Yeshe was growing weaker. I looked at her and said, "I think he will wait for you to come home from your trip, don't you?" She agreed, as we both knew he wanted to be with her. Before she was to leave, however, we had to find a solution to something many horse owners struggle with at the end—where would we put his body? The caretaker suggested burying him under the manure pile in their back acreage, as the warmth kept the ground there unfrozen all winter. The owner knew this was not a good idea, and searched for someone with a back hoe to come to her property. I suggested that since humans are buried in the winter we should contact someone at a cemetery to come. She was able to arrange for someone to come the next day to make a place for Yeshe beside his beloved companion in the front field.

Alone with Yeshe that afternoon, I asked my friend Tracy Vroom, TTouch and craniosacral instructor, and also a shaman, to work with Yeshe as well. Tracy is an advocate for retired racehorses and owns several Thoroughbreds. She did a shamanic journey with Yeshe, and she told me many details of her conversation with him. He was first very grateful that his owner was allowing him this time, as he had important reasons for waiting. He told Tracy that what he had seen at the local tracks was horrifying—so many horses in pain, abused, suffering profoundly—and that he had never been able to recover emotionally or trust people fully again. He chose instead to open his heart to only his palomino friend. He was so thankful that his owner simply let him live with her, not riding him or asking anything of him for his entire life, as he felt he had nothing left to offer. Tracy wrote his story and shared it with people in her network; it was so important to Yeshe that his story be told.

I returned to work with Yeshe the morning of his owner's return from her trip. He was growing very weak, and the vet felt he did not have much more time. I sat next to him, listening to the long shallow breaths he took, and thanked him for being my friend. I used frankincense, known to help spirits when they are passing, on his crown chakra. It was the last of his chakras spinning clockwise. I hoped the frankincense would help him to pass away peacefully. I did craniosacral stillpoints on his body and could feel the life force weakening in his craniosacral rhythm. I also used the very high-frequency sounds of my "angel" tuning forks to help raise Yeshe's vibration to the higher spiritual plane for passing away smoothly. He particularly had enjoyed the vibrations of the bigger forks on his body and hooves in the past, and I could see his ears pricking forward to the sounds of the angel forks.

Finally, I used to my cell phone to call Tracy from Yeshe's stall, and together, we connected with the ancestral herd of horses, asking them to bring him to the other side. I asked aloud for each of the many horses I'd known who had died to come to escort Yeshe. I called gentle Spooky and had a clear picture of her blue eyes and pink muzzle. Yeshe lifted his head and nickered softly in her direction. I called Goblin, and he gave a bigger whinny for the pretty chestnut mare. I called Judy's ponies, Betsy and BB, and he nickered to them as well. I called Richard, and Yeshe gave a snort to greet him. I spoke of Hatchet, another chestnut Thoroughbred who had raced, and Yeshe made muffled whinny sounds, seeming to have a conversation with him. I called Burgers, and I could feel his grounded energy around us. Yeshe sensed his deep brown eyes looking into his own closed eyes. Finally, I called Yeshe's beloved palomino friend Bodhi, and he responded with the quiet nickers horses use to greet each other. I knew then that he would follow his friend and the rest of the herd. It was clear, as his breaths become less frequent, that Yeshe was in a state of deep peace.

Many people who have had a "near-death" experience report seeing their deceased loved ones coming to greet them as they feel the pull of the "white light." I have no doubt that Yeshe could see and feel the horses I called to us, especially since he greeted each new horse as I called his or her name and described to Yeshe what they looked like so he could recognize them. Many people have also reported that relatives "on the other side" have told them to return, as their time has not yet come.

Soon after I left Yeshe, his owner returned, and Yeshe passed away with his head in her arms, just as the place for him in the front field next to his friend was completed. His owner had chosen his spiritual name for him thirty years before, and it now reflected her wisdom in honoring his wishes, and for following her heart in his final days.

Being with our animals when they "cross the rainbow bridge" requires all of the strength we have in us. The way to the rainbow bridge is not always a trip down the yellow brick road. As Bernie Siegel says, "Dying is part of living," and, "Remember, no one gets out alive." It is an honor that our animals share this final journey with us, and I think it's important for us to share our stories of this process with others so that we can be prepared, and make choices about what is best for our animals and ourselves. I have been with so many animals and people at their lives' ends, and I have provided hospice care for many animals. The time with our animals in their last moments is precious, and we must have strength and peace to be of greatest benefit to them.

Chapter 36

Joyous Dancer
Intrepid Trystan

Sally's Intrepid Trystan, eight weeks old, on his first night in his new home.

"Oh, I know they're not little people in fur jackets; they're enchanted pixies."
— Becky Roller about her corgis, Rudy and Maggie, *Woman's Best Friend*

It was becoming apparent to Judy and me that Comet's gait was deteriorating, and that it was very likely he had degenerative myelopathy (DM, similar to Lou Gehrig's or ALS in humans). I was not concerned about caring for Comet, having learned so much in caring for Winston when he had DM. But Comet definitely did not like the cart, and he was showing DM symptoms at a younger age than Winnie. Comet was a much bigger dog as well, which would make it difficult for me to carry him when that became necessary. Comet was still doing fairly well, and I am thankful that I had a long time to get used to the idea of his impending disability.

I decided it was time to get a new corgi puppy so that Comet, like Winston, would have plenty of time to teach him what he knew, and in that way, my dogs would all be connected to one another. It was a year after my cancer diagnosis and treatment, and it felt like a good time to get a puppy. I searched the Internet, called some breeders, and asked my sister to keep a lookout for corgi puppies. As Christmas approached I was feeling discouraged, but was hopeful that the spring would bring more litters of puppies or rescues for me to find a new dog.

Comet and I made the drive to New Jersey for the holidays, and on Christmas Eve, my mom was in a frenzy getting ready for breakfast and dinner to be held at her house the next day. She was rustling through the cupboards and moving boxes and jars when I said, "Are you looking for something?" She said that she could not find any cornflakes for the top of a potato casserole that my niece particularly loves. She was resigned to use a frosted type cornflake instead, which sounded awful to me. So I offered to make a trip to the grocery store to pick up anything that would be better. She demanded only the usual cornflakes, nothing strange, and I said, "Sure," heading out the door with Comet coming along for the ride.

The store was packed with shoppers getting their final items before the early closing for the holiday. I searched the cereal aisle, found a few types of cornflakes, and read the ingredients. They had nearly the same amount of sugar as the frosted ones. This was very troubling to me, having switched to an all-organic vegetarian diet since I had been diagnosed with cancer. I instead grabbed a box of healthy organic flakes and headed for the checkout line, my mom's demand for only her usual flakes rattling around my mind. I paid for the flakes and made my way to door. I was confused, going out through the "in" door in this unfamiliar store. A woman coming in pushed me aside with her cart, grumbling in her hurry. But flattened against the wall, I saw next to my head a sign with photographs of baby corgis! I read the sign for corgi puppies for sale carefully, seeing a picture of a tiny pup with a white nose like Winston, and called the numbers on the sign. The red male was still available.

I raced back to the car, telling Comet, "I think I found your little brother!" He stared at me, unimpressed, since I had been telling him we'd get a little brother for months. The puppies were at a house just a half-mile from where I had lived in high school. A man stepped out onto the snowy lawn as I stood with Comet looking at the Quarter horses in the corral next to the house. I introduced myself, and after a few minutes spent talking about the horses, the man told me that he knew and worked with some of my old riding friends. We stepped inside with Comet and were surrounded by a bustling group of tricolor corgis and one red male, Buddy, the father of the puppies. The man told me that Buddy was a good herding dog, working some of the cattle at the rodeo with him sometimes.

Comet towered over all of these small corgis, and surprised, I squeaked out, "They're so small!" I met the man's wife, and they introduced me to the herd of corgis one by one, including the new mother, Zoey. They were all friendly and happy, and Comet seemed to like all of them. The man returned from the basement holding the little red male with the white nose. He was covered with gray fluff, and the man assured me that the gray was the puppy fur on all red Pembroke pups, and said that he would grow up to look just like Buddy. I held the little guy, noticing he had a spot on the top of his head, called a fairy kiss in the corgi world—those favored in particular by the fairies were given this special marking. Winston's markings, with a big white saddle over his shoulders, meant that he was a corgi steed for fairies to ride, and Comet's stripe up his face like a harness indicated his skills were in pulling fairy carriages. This little pup had Winston's white nose and Comet's stripe, with that fairy kiss that made him special. I knew he would be my next corgi.

"You're lucky," the man said. "This guy was adopted this morning, but came back because the people decided they wanted a female instead."

"No," I answered. "They brought him back because he is meant to be my dog." I then learned that he had the same birthday as Jack, another good sign. The man gave me the pup's papers and medical records and introduced me to my puppy's sisters. My pup especially loved to play with a black and white female with one blue eye. They said they were keeping her, and her name was YinYang. I told them that if they ever changed their minds about selling her, they should give me a call first, as my pup loved her and she was beautiful. They also mentioned that the puppies had been sleeping with their toddler daughter and had also been on many car rides, even riding in the carriage with them behind their horses. I could not have asked for a better start for my puppy.

I named him Trystan, a Welsh name I had chosen months before, reminiscent of Tristan in the book *All Creatures Great and Small*. It seemed to fit him. He snuggled with Comet in his special place on the floor of the car under the back seat for the ride home. I was sure my mom was starting to worry about the delay in getting her cornflakes.

I walked in, apologizing for taking so long, telling my mom, "Well, it was worth it. I have a surprise." I returned to the car and carried in little Trystan. My mom gently stroked his head, exclaiming how cute he was, and how tiny. We agreed that he was smaller than even Winston as a puppy, which was starting to seem like a good thing to me. When my sister arrived a few minutes later, she inspected his health records and his body and discovered that—as happens sometimes with puppies—he had fleas. My mom flew into a panic, fearful of a flea infestation in her house. Judy filled the kitchen sink, found the right type of soap, and Trystan had his first bath. He didn't seem to mind at all, nipping at the towel during his rubdown and rolling onto his back for a post-bath inspection. No more fleas.

We found some toys and balls for him, but his favorite activity was nibbling on the feathers of my mom's schnauzer's legs. She tolerated this well, nosing him when he got too rough, as he wiggled on his back making small yips. Comet was somewhat standoffish with him, but after a few hours he began to play tug with him with some of the toys my mom had for her dog. We didn't have a crate, so Trystan slept in bed with Comet and me with no accidents, much to my mom's relief. Like Winston, he had almost never had an accident in the house, owing to frequent trips to the yard and a careful eye on his drinking, sleep, and play times.

Trystan is exhausted after the long drive from New Jersey to Massachusetts and from playing with his new toys.

He had a grand time tearing up wrapping paper, scampering around the pile of gift wrap and trailing ribbons behind him, and meeting some of Judy's Cavalier King Charles spaniels the next day. She had stopped by her office to bring him a supply of puppy food, treats for puppies, and toys. He became friends with her dog George immediately. Gwen held Trystan on her lap much of the day when he wasn't on my lap. His happiness spread to all of us, and although getting a puppy for Christmas is rarely a good idea, for me this was the perfect time to get a new corgi.

I was sad for him coming home to live in my house with just Comet and me for company, after leaving his family and all of the dogs at my mom's. I carried him for a tour of the house, showing him the corgi paintings on the walls, the collection of stuffed corgis (a mistake, as later he would pull them down and try to get them to play with him), and the basket of his toys and his food and water bowls. Comet showed him where to do his business outside, and informed him that he did not wish to share his bed with a squirmy puppy. Comet showed him how to walk on a leash and how to go up and down stairs, always a challenge for a short little corgi puppy. Jack babysat for him one weekend when I was away, and he taught him how to go up and down steps without carpet. He was touched that Trystan shared his birthday and they instantly bonded, as Jack stepped into the role of Trystan's dad and Trystan loved licking him with kisses, and barked happily whenever Jack stopped by to visit him.

Trystan fit perfectly into my life with Comet, although it was gradually becoming clear that Comet was not feeling the need to help with Trystan's training. He ignored Trystan's munching on my shoes or the rug. Since I was working at home, I was able to take care of Trystan without needing Comet's help.

Comet is showing Trystan around his new yard.

Trystan was fascinated by everything in his new yard.

Trystan hiding form Comet.

When Trystan was about six months old, I set up a booth advertising my work—Tellington TTouch Training and craniosacral therapy—at a local fun dog show. I decided that Trystan's cuteness would bring people to my booth, and that I would enter both dogs in the show's costume class. I found a onesy with yellow dogs printed on it that fit Trystan, got him a pacifier and a toy baby bottle, and borrowed a friend's antique doll stroller. Comet dressed as a nanny in a big blue hat covered in silk flowers, wore a dowdy dress, and carried around his neck a beaded purse with a handkerchief poking out. He also wore a pearl necklace. The boys won the class, posed for countless pictures, and had a great time. The judge particularly loved Comet's costume, saying she'd like to borrow his evening bag and pearls sometime.

Comet, dressed as baby Trystan's nanny, practicing for the Northampton dog show when Trystan was four months old.

The following year, the corgis wore baseball outfits, complete with a tiny bat and catcher's mitt and backwards baseball caps on their heads. I had to cut holes in Comet's to fit his large ears. With the Red Sox in great favor here, the costumes were another hit with the audience.

At the show the next year, Comet was losing his ability to walk, so I filled a wagon with sand and sea shells, dressed the corgis in sundresses from the children's department, got them tiny sun hats, and sunglasses for Comet. I added a beach ball and squeaky inner tube, and carried a pail and shovel myself. Again we won the class, posed for pictures, and got many comments from people thanking us for reminding them that summer would come, since it was a particularly long New England winter that year. As I pulled the wagon out of the ring, the blue ribbon hanging on Comet's collar, I knew that would be the last time he would make it to that show with his growing health problems.

Comet (left) and Trystan playing with YinYang and Buddy (right), Trystan's sister and father, at a reunion playdate when Trystan was a few months old.

A few months after the first show, Trystan began attending puppy classes with me and Comet to learn basic manners and to have some play time with dogs his age, even though they were mostly much larger than he was. He learned quickly, watching Comet demonstrate what I wanted first. I knew from my years with Tellington TTouch Training that animals do indeed learn from watching others, and Comet enjoyed the extra treats and being a star in a class of pups who were just learning.

It was eventually time for Trystan to meet the dachshunds, Aiden and Peanut, who live with Jack's partner Ron's daughter, Heather, and her wife Larissa. We spend a lot of time together, and it's important that all of our dogs are able to get along. The dachshunds were not always friendly with other dogs, but they were always fine with Comet.

Comet and I got out of the car in the backyard at their house, and Trystan scampered along behind us. Heather tried to first just let out Peanut, as he is friendlier, but Aiden squeezed out as well, and both dogs galloped at top speed at Trystan. Trusting, he just stood there, until Aiden decided to attack him. Trystan ran under a car in the driveway, but the short dachshunds followed right behind him. Heather and I were horrified to hear the barking and crying and growling coming from under her car. We tried to squeeze under the car to rescue Trystan, and Heather managed to grab one of her dogs, when suddenly a flurry of orange and golden hair settled the argument. Comet had scrambled under the car to help Trystan, chasing the dachshunds to the back of the yard where he kept them cornered. Heather picked up Trystan and we inspected him closely—no injuries, but he was very afraid. We put a long leash on Aiden so that we could keep him away from Trystan. Soon Trystan, Peanut, and Comet were happily playing in the yard.

Comet keeps a watchful eye on Trystan, nearly a year old, during long hikes.

But this incident changed Trystan, and I now know that there are times in a puppy's development when situations have a great impact on their emotional growth. At the time I thought Trystan was old enough to manage, at least with the friendly dachshund, Peanut. Heather and I did not plan to have him meet two new dogs at once, or to even meet Aiden at all that day.

Trystan's full name is Intrepid Trystan, because he was so brave, venturing off to explore the woods, the house, and all of the new things around him with courage. But after this he became timid, and Comet became his protector. Even when Comet could no longer walk, Trystan checked in with him whenever a new dog entered our lives. Thankfully, after five TTouch classes, Trystan has found most of his courage again. It is a continuing process for him to feel safe with a new person, to adjust to the other dogs around him, and to feel safe in a crowded room when I am not with him. He and Peanut have become close friends, though he and Aiden merely tolerate one another.

Soon it was Trystan's first summer, and the three of us went to the beach. Trystan, like any puppy, loved chasing the waves. Comet has always preferred wading to swimming, and little Trystan followed behind him in the quiet waters of the bay in Provincetown. Fortunately, there are many corgis at the beach where we go, and one morning on our walk on the beach we met a corgi, Bexley, who is a strong swimmer. Trystan loved him and he boldly swam out into the deep water, following the other corgi to get his ball while Comet barked next to me, supervising everyone. Trystan was an excellent swimmer from the start and ever after this day, he paddles out for a swim even in rough water. The dachshunds were at the beach that week as well, and the two of them and Trystan ran and ran, seemingly recovered from the incident that spring. The three of them loved to swim out after tennis balls while Comet and I waited on shore.

That summer, I set up a TTouch Confidence Course for Trystan with poles to walk over, different surfaces, a labyrinth, and for fun, a little jump. He followed Comet through each obstacle with no problems. He continued to play with our Yorkie neighbor and the pugs across the street. He went to dog daycare two days a week to play with his pals in the small dog group. Trystan passed his Canine Good Citizen test. And unlike Comet, he showed little interest in working with my craniosacral clients, although he did love to greet them at the door when they arrived for their sessions. As Comet's mobility decreased, Trystan came with me to doctor appointments and to cancer support group meetings, both locally and with Bernie Siegel. A few years later, when Trystan accompanied me to a job at a veteran's home, he would be drawn to the patients with cancer, perhaps sensing something in them he had learned from these meetings with me. And it would be my patients with cancer who evoked Trystan's healing skills.

Chapter 37

Dancing Into Eternity
DM Test, Holistic Health Conferences, Tuning Forks

A Fiord pony and I demonstrate a TMJ release at the Holistic Equine Expo. Photo by Maureen Harmonay.

"The power lies in the wisdom and understanding of one's role in the Great Mystery, and in honoring each living thing as a teacher."

— Jamie Sands and David Carson

"The path to God is whatever path you're on ... just follow your nose."

— Rover's Guide to the Universe, *Dog Gospels*

In 2008, a few years before Trystan was born, a test became available for DM (degenerative myelopathy), and after I got Trystan, I decided to test both of my dogs. Judy and I knew what the results would be for Comet's test, and I knew that I would have a hard time facing another of my corgis having DM. Molly, fortunately, never had it. I waited anxiously for the results to come in the mail, certain that I wanted to know now, while Trystan was young, so that I could do everything possible with his diet and exercise program to keep him healthy. When the results came, I nearly cried in happiness that Trystan was DM clear! I hugged him close to me, knowing that he would never need a cart, and he would be spared the difficulties of this disease. I called the people I had gotten him from to tell them how fortunate they were to have been breeding dogs without this disease, only to learn that Trystan's mother had died the year before. Trystan was already neutered, as I had thought I could count on getting another one of Buddy's and Zoey's pups, but now I learned that would not be possible. The man assured me that they had a new female, and were planning to have more litters in the future, but the news that Trystan was DM clear was overshadowed by sadness that I could not get more corgis exactly like him.

We all love our dogs as much as we possibly can, knowing their time with us is short. I am always aware that I will have more dogs coming into my life, which is some consolation for the brevity of time I have with each dog. I am always wondering where my next dog will find me, and I am glad that Trystan's dad will sire more puppies in the future.

As Trystan turned two, becoming a rambunctious teenager, his best playmate, Comet, was becoming more immobile. One day, as Comet lay on the floor, Trystan began to run around him and the chair next to him, nipping at Comet's toes as he raced by. Both corgis got more excited with this game, and Comet started barking and nipping at Trystan as he ran by, circling and circling. I smiled. It was the same game Comet had played with Winston in his cart. Had Comet somehow explained to Trystan how to do this? Did Trystan invent the game on his own from some deep instinct to herd even an immobile dog? Or was Winston, from across the rainbow bridge, showing Trystan how to play with Comet? This game continued for years. I could always see Comet's spirits elevated by Trystan's game.

I was invited to speak about craniosacral therapy and Tellington TTouch Training at a holistic equine health expo in my area. Sadly, Comet was not up to the trip to assist in the booth where a friend and I would be offering craniosacral sessions. I also did demonstrations with horses from a rescue group in our area. It was an unusually warm spring day, with bright sun, and many people came to learn about holistic care. One of my demonstration horses was a senior Appaloosa gelding. I had a group of young women who worked with the horse at the rescue watching me, as well as some other professionals from our area. The horse was a quiet gentleman, who had some old injuries to his stifles, as evidenced by his discomfort in that area and the lovely leg stretch releases he did. I was showing the diaphragm releases and a general approach for a craniosacral session when I had my hand near his heart. I could feel a significant heart murmur. I pressed my ear against him and confirmed what I had felt. I continued my demo, and asked one of the girls watching to bring the vet over for a minute, with a stethoscope, please. He was the same vet who later helped with Yeshe's passing. I could see him look over at me, puzzled, before coming over to meet my Appaloosa. I asked if he wouldn't mind taking a listen to the horse's heart, as I suggested to people how important it is to work with veterinarians as well as using complementary care with our horses.

Demonstrating craniosacral therapy with Buster at the Conference for Complementary Care for Animals. Photo by Maureen Harmony.

The vet, someone I worked with quite often, knew what I was getting at, and turned to the group to explain that indeed this horse had a rather significant heart murmur, and then he suggested that the girls not ride him at all, and certainly not at the trot or far from the barn, urging extra caution on warm humid days, or frigid cold days. He, like me, was impressed this horse had enjoyed a long life. I showed the girls some

TTouches to practice with him, and said that perhaps he could be a TTouch practice horse instead of riding horse. They loved this idea, as his gentle nature had already won their hearts. I made sure they had plenty of practice and handouts to refer to, and at the end of the day they thanked me for helping their friend.

Later that year, Comet, and little Trystan as well, came with me to the "Conference for Complementary Care for Animals." I had been asked to present a two-hour lecture and demonstration of craniosacral therapy for animals, as well as an hour lecture about my newer work with tuning forks. I had been using tuning forks to assist in orthopedic manipulations for several years. I also used the sounds and vibrations of the forks to work on chakras off the body and to clear energy from old injuries. I had good success using tuning forks to help animals after trauma or surgery, and to make spiritual connections for them when they were "crossing the rainbow bridge." People were fascinated to learn about the lower frequencies of disease states, and the higher frequencies of healthy tissue in various places in the body. The dogs in the room all turned their heads to the sounds of the forks, even when the people in the room could not hear them. I showed everyone how I use the high frequencies of the forks to elevate the low frequencies of restrictions in the physical body, as well as in the field around the body. Resonance, which occurs when one key on a piano is played and the other keys vibrate with it, explains how the higher vibrational tones of the forks improve the health of bodily tissues by increasing their frequencies.

At the Conference for Complementary Care for Animals, I demonstrated Vibrational Therapy with Max. Photo by Maureen Harmonay.

Comet, becoming so fragile, cheerfully demonstrated the use of the universal healing fork on his paralyzed limbs and sore shoulders. At this point in his life, his favorite healing method was indeed with the tuning forks or my sister's cold laser treatments at her veterinary office. She and I have thought that at some point we should try to measure and compare how the tuning forks and the cold laser effect tissues, prompted by the slowing of the progression of DM we saw from both modalities for Comet. He especially liked Maureen Harmonay, an animal communicator who had organized the event, and he licked her hand affectionately when she thanked him for his demonstration. As the people in the room clapped their appreciation, Comet woofed too. It was his last public appearance, and he finished with his usual good humor and well timed barks.

The next year, Maureen organized a conference called "Animals in the Afterlife." She presented case studies of animals she had worked with as a communicator, after they had passed away, and had compelling stories from the animals' owners confirming the accuracy and details the animals had given her in their stories. Other presenters told stories of how their animals had come back to them as a new kitten or dog, showing pictures of remarkable resemblances. They told stories of their new animals who, as with a malamute I had met years before, took on the habits and quirks of the animals that had come before them, indicating some sort of communication or connection.

As the keynote speaker, I first shared my own "near-death" experience. I knew that it was important for people to hear that dying is not a dark and frightening experience, but rather a peaceful and light filled process. And at this conference, I wanted to emphasize the interconnection between all beings, since so many people feel deeply connected to their departed animals, as well as with the animals who share their lives.

I continued my talk, and recounted the stories of some of the many animals I have known at the end of their lives. I had worked with a slim frail whippet. His owner had brought him to me, uncertain what she should do as so many were telling her to have the dog put to sleep. She sensed it was the wrong choice as she told me about the tremendous upheavals in her own life at this time. I could feel the whippet's anxiety go up as the dog's person told her own story, and I knew he wanted to stay with her. I used a pendulum to ask the dog yes and no questions, and showed the owner that indeed, according to all I could see, the dog was not ready. I received a call months later, and the woman told me her dog had passed away just after she had found a new job and relocated to a new apartment. The fragile whippet was able to stay with her until the changes in her life were completed.

I told the story of a very old Pyrenees dog, Major, whom I was with as he died, and how he was surrounded by the person's cats for hours up to and after his death, spirit guides for the old dog. They stayed with him three days. The owner was familiar with the three day waiting period described in *The Tibetan Book of the Dead* and felt she should wait that long before moving him, and her cats apparently agreed. As soon as the time was up, the cats resumed their normal activity.

Major, a senior Pyrenees whose life story I shared at the Conference for Animals in the Afterlife.

I also told the story of a cat named Percy, whose owner had wanted to be with him when he died, but he had other plans. She followed him on his short trips outside, stayed next to him in the house, and finally was on the phone with an animal communicator trying to figure out what to do next. The animal communicator asked the woman to go to her bird in the next room, as he had a special message for her. The woman waited for the bird to offer something, but he did not. She went back to her cat, only to find that he had passed in that moment, heeding the call of the ancestral pride, not wanting her to be with him in the end.

Once, I recounted, I found a dead fox by the side of the road on my way to work with a chestnut senior horse named "Red," who was struggling with EPM (equine protozoal myeloencephalitis, a severe neurologic disease in horses caused by a parasite). I had stopped to check the fox, still slightly warm, and moved her to the side of the road. The horse's owner gave me a bag to bring the fox's body back to the woods for burial, so that her mate would not be killed sitting by her in the road. Two days later, the horse's owner called to tell me that she had put down her horse Red, and on the same morning, she had seen a fox in the pasture. In fact, she added, she had named her horse Red after seeing a red fox in the paddock the day she had brought him home. She had not seen a fox in the pasture for nearly three years since then. What is the message of the foxes?

Foxes, among other things, are associated with an ability to see spirit, and see beings such as fairies and elves that live between worlds. Their fur is associated with psychic energy. And in some cultures, the fox helps the dead find their way to heaven. It seems the fox was the perfect animal to assist Red's owner with making the choice to end his life.

I told the story of Burgers, and how I had asked him many times in his older years to pass away on his own when it was time. For many days after his passing, the barn manager and others at the farm heard the galloping hooves of a herd in the pastures, even though all of the horses were in the barn. And several people heard the sound of Burgers' hooves galloping around the pasture as I followed his body across the field to his resting place. These experiences all point to the possibility that our animals stay with us, that the line between "here" and "there" is blurry and fluid.

Next, I told the story of the courage of Yeshe's owner in allowing him to choose his own path in the end, with medication for pain and discomfort. I educated the audience about the plight of racehorses, passing on Yeshe's words, and many people in the room understood, as their own horses were rescued racehorses. Several animal communicators in the room later told the group that they could see racehorses galloping around our group, strong and free, with a small bay gelding in the lead. That day, many heard Yeshe's words clearly.

Finally, I told the group about Bernie Siegel's book *Buddy's Candle*. It is a children's book about a boy who has leukemia and needs a bone marrow transplant. He finds a dog and names him Buddy, only to find that he has cancer too. The dog's enthusiasm for life, even undergoing his own chemo treatments, encourages the boy and his family to live each day fully with happiness. The boy recovers, but Buddy dies. The veterinarian tells the boy that dogs have shorter lives because they already know about love and forgiveness, which the boy understands. Missing his dog, the boy goes to sleep asking for Buddy to help him. He has a dream about a dog angel who comes to tell him that death is like a "new beginning, a commencement, or a graduation." The angel shows the boy a parade of animals in heaven carrying burning candles all except his Buddy, whose candle is unlit.

The boy offers to light the candle, and Buddy explains that they do light the candle however, the boy's tears keep putting out the light. The boy promises Buddy that the next time he feels like crying, he will instead think of the love between him and Buddy so that the candle will burn brightly. The angel also promises the boy that Buddy will come back to him sometime. At the end of the story, the boy goes to a shelter where a dog immediately recognizes him. The boy knows it is old friend coming back to him as a new dog. The boy learns in the end that tears are all right, but it is important to "let your light shine brightly every day," and that "the most permanent candle is love."

There is a universal life force, a Oneness that Larry Dossey M.D. writes about in his book *One Mind—How Our Individual Mind Is Part of a Greater Consciousness and Why*

It Matters. He describes "another level of consciousness, an all encompassing, infinite dimension of shared intelligence." Dossey describes lost pets who made seemingly impossible trips home to be reunited with owners, as well as telepathic connections or communications between people and their animals. He includes stories of dolphins saving other animals or people, suggesting an inter-species empathy. This empathy works both ways—we feel empathy for our animals, and they feel empathy for us. Dossey explains that empathy allows us, animals and humans, to tap into the higher infinite dimension of consciousness that is the One Mind. Acclaimed biologist Carl Safina echoes Dossey, "The greatest story is that life is all one." One of the greatest gifts of sharing time with our animals is being able to experience this shared consciousness with them, both during and after our time on earth with them.

Chapter 38

Spirit Dance
Comet Crosses The Rainbow Bridge

Sally's Charismatic Comet, nearly 14, enjoying a day at the beach in Provincetown.

"All animals except man know that the ultimate of life is to enjoy it."

— Samuel Butler

"... love knows not its own depth until the hour of separation."

— Kahlil Gibran

275

How can anyone describe the passing of a beloved dog? There is a deep, profound sadness that no words can capture when one experiences the loss of a dog. Perhaps we never have such a close connection to another living being as we do with our dogs, as we open our hearts fully to them. No one knows us like our dogs do; no one loves us like our dogs do; and no one leaves such complete sense of emptiness like our dogs do. The only way I have gotten through the deaths of my corgis is with the love and life of my new corgi, constantly at my feet or on my lap, to ward off the sadness and loss. I can't even imagine having only one dog, and then finding myself at that day when I am alone in a dog-less house. Like the boy in *Buddy's Candle*, I need reminding to see past the grief—my new corgis remind me to replace the sadness with the love I felt for my departed corgi, and the love I feel for the corgi still with me.

Comet, age 15, enjoying some sunshine on a late summer day.

Comet thrived through his final months, thanks to Judy's exceptional veterinary care and unconditional support from me to keep his body comfortable and his spirit bright. He loved to lie in the sun on the deck and survey the forest and stream beyond the yard, listening to the birds. He had a final trip to the beach in Provincetown, to feel the sea against him as I supported him so he could allow the tides to pull his paws in and out as they rolled against us. He wiggled in the warm September sand, scrubbing his cheeks against the cool wet patches. I bought him a better bed, a thick blue velvety one that rolled around him like a hotdog bun, keeping him upright like a sphinx most of the day, and I could flatten it for him to lie on each side as well. He loved his soft new bed, giving it a thorough sniff for inspection, noting its new, unused smell, perfect for a senior corgi.

Comet following Burgers on the trail. Photo by Helena Sullivan.

Since he now required his bladder to be expressed, as he was unable to pee on his own, he was able to avoid the many clean ups he did not always like. He loved the fluffing with the towel after a rinse, and I continued to do this for him when I changed his bed, as he was unable to move enough to scratch himself. Comet was having a hard time sleeping at night, starting to bark and whine in the early evening each day. I tried various calming remedies: pills made of colostrum, herbal capsules, and essential oils. My sister explained it was like sundowning in humans, which, from my work as a physical therapist with Alzheimer's patients, made me realize that there was something Comet needed. My work with elderly people had shown me that there is always a grain of truth in whatever is causing their emotional distress. I had to figure out what Comet wanted.

I called one animal communicator who said that he was like a nervous elderly woman, needing to check the locks a hundred times, afraid of the dark, fidgeting and perseverating over intruders. This did not sound like Comet, so I called Maureen Harmonay, who I had met initially at a holistic horse health conference, and who knew Comet from his attendance at her Conference for Complementary Care for animals. She gave me invaluable information about Comet's needs and concerns, and her input made his last weeks on earth much better.

Maureen said that Comet was lonely at night, a little afraid, and needed company. I gave him a blue nightlight so he could see his surroundings but still have darkness for sleeping. I brought his big stuffed lamb from his fourteenth birthday close to his bed so he could see its sweet sleeping face. I played soft music for him all night and set up Tibetan salt lights around the kitchen, hoping their soft golden glow would settle him. And Trystan and I made a point of saying goodnight to him, telling him about the delicious food he would have in the morning, and that we could hear him upstairs if he needed anything, and that we would all be together in the morning. The first night after I talked to Maureen, Comet had a good night's sleep, with no barking or distress. He just needed to be heard and understood. He never again showed the distress he had before I had conferred with Maureen.

Maureen also said that Comet wanted to feel extra special—he wanted a party. She said Comet told her that I could not have done the work I do if it weren't for him, that he was very important and everyone should know that. He had worked in New York after 9/11, was a famous craniosacral corgi, had sniffed a dolphin, had been in airplanes, and had had many jobs in his lifetime working next to me. His sixteenth birthday was coming up in December, and Maureen said that he would like his party sooner, right away, that this was very important for him. I set plans into motion for the third Sunday in October, to give us two weeks before little Trystan's fifth birthday party. I invited Comet's best friends, Jack and Ron, Heather and Larissa and the dachshunds Aiden and Peanut, Becky, Susanne and Suzanne with their dog Chaco. I ordered a gluten-free almond raspberry cake from my natural food store, stocked up on Frosty Paws dog ice cream, one of Comet's favorites, and purchased a supply of healthy meaty dog treats for the party guests. I got Comet's Happy Birthday party hat out, and bought him a blue ribbon that said "birthday boy" on it. Comet had a bath, and all of his things had a wash. His stuffed lamby and Trystan wore party hats, and we had paper plates and cups with dogs on them. I gathered some chairs and stools around Comet's place in the kitchen so people could visit with the birthday corgi.

His party was a huge success. Comet, who had seemed very weak in the morning, eating only a little for breakfast, rallied and woofed greetings to his friends. He wore his hat with aplomb, enjoyed his birthday cake and some Frosty Paws, and looked bright and happy. Suzanne sat next to him, stroking him and complimenting him for over an hour on his handsome good looks, soft golden coat, and his courage. Ron brought a new bottle of lavender clean up spray. Jack gave Comet many kisses, and Becky and Jack made a toast to him. Trystan seemed to understand and took a back seat all day, not demanding that everyone throw his squeaky toys for him. Comet ate the delicious treats people brought for him, and enjoyed a few kisses from Suzanne's dog Chaco. The dachshunds could not make it, so Comet was relieved of peace-making duties with the feisty Aiden and the other dogs at the party. It was clear to everyone that he knew this party was for him, his sixteenth birthday party, just a month early. He smiled corgi grins, got butter cream icing on his nose and paws, and barked as we all sang "Happy birthday dear Comet, happy birthday to you!"

Comet awaiting a piece of his almond raspberry sixteenth birthday cake.

Jack was the last to leave, giving Comet more kisses and telling him he was the most handsome dog in the world several more times. Comet woofed goodbye when Jack stood up to go.

Comet wearing his special birthday ribbon.

After the party, Comet did not want dinner, since he had been eating all afternoon. He was tired, and I left his blue ribbon pinned to his collar on him until late in the evening when Trystan and I bid him goodnight with final birthday kisses. Comet surely had gotten exactly what he wanted.

The next morning, I called Maureen to thank her and tell her how happy the party had made Comet. He had a bit of egg for breakfast, some licks of water, and rested contentedly throughout the day. I opened the window near him for a while so he could smell the outside world. When it got to be dinnertime, he showed no interest in food, not cheese, not eggs, not tuna, or turkey, or Frosty Paws. He ate a few special meaty treats. I had to syringe water into his mouth. His eyes looked far away for hours, and then when I hugged him and sang his corgi songs to him, he'd come back to me. I had to leave to teach yoga that night, and we had a short class because I was worried about

Comet. Trystan and I sat with him for half an hour before bed. I left for work Tuesday in the morning, Trystan coming along as usual, after a long snuggle with Comet, who had refused all breakfast except syringes of water.

I raced home, even later than I had expected to be, and immediately ran to Comet to take care of his bladder and reposition him. He looked very far off indeed, his eyes glassy and his head nearly limp. I got a stethoscope to check his heart, which was weak.

More syringes of water, but Comet was barely able to swallow. I offered him every enticing food I had, but Comet refused to eat. I sat next to him, eating some soup, knowing what was coming, wishing it to be otherwise.

I called my sister who said to stay with him, keep him comfortable, and call her if I needed to. I carried Comet on his big blue pillow bed, and put him next to the sofa where I sat stroking his ruff, with Trystan next to me. Comet's eyes widened and he gasped for air at times; I knew he was struggling. I lit candles, got the frankincense, and rubbed a drop on his third eye, as frankincense is known to ease the transition to spirit. He seemed calmer for an hour. Then he began to bark, his mouth opened, his eyes widened; he took one breath, and he was gone. I curled my arms around him, crying, and stroking him, talking to him, telling him again what a perfect dog he had been, would always be, that I would always miss him, and that I would forever know he would be with me when I needed him. He had always been with me when I needed him.

I sent the sad text messages to Jack, my sister, Comet's friend Nikki, and Dr. Mark Restey who is a gifted holistic vet and friend of mine who helped Comet for many months. A few minutes later Mark called me, and he reminded me that I had never let Comet down, and that no one could have taken better care of him than I did. We hung up, and I found the beautiful wooden corgi angel someone had made for Comet, and put it on his heart. I surrounded him with drops of frankincense on his blue pillow, and made an altar holding his baby picture, candles, his big picture of a corgi that looked like him, flowers, and his collar still with the birthday blue ribbon attached. I trimmed that bunny soft hair from his neck and behind his ears. I sat next to him, quiet, with Trystan coming and going, giving Comet kisses, and then finally one long sniff over his whole body. "You know, don't you?" I said to Trystan, hugging him close.

As I sat close to Comet, I thought back over my time with him, and wondered how it would be to teach a craniosacral class or TTouch class without him. I knew he would be there in spirit, but I struggled to sense something else from him. It suddenly occurred to me that maybe I should keep his skull, and he would be there forever to help people find the bony landmarks. One of his favorite parts of the course was to pose on the front table next to a coyote skull exactly his size, and show the furry landmarks that corresponded to the bones on the coyote skull. He would change his facial expressions to suggest the movements of the bones even, pinching his nose and widening his eyes, tilting his ears. I called my sister to ask her about keeping his skull.

She was horrified. She said she could not help me with this and could not believe I could do it. I hung up, questioning my idea.

Comet pauses in a meadow near the barn. Photo by Helena Sullivan.

The longer I sat with Comet, asking him to give me some direction with this, the more sure I became that this was indeed the right thing to do. I felt a blanket of peace cover my spirit when I imagined a box with his skull, a piece of him that I could always touch, that would be a part of so many people's learning. Yes, it seemed horrible, but it was what I had to do. I called Mark, who is a shaman as well as a vet, and he had the opposite response to my sister. He said that if this idea, unusual as it was, came to me at this time, it must be right, must be what Comet wanted. He suggested that I call Tufts Veterinary School, saying that he was sure they would be able to help me. I knew he was right.

That night, Trystan and I said goodnight to Comet as usual, leaving candles burning for him, and a light on in the kitchen. Trystan snuggled close to me as I listened to harp music, unable to sleep. His quiet breath in and out seemed so fragile and transient to me; he was still a puppy really, and now he was my only dog—how would we manage alone, the two of us? I cried most of the night. Sometimes it seems that no one can help you when your dog has gone across the rainbow bridge.

Early the next morning, Heather, who loved Comet so much, called and asked how she could help. I told her I was waiting until eight to call Tufts. She said she would take care of this for me, finding the person in charge of the anatomy lab, finding out what kinds of permission I would need. Jack called, offering any help, crying too, not shocked by my idea to keep Comet's skull. He said he could drive me to Boston. I said I would also need someone to drive me, Trystan, and Comet to White Rose in Vermont, where they would cremate him. He said he could do all of this. Heather called back with information from Tufts—Joe, director the anatomy lab, and his department head were the people I needed to call. I explained to them that I teach detailed anatomy in my small animal craniosacral class, and that I felt Comet had volunteered to help me with this, and that I would need someone to preserve his skull for me. They called back a few hours later and said that we could bring Comet to them the next day. I was relieved to have one more night with Comet on his blue cushion in the kitchen.

Jack arrived the next morning, cold icy rain falling outside. Unslept, I was functioning but inconsolable, afraid to have Trystan out of my sight. I carried Comet to the car, still on his blue bed, and found a box for him to be in on the ride back from Tufts. Trystan and I sat in the front as Jack drove us all down the turnpike across the gray, wet landscape. We found the back door of the anatomy lab area, and I went inside, waited in the office I had been directed to, nervous, missing Trystan who was in the car with Jack and Comet. Joe came in, bowing, saying "namaste" to me. This action unmistakably showed me Joe's respect for my situation and for my beloved Comet. We went to the car, and I carried Comet inside, leaving his bed in the car with Jack and Trystan. I placed Comet on the steel gurney, all too familiar to me from anatomy classes and time spent in large veterinary facilities. Joe gave me a few minutes, and I told Comet how much I loved him, how brave he was, how beautiful he was, stroking his bunny-soft fur one last time. I knew that once he was in the box I had brought, I would never see him again. I left the room as Joe came in, and sat in the office to wait.

A few moments later, Joe came out carrying the box, and I mumbled something about how fast that was. He was grave, said how sorry he was for my loss, looked deeply at me, and I knew that he was a very kind man. He carried the box to the car in the pouring the rain—I could not carry it as I did not want to feel the weight change, realizing that part of Comet was still on that table. Jack jumped out and thanked Joe, and we drove back down the highway to my house. Jack carried Comet's box into the garage where it would be cool overnight. I mumbled that I was worried that Joe had been so quick, that it really could mean only one thing, which I could not say, that some of Comet would be at Tufts. Jack, as much as this whole business could have been upsetting to him, simply said, "I'm sure you did the right thing for Comet. You know how much he loved your classes together." I brought some flowers and his wooden corgi angel down to the garage, with his stuffed lamb, to keep Comet company.

Another sleepless night. Jack arrived in the morning, dressed up. When I asked why, he said, "Well, one ought to dress for a funeral," matter-of-factly. It was slightly funny and true and exactly right. He put Comet in his box into the car again, and Trystan and I once again snuggled in the front seat. It was still gray and rainy, but the ride to White Rose was much shorter than the trip to Tufts had been. As we pulled off the main road into the White Rose driveway, we could see beautiful manicured gardens, and stone statues of dogs, cats and other animals lining the driveway, nestled into the gardens. It was a bucolic place, settled in between the surrounding hills with great trees around the property. We parked by the building, where even more stone animals and benches and flowers surrounded the portico. Jack carried Comet and the box inside, and I put a leash on little Trystan.

Inside was a lovely room, with antiques and oriental rugs and a display case with different urns, keepsake boxes, paw print frames, necklaces and other items one would want to help remember a departed pet. A young woman greeted us, and we placed Comet's box on a table covered with a tapestry suited to his Celtic origins. Soft harp music was playing. We made the arrangements and I chose a rosewood box for Comet's ashes. We sadly left him there, knowing that this was the best possible place for him to be now.

Comet, in his prime at age five in Provincetown.

We stopped on the way home for macaroni and cheese, as Jack had said, "I need comfort food." It was the first I'd eaten in a few days. Trystan, undaunted, was delighted to lick the cheese from the lid. I murmured to Jack, "Don't the ladies in the church often bring you a lunch with macaroni and cheese after a funeral?"

I counted the days until Comet would come home again, in the small rosewood box. I felt then that I would feel some greater peace. After that, I would count the days until his skull came, a few weeks later, in a lesser box, and then I would know all was right, as much as it can ever be when your dog has gone over the rainbow bridge, to another place, a place where you can no longer stroke his fur or watch him run in the waves at the beach, or hear his bark.

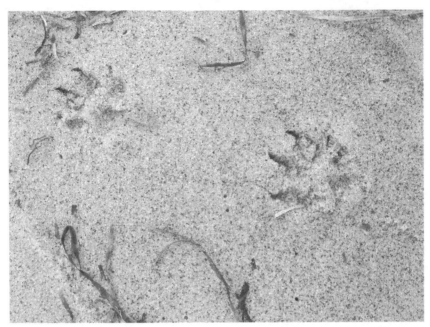

Comet's paw prints.

Trystan and I sat desolate in the living room the next night. We stared at each other. I heard a small bark. I looked out into the dark street for a dog, but it was empty. I heard another bark. This time Trystan turned to look where Comet's empty bed was in the kitchen by his alter. A third time, we both heard the bark, and Trystan jumped off of the sofa to inspect Comet's bed. We could feel his presence. But for Trystan's response, I would have thought my exhaustion was catching up to me. This happened several more times over the next months, each time with Trystan looking to see if Comet was there.

I recalled a man at the Alaskan Malamute rescue retreat years before who had come to my talk, asking if it was possible that his new dog was somehow in communication with his dog who had died a few months earlier. The new dog had taken up the old dog's habits, getting his leash at a certain time each day, a particular way of barking at squirrels, arranging himself on the living room sofa the same way. Without hesitating, I said, "Of course; of course your old dog is helping your new dog learn how to be with you. He's showing the new guy around." Others in the group nodded in agreement, quietly sharing similar stories. The man's new nine-month-old pup sat alertly next to him during this conversation, looking over at me and Comet. The man burst into tears of relief and happiness. He loved his old dog so much and was overjoyed to hear that there was somehow a connection between his dogs, so that a part of his old dog would still be with him. This is what we all want really, to never see the end of our time with our beloved dogs.

Comet visited me and Trystan with his small barks for a while, and then, at some point, he didn't. When his skull arrived in the mail, I called Trystan, and we opened the package gently, together. I carefully unwrapped it, noticing the slightly crossed lower front teeth that were part of Comet's smile. Trystan sniffed everything carefully, and looked up at me and back at the skull. Could he smell something of his old pal in the bones? I could not really tell. I wrapped it back up carefully, and placed the box on Comet's blue pillow bed in my room, with his lamb toy on top of the box. I wondered how it would be when I was teaching a class and unwrapped Comet's skull for the first time. I moved his alter from the kitchen upstairs to my bedroom, with the corgi angel, his pictures, his rosewood box, and his blue ribbon collar. Finally, Comet was home again.

(As I am writing this, Trystan is making little barks and looking over at the front door past the papier maché corgi—what does he see or hear? Are Comet and Winston stopping by? I wish I could know for sure.)

Chapter 39

The Dance of Courage
Trystan and TTouch

Linda Tellington-Jones with me and Comet at a Companion Animal TTouch class.

"It came to me that every time I lose a dog, they take a piece of my heart with them, and every new dog who comes into my life gifts me with a piece of their heart. If I live long enough, all of the components of my heart will be dog, and I will become as generous and loving as they are."

— Anonymous

During the last years of Comet's life, it became clear to me that Trystan, like Comet and Burgers, would benefit tremendously from going to a TTouch class or two. He was lacking courage and confidence, and I was concerned that with Comet's decline, this would only increase, as Trystan would not have his "big brother" to look to for guidance and support. I set off to assist Linda Tellington-Jones at a TTouch class for companion animals in Rockville, Md., organized by my friend Pam Wanveer. I shared a room with Rose Reece, a woman from Pennsylvania, who agreed to work with one-year-old Trystan, as it was her first training and she could not bring her own dog, a Sheltie named Mickey, until her next training. She was already a dog trainer, and also starting the path to becoming a TTouch practicioner.

Comet, always a wader, watches as Trystan floats out to the deeper water for a swim.

Trystan loves to swim more than any corgi I've known.

Rose's business is called Training from the Heart, and the name is a very apt description of her work. Upon meeting Rose in our hotel room, Trystan immediately liked her, feeling her warmth and open heart as she got on the floor to greet him. I thought this connection with her would him feel more confident as they worked together over the week. She brought him delicious homemade treats (featuring coconut, a favorite of his) and took him for short walks in the hotel to get ice or visit the snack machine. Generally Trystan is very timid in a new place without me by his side, but he trotted beside Rose as she spoke to him matter-of-factly about points of interest along the way. The next day we all set off for our class, a short drive from the hotel.

I had been working with Linda Tellington-Jones for over 25 years at this time, and had attended more than 30 clinics for horses and companion animals. After a brief introduction, Linda reminded us, "Our animals are here to teach us to dare to open our hearts. They are essential to our spiritual survival."

Trystan in his TTouch class in 2011 demonstrating the TTouch "suitcase" leash wrap.

She described how the circle and a quarter we use in TTouches activates the forebrain, allowing us to come into a place of heart coherence, reducing stress, enhancing our breathing, and bringing us to a state of appreciation and a place of peace. Linda reminded us that "heart coherence, as researched by the HeartMath Institute in Boulder Creek, Ca., is achieved by controlling one's breathing and quieting one's thoughts while coming from a place of gratitude ... there is value in learning to monitor emotions, giving thanks for small things, and smiling." One or two Heart Hugs, done with the hands gently placed over the heart and moved in a circle and a quarter, "can bring a person or animal from a place of panic to a place of reason" Linda added. We practiced Heart Hugs on ourselves and noticed changes in our bodies. I could sense a shift in the energy of the room as the frantic rush to get to the class left everyone's body and we were all filled with love for our dogs. Since then, I have used Heart Hugs as a way to open or close the yoga classes I teach, seeing especially the calm that Heart Hugs bring to the elder residents living in a dementia unit when we close our eyes and count three things in our lives that we are grateful for.

Linda next explained that the combination of bodywork and the leash work in the Confidence Course would bring about "the possibility for dogs to think, increasing and enhancing the intelligence of dogs. This means they will respond in an appropriate way in many situations, and have the ability to adapt and be flexible, which also translates to the person working with the dog."

Trystan checking in during a walk.

Linda's words reminded me of Lassie, who was able to find Timmy and help him in many circumstances. She suggests that we talk to our dogs as if they understand us perfectly, as Lassie did, in complete sentences, using "please" and "thank you." Not only does this help us to keep breathing, but we create a clear picture in our minds of what we'd like the dog to do. Don't we all dream that our dogs can be like Lassie?

TTouch increases the level of communication and connection with your dog, which is much more than the principles of positive training. "With our equipment (harnesses, wraps, sliding handle leashes) and TTouches," Linda added, "we have found a way to work with dogs so that they want to work with us. We make it fun for them to be with us, because we appreciate their intelligence and respect them."

I smiled at Rose sitting next to me, and she smiled back. I could see how excited she was to be hearing these words from Linda, just as I had been at my first clinic with Burgers. Training from the heart, after all, is about connection, a dance partnership, not about blind obedience.

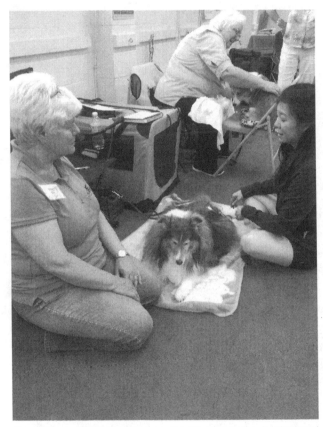

Rose, shown far left, with her dog Mickey. In the background, Trystan is working with another TTouch student.

We practiced TTouches on each other, and then with the dogs. Linda reminded us, "Whenever you touch your dog, touch with respect." The origins of respect come from "to be esteemed" and inspect, which is "to see," so we touched our animals with deep appreciation and connection. As Linda teaches in the horse classes, it is important to smile during the work, to give the dogs a sense of their beauty and preciousness to us. Also, smiling activates oxytocin and serotonin, two hormones linked to the good feelings we have when we are connecting with our animals. Smiling also relaxes our bodies.

As I helped new students around the circle practicing TTouches on their dogs, I could see Rose working with Trystan across the room. His eyes were closing in relaxation and pleasure as she worked around his ears and shoulders. Although he glanced my way a few times at the start of the session, he seemed to be adjusting to spending time with someone else who also knew the magic of TTouch.

One small dog in the group was considered "reactive," barking fiercely and lunging towards other dogs when they got near her. Linda reminded us of words from *A Course in Miracles*: "Aggression comes from a place of fear and is a cry for help."

I could hear people exhale around the room as they listened to these words, and the dog became calmer, too. Over the week, she wore wraps and experienced many TTouches on her body to help her learn to remain calm. We got her delicious treats as well, as in TTouch we use treats to help dogs stay in the "rest/digest" state of the parasympathetic response, instead of the "fight/flight/freeze" state of sympathetic arousal.

We put her in a place where she knew she was safe with barriers around her. She could watch the group from the front open area and see if any dog was near her. Everyone in the group made comments to her that she was safe throughout the days of the class, and anyone walking near her with another dog made sure to tell her first that they would be coming by with a dog. Sometimes she retreated back into her enclosed space, and sometimes she sat watching dogs go by, vigilant if they were to get too close, but much less reactive. It was amazing to see how she was able to sleep on her person's lap on the last days of class, with other dogs resting nearby next to their people. Like Trystan, she lacked confidence. She also needed to know that she would be safe around other dogs, trusting her person more to maintain a safe environment for her.

Linda introduced using wraps with dogs. We use colorful dyed ace wraps in 1-inch or 2-inch to 4-inch widths, wrapped gently around the dog's chest and behind the front legs, to give the dog a better sense of her body, a sense of boundaries, and allowing the dog to walk in better balance. Practitioners put wraps on some of the wiggly dogs in the room to help them settle, and timid dogs like Trystan seemed more outgoing with a wrap on them. Linda cautioned us to never leave a wrap on a dog we are not with, and to make sure no knots or pins on the wrap are directly over the spine.

Wrapped in a 2-inch saffron colored ace bandage, Trystan perched on Rose's lap, smiling and looking around the room. We had placed several colors on the floor and let him pick the one he preferred. Others had also done this, and it was interesting to see the colors the dogs chose—a chocolate brown dog in a teal wrap, a gray dog in a raspberry wrap, a black dog in a red wrap.

Colors, of course, are a reflection of different vibrational frequencies, and as I knew from my work with tuning forks, some colors increase energy and some colors calm energy. While red seems a vibrant color, it is also the color of the root chakra and the red wrap did seem to be helping the black dog stay more grounded. We were fortunate to have a rainbow of wrap colors in this class, dyed with care by Jamie G., with matching baby safety pins. We also tried wraps on people, learning particular ways to place them for sore shoulders, headaches, and back pain.

We next looked at different types of equipment for the dogs. The Freedom harness has been a favorite of TTouch practitioners for years, as it really helps balance a dog and discourage pulling. When a dog pulls, injury can occur in the spine, the shoulders, and the stifles in the hind legs. Aside from a big dog possibly injuring the person on the other end of the leash, pulling is dangerous for the dog's health as well. Today, Robyn, Linda's sister, has developed some innovative harnesses and leashes that are useful to discourage pulling dogs. We also discussed using step-in harnesses for certain body types.

Prior to the development of the Freedom harness, TTouch practitioners often used a "halti," or head collar, to give the person a second attachment to the dog besides to the collar or harness. We always used the halti with the leash also attached to a harness, and rarely, to a collar. We used the halti just to redirect the dog's head. It is very different from a "gentle leader" in fit and action, as it does not tighten around the nose. First Winston, and then Comet, had worn "snoot loops," as they fit the pointy nose of a corgi very well, and they helped discourage barking when my dogs were too excited in a big room full of other dogs. Linda reminded us that walking any dog with a head harness, like a halti or gentle leader, with only one point of attachment, can cause serious injuries to dogs' necks and spines. Trystan looked happy in the little blue Freedom harness Rose put on him. When she took him outside for a "break," he did not pull at all, which can sometimes be his tendency in a new place.

My mother's schnauzer, Shatzi, had worn a "gentle leader" for years, with the leash, including a heavy snap, attached to it. The snap and leash put pressure on her neck and face that was very uncomfortable, but because she is a reasonable dog, she allowed my mom to put it on her, although she clearly did not like it. When I asked my mom about this, she said a trainer told her to use this, and she felt concern that Shatzi didn't like it, even though without it, the big dog pulled my petite mom very strongly.

I ordered her a Freedom harness, which came with a leash that attaches at the front and the top of the harness, with a sliding handle for my mom to hold. She took Shatzi for a walk and reported to me with relief and excitement, "She didn't pull at all. It's easy to see she's much happier in this!"

Many people she saw on her walks had noticed the calmer dog in the raspberry harness, and my mom showed them how the harness was helping Shatzi not to pull, and several of them said they would also get one for their dogs. We saw more examples like this success with different equipment with some of the dogs in the TTouch class that week.

Trystan enjoys being stroked with a TTouch wand, which helps ground him and give him a sense of his body.

Linda pointed out that there is no universal "right" equipment for all dogs, but that instead, we needed to understand the benefits and limitations of our various options and to learn which may work with different types of dogs. In the past, I had taught dog caretakers to walk with two hands on the leash, one going to the halti, and one controlling the leash attached to the harness. This was awkward and hard for some people to manage. The advent of the TTouch sliding handles and the Freedom harness with two points of attachment and a sliding handle leash made it much easier for a person to manage the leash and not put unintended pressure on the dog.

The next day, we set out to use the new equipment on the dogs at the clinic as we worked with them on the Confidence Course. This is not an agility course, in that in TTouch, we want the dogs to go over the obstacles slowly and with care so that they can learn about proprioception and balance. The most important aspect of the course is the labyrinth, just as with the horse work. There are also different surfaces, such as carpet, screens, grates, and foam, for the dogs to walk on. And we use a raised board, like a balance beam for dogs, for them to learn about balance.

At this class, we set up a star as well, flat boards arranged in a fan shape with one end raised up, so dogs can walk through a section lifting their legs quite high, and the other end set so they can just step over the boards. We also set up some cones for dogs to weave around, as well as flat boards set up like cavaletti for horses, and a ladder of plastic pipe for the dogs to walk through. All of these elements teach the dogs to think and make careful choices.

I have worked with reactive dogs who, when being TTouched in the corners of the labyrinth, have been able to focus much better, with no lunging and barking. The Confidence Course is one more way that TTouch helps dogs to think and respond, rather than react.

Rose set off with Trystan, in his new blue Freedom harness and who was now wearing a much longer leash so that Rose did not have to bend over and put herself out of balance to walk with him, to try the course. Although he has an agility course at home with jumps, a loud banging teeter-totter, and weave poles, there was no guarantee that he would be comfortable on the Confidence Course with a new person.

Rose found that Trystan started off just fine walking over screens and carpets, but the narrow ladder confused him. Owing to his short size, he had to really figure out where to place his front and hind paws to navigate the ladder. He stopped in the first section, looking confused and searching the room for me. Linda suggested that Rose try some TTouches on him and add a wrap around his chest and behind his front legs to help him have a better sense of his body.

Linda asked the group to see what was happening to Trystan's posture as he stalled in the first section of the ladder. She reminded us that if we can change the posture, we can change the behavior. Trystan was afraid, rigid, eyes wide—although as a reasonable dog, he was still trying to do what Rose asked and continue through the ladder.

With the wrap on, he began breathing steadily again, and the TTouches helped him rebalance so that he had his weight evenly over all four legs instead of crouching over his front legs in fear. Linda added, "Also, if you can change *your* mind, you can change your dog or horse." She asked us to all hold a picture of Trystan trotting easily through the ladder confident of where his paws would land, and we could see a shift in his eyes as if he "heard" our thoughts.

The concept of "change your mind, change your dog," encompasses so much. When you change your mind, you actually *open* your mind to your dog's possibilities—for health, for different behavior with other dogs, for a new way to be in stressful situations, for a new way of moving.

After trying Linda's suggestions, Rose guided Trystan easily through the ladder with a spring in his steps, over a screen, and up to the start of the labyrinth. She offered him some treats in the first corner, and he eagerly ate them. She continued through the labyrinth to some poles to walk over and some cones to walk around. When Trystan got to the end of the room, he searched to find me and couldn't see me. He became more nervous and would not eat the treats Rose offered him, as he was very concerned that he could not see me. Linda asked me to walk near Rose and Trystan, gradually adding more distance, so that he would see that I knew he was safe with Rose. It took a few more days of work, but by the end of the class, Rose was able to take Trystan around the Confidence Course, near some bigger dogs, and outside, without Trystan needing to see me or check in with me. This was a huge step forward for him to gain greater confidence.

As we reviewed bodywork, Linda introduced ear work, mouth work, and tail work with the dogs. We had noticed that one nervous lab wagged his tail rapidly and constantly as a coping mechanism for stress. It was very different from the relaxed wag of a happy dog greeting us. Trystan, as a corgi, has a docked tail, as did a spaniel and a pointer mix in the group. We discussed the implications of this for the dog's balance, and I have talked with people who do agility with several different breeds who have suggested that the tail acts as a rudder for dogs running at top speed, and that those without tails require superior balance to reach high speeds.

Tail docking is very traumatic to a dog's system and emotions, and I have known reactive dogs, fearful of things behind them, whose owners can trace the fear back to the time when the dogs' tails were docked. With kirlian photography, we can see the energy pattern where a dog's docked tail would be. I know from the detailed anatomy of the spinal cord that I teach in my craniosacral classes that tail docking actually cuts into the central nervous of the animal, and could be a factor in some dysfunctions in the dog's spine and nervous system later in life. (One corgi breeder I've spoken with believes tail docking could be a factor in DM symptom development, even though DM is also known to be an inherited disease.)

Linda suggested that one reason perhaps that Trystan lacked confidence was that he did not have a good sense of his hind end because he did not have a tail. I thought back to how he wiggles his hind end and seems to enjoy moving the tail on his skunk costume to feel the sway of the tail. Clearly, he has the somatic memory of a tail.

Rose carefully did TTouch circles on Trystan's hind legs and rump, doing tiny "raccoon" TTouches near the base of his tail. She gently stroked the hairs growing from his tail, and made sweeps up through the air where his tail would be. Dogs, like people, have phantom limb pain, and TTouches are very helpful to address pain. Also, hair develops from the same embryonic tissue as the central nervous system, and so the hairs on Trystan's tail are a direct link to his central nervous system. For this reason and others, working on the tails of nervous dogs can be one way to help the dog become calmer, again engaging the "rest/digest" aspect of the nervous system. At first, Trystan tried to sit down to hide the bit of tail he has, but as Rose did careful circles with the hairs there, he relaxed and rolled to his side on her lap. Rose, as Linda suggested, was reminding Trystan's tail of "the potential for ideal function." I could see that this work was one more piece of the puzzle for him to improve his confidence.

Many of us in the room felt anger at the custom of tail docking and at the people who continue to dock dogs' velvet soft ears and beautiful tails. Since her move to Hawaii, Linda has spoken to every TTouch class group about the value of Ho'oponopono. This is a Hawaiian prayer, described wonderfully in a book by Ulrich Dupree, that includes four phrases: I'm sorry; please forgive me; thank you; I love you. Instead of feeling anger at puppy mills, abusive situations, or actions of animal cruelty, this prayer of reconciliation and forgiveness offers a way to make a shift in yourself, a way to meet anger and violence without adding more of the same. We are asked to find forgiveness, which is not acceptance, and offer thoughts of a better way to the people responsible for violent actions.

Dupree describes remarkable recovery for criminal patients in a mental hospital using the power of this prayer. It gives us strength in a situation where we may feel hopeless and helpless. The lessons of Ho'oponopono are derived from an understanding of the unity of everything in the universe, of the interconnection of all beings. As with my tuning fork work, the idea of resonance here means that nothing can happen in the world that does not affect the observer—Ho'oponopono offers us the chance to influence problems by raising our inner vibration and allowing that resonance to increase the vibration of all it touches.

Violence and anger are low vibrations; forgiveness and love are high vibrations. By applying Ho'oponopono to situations around us, we can create change. This goes along with Gandhi's idea of being the change you want to see in the world. As I breathed out forgiveness for the person who docked Trystan's tail, knowing that he did it out of lack of knowledge of alternatives, I watched my corgi's eyes soften as Rose gently TTouched him.

In his book *The Spontaneous Healing of Belief: Shattering the Paradigm of False Limits*,

Gregg Braden describes how a group's belief and feeling can influence others. In 1982, during the war between Lebanon and Israel, meditators were asked to "feel" peace in their bodies and believe that peace was present within them, not just imagined in their minds or prayers for peace.

At specific times on specific days, the meditators were positioned throughout the war stricken areas of the Middle East. The remarkable result was that during those times, crime decreased, terrorist activities ceased, emergency room visits declined, and the incidence of traffic accidents dropped. This means that "when a small percentage of the population achieved peace within themselves, it was reflected in the world around them." In fact, researchers were able to calculate the number of people required to feel peace to influence the world, and it was 100 people for a city of a million. (Results of this International Peace Project in the Middle East were published in 1988 in *The Journal of Conflict Resolution*.)

This example illustrates that our thoughts and feelings do indeed affect those around us, including our horses, dogs, cats and other animals. It supports the idea of Ho' oponopono as a way to bring love and forgiveness to the world. We are all connected through the quantum field, and what we think, especially what we *feel*, does have an impact on the world outside of ourselves.

When Rose asked Trystan to come out of his blue soft carrier on the final day of our class, she did not have to use our white wands to entice him with TTouches. She just extended her hand with the palm facing her so as not to be threatening to him, and he stood up, stretched, and walked over to her. This was a big step for him, showing that he was learning to trust other people, and he responded to her patience in not just pulling him out of his crate for the previous few days, by finally reaching out to her. This was the first step in hands-connecting-with-paws to begin the dance of cooperation and partnership.

Chapter 40

Miraculous Dance
Winnie and Equinisity

Winnie and I share a special bond.

"When the time is right, it will all come together, and you will see the whole perspective, and you will see how much I love you."

—Liz Mitten Ryan, *One With the Herd*

"The Zen moment is when they and we forget ourselves and become joined in the spirit of truth and dance."

—Liz Mitten Ryan, *One With the Herd*

After Burgers "crossed the rainbow bridge," horses shared my life as clients for craniosacral therapy, TTouch, reiki, and other healing modalities. I did not expect to find a deep heart connection with another horse. And then I met Winnie, a beautiful dark bay warmblood who lives at Gateway 2 ranch outside of Kamloops, B.C. Like Burgers when he was older, she has a star on her forehead the shape of a squirrel holding a nut, and one white sock behind. And reminiscent of my beloved first corgi Winston, her name is Winnie.

I went to an Equinisity retreat at Gateway 2; after carefully reading about the horses in books written by Liz Mitten Ryan, the farm owner, I knew the horses fairly well, and expected to connect with Epona. She is a big palomino mare who, Liz told me, performs craniosacral therapy. I felt an immediate rapport with Epona when I saw the stunning pictures of Liz's herd in her books. In fact, Epona and I met as colleagues. It was Winnie who filled my heart with a depth of emotion I have only rarely encountered in my life.

Epona and I met as Craniosacral colleagues. Photo by Liz Mitten Ryan.

The horses at Gateway 2 have been kept in a herd of family members their entire lives, and have known only kindness and cooperation with humans. As Ginger Kathrens also discovered in her work following the life of the mustang Cloud and his herd, family groups are an important aspect of equine social order. It is significant that at Gateway 2, horses have their families intact. They wander over 350 acres and come to a wide, open barn in the mornings to eat hay and meditate with the people who come to the farm.

The horses do healing work. They move energy to shift peoples' emotional and physical wounds, working together inside of the barn, and throughout the paddock outside the barn. People sit on stools or the barn floor, or stand quietly against a wall, and the horses come close to them, breathing gently next to their faces and hearts. Often the horses lie down in the thick layers of shavings, meditating together with the humans in their presence. Liz also believes, and I have to agree with her, that her horses are connecting with beings around the world, elephants, whales, and dolphins in particular, to bring peace to our world. Others who are sensitive to energy, such as my friend and animal channel Sandra M. who shared my time at Equinisity, have told me that they also can feel a deeper connection from the horses to the earth, and to other animals across the globe.

Liz says, "These spiritual retreats offer reconnection, revitalization and healing, dispelling illusion, shifting consciousness, and tuning and raising personal and universal vibration."

Speaking for the herd, she adds, "There is only one consciousness in all life ... all thoughts, emotions and inspiration flow from this higher consciousness and express through the diversity of all creation."

It is a profound experience for everyone who participates in the healing work there. In fact, I believe that every horse or animal can do this healing work, but not everyone allows their animals the freedom to show them what they can do. Liz has spent long, quiet hours with her horses to understand their needs and wants, and sees clearly how they do this work.

I had spoken with Liz on the phone about my work with horses and my corgis assisting in craniosacral sessions with me. She knew immediately how this happened and how effective it is to work with animals in healing sessions. After our conversation, I made plans to go to her farm, meet the horses, dogs and cats there, and explore the healing work her animals were doing. My visit coincided with a filmmaker's trip to Gateway 2 to record the experiences of my own and seven others' journeys with Liz's horses.

I arrived several hours early and I ventured into the paddock to meet the horses. First I went to Epona. She pricked her ears at me, and we greeted each other with breaths and a quiet gaze. We had a connection, and I knew she had heard my messages to her before I arrived. My new friend Leslie called me over to meet the foal, Hyperion, and his mother, Serene. We greeted Serene with compliments on her handsome son, and were delighted to be able to scratch and rub Hyperion as much as we, and he, wanted. Only a few months old, he was charming and adorable.

As I looked across the paddock, my eyes met the eyes of one of the many dark bay mares there. She was standing with her daughter Prospera, a half-Andalusian, in a small area away from the rest of the herd. I walked slowly over to her and gently reached out to touch her shoulder with the back of my hand, feeling her thin skin and fine hair—she was an exquisitely sensitive horse. Liz told me her name was Winnie, from the first group of mares she had brought to the farm nearly twenty years ago. I said hello to Winnie with soft breaths near her muzzle. Immediately our breaths fell into synchrony and we were in heart coherence. I felt myself pulled deeper and deeper into this horse's soul as I gently rested my hands on her shoulder. I was moved nearly to tears by the connection I was feeling with Winnie.

The next day, when I met Winnie in the small paddock where she prefers to rest in the mornings, I again breathed "hello" near her muzzle and looked into her eyes with appreciation for her spirit and beauty. I became aware of tension in her head, above her eyes, and noticed the holding patterns in the muscles there. I realized that my craniosacral skills could be beneficial for her, so I silently asked if she would like me to work with her. She lowered her head into my hands with a long exhale.

I followed the motions of her head as I released all of the sutures in the bones of Winnie's face. I felt tension in her jaw and around the orbits of her eyes in particular, as the sutures released fully. Her jaw melted through my hands connecting into the earth as Winnie first slowly lowered and then lifted her head, fully aware of the fulcrum my fingers created around the bones in her jaw. When I glanced to the side at her offspring, Prospera, I saw that her muzzle was close to Winnie's shoulder, following the line of her neck, and connecting with my hands. It was apparent to me that she was helping me with the work I was doing with Winnie.

As I finished with a thoracic inlet release on Winnie's neck, I could feel Prospera's muzzle meeting my hand under Winnie's neck. Winnie slowly yawned and shook her head slightly; I knew she was feeling better after the work. I walked away to let her rest and process the work with her beloved Prospera by her side.

Liz suggested I sit near Epona, the horse she had told me does craniosacral work. I positioned myself quietly on a stool under her muzzle, placing my hands over my heart, sending love and appreciation to Epona. As we came into heart coherence, our breathing and heart rates in synchrony, she lowered her muzzle close to my head, resting her chin on my forehead. I was fully aware of the depth of the energetic connection between us and I could feel my body making corrections and adjustments as Epona's neutral presence washed through me. Would I call this craniosacral therapy? In many ways yes, as Dr. Upledger himself often said that one of the most important things a therapist can contribute to a session is a neutral presence and an open, loving heart.

Clearly Epona's work met these criteria.

Cavalia founder Frédéric Pignon echoes this idea, "It has always amazed me how quickly a good chiropractor or osteopath convinces a horse that he is important to him. The horse understands in no time at all that the osteopath will relieve him of his aches and pains and therefore accepts him as a friend." With the horses at Equinisity, it is the humans who quickly see that the horses are offering healing to them, and the horses make an immediate connection with the people who go there. After thanking Epona for her time with me, I quietly made my way to one of the "healing tables" Liz has in her paddock area, to process my experience with Epona and perhaps rest a bit.

I lay on the table in the sunshine, reveling in the clear blue of the sky and the mystical formations in the white clouds overhead. We had noticed a shape like angel wings in the sky earlier that morning, and I watched as bits of angel feathers became dogs, rabbits, and waves in the sky. I became aware of shifts in my body, my right leg readjusting its position on the table, and subtle alignment in my sacrum. I turned to look beside me and saw Merlin, a pony, next to me, eyes slightly closed, muzzle near my left shoulder. He had chosen to connect with me and continue the rebalancing work Epona had started with me. As my body felt heavier on the table, Merlin walked to the end of the table by my feet. I could feel a shift as our paired energy balanced my pelvis, and subtle shifts in my left ankle felt like a craniosacral regional tissue release. As I took a big breath in and out, Merlin felt his work was done, and moved over to the table next to me. I thanked him for our time together, but had a distinct impression that it was "all in a day's work for him, not a big deal."

I did discover his playful nature when we worked together in the following days over the course Liz set up for working next to the horses without halters, trotting through hanging pool noodles and over raised earth-filled tractor tires, and stepping around hula hoops. Merlin loved to trot and race with me and others around the course, and across the pasture.

The next day, Winnie did a remarkable thing with me. I had met her outside the large open barn, and I had worked with Prospera's sore shoulders a short while, and done some work with Winnie's sacrum and hips, as she was off in her hind end. I walked over closer to the barn door and took a place on a stool just outside the door. Inside the barn, just behind me, a woman named Arie was seated, meditating with the horses in the barn. Winnie and Prospera came across the barnyard to us, and Winnie took two steps past me and rested her head near Arie. At first, I was unaware of my continued connection to Winnie, but when I shifted on my stool considering getting up, she moved a foreleg to block me. And then I became aware that she was requesting my neutral presence as she needed support for her work with Arie. As always, Prospera stood quietly by her side. I could hear Arie crying, first muffled, and then later tears and shaking erupting from far within her heart. Winnie rested her muzzle in Arie's lap, as Arie leaned her forehead into Winnie's head. After maybe twenty-five minutes,

Winnie lifted her head, and the horses in the barn started to move outside.

When Arie and I spoke to Liz after this, Arie said in her still unsteady voice that she was so thankful for the opportunity to cry with these horses over the recent death of her young son named Bodhe. She had been unable to fully grieve as she struggled to pick up the pieces of her life and find the spiritual guides she needed, including a woman who had suggested she go to a place with horses to reconnect with herself and find healing. Liz and I listened closely, and then Liz told us that Winnie had lost a foal several years before; of course she understood Arie's grief. It was a profound moment of realization for all of us. And I felt that Winnie had requested my support as this was a struggle close to her own heart. She had clearly asked me to stay as a participant in this "session" where she and Arie shared so much.

Later that week, it was raining and quite cold for June, so the horses and the people stayed in the warm, dry barn that morning. One horse in particular, Picasso, had been following me, and pushing his nose into me, and I felt he was asking me to do some craniosacral work with him, as he was rather sore behind. He stood quietly near the barn door with his friend Mica standing in front of him. I greeted him, and gently placed my hands on his sacrum. As I released some layers of restriction there, I positioned my hands over his left sacroiliac joint. As the tension released, I felt him sinking beneath my hands as he carefully lay on the ground, extending his left hind leg to the side for me to reach more easily. I worked my way down the leg, through the stifle and the hock, noticing that Mica had her muzzle on his poll. I tuned into a connection with her and felt a surge of energy through Picasso's spine from her muzzle into my hands, extending back into the earth. As the left leg released, I went back up to Picasso's sacrum to do a lumbar decompression.

When I shifted to reach up to his withers with one hand, I became aware of another horse's presence behind me—the mare Magic. She stepped closer, bringing her muzzle to rest on my hand over Picasso's sacrum. At that moment, I could distinctly feel Mica's work as she used her muzzle to put a gentle traction on Picasso's occiput over his poll. Magic squinted at me and moved closer in, and I felt she wanted me to move over. I did not want to leave Picasso, so I watched her closely as I moved both of my hands over his withers, spread like butterfly. Immediately, Magic rested her muzzle on Picasso's sacrum where my hands had been. As I kept my place at the withers, I could clearly feel Magic and Mica balancing their energy to do a textbook dural tube glide with Picasso on his spinal cord. In disbelief, I looked closely and even saw the two mares swaying together, as they worked with me, freeing up restrictions for Picasso. He, meanwhile, slept deeply, his muzzle resting heavily on the shavings, eyes closed.

I refocused my intention, and for several minutes, two horses and I worked together. Mica was the first to release her muzzle, carefully lying down next to Picasso. Next, feeling the subtle "pushing away" energy, I released my hands and turned to face Magic's muzzle still resting on Picasso's sacrum. I watched as she slowly slid her muzzle down his spine to his tail, noticing that she paused a bit longer where there were greater restrictions. She made her way to the base of his tail and moved her muzzle away in a slight swoop, as I sensed a shift in the energy around Picasso. Then she slowly entered the barn and also settled down in the shavings next to Picasso. I sat next to the group for about twenty more minutes. It was remarkable to me that not one, but two horses, had joined me in this craniosacral session. And both of them had watched what I did with my hands, and then replicated it perfectly.

Mica working with me on Picasso before Magic joined us. Photo by Liz Mitten Ryan.

They say that in craniosacral therapy, one is swimming in the sacred space of the life force of another being during the work. The longest of the craniosacral rhythms may in fact be the last detectable motion in a body after it has been deemed no longer alive. On that morning with these three horses, I had experienced something profound as we shared a time of such deep connection not only to each other as therapists, but to Picasso as well. It was an honor for me to have had such an experience with these horses.

Each morning of the retreat, I first went to see Winnie and spend some time with her, just "being," or maybe doing some work on something that had been stressed over her nightly rambles across hundreds of acres. She is not a young horse as she approaches her twentieth year. She chose to work with Arie a few more times as well. Each day when I placed my hand on Winnie's shoulder, in the area of her eighth chakra, said to be where animals connect to humans, I could feel our hearts joining and being pulled into a blanket of comfort and unconditional love. Each time, I was close to tears, but not because my heart was breaking, but because my heart was so full of love. I felt as if I had known her love as long as I had known anything.

On one of our last nights there, we made a fire to release whatever each of us had to let go of, and to ignite our intentions. As we made preparations for the fire, the herd came into the small valley outside the Spirit Lodge. People played drums and rattles, and others walked silently into the field to see the horses who had shared their lives for a week. I played my flute, walking though the grass beside the pond, in the place that Liz had told us was favored by native people many years ago. My eyes found Winnie in the herd, and I played my flute to her, hoping to find a song that would be Winnie's song. As I got closer to her, she raised her head between bites of grass to listen and watch me. The drumming grew quieter, as some horses seemed concerned about the loud rhythms carried by the still night air.

As the night settled around us, it felt that Winnie, Prospera and I were alone with the music of the flute. When I was six feet from her, Winnie kept her head up from the grass, eyes watching me, and I stopped playing. I approached Winnie, and rested my hand on her shoulder. She snorted, and hugged me with her neck as Prospera nuzzled my back. It was as if I had never been closer to another living being, with the miles of stars surrounding us, the fragrant sage beneath us, and the quiet sounds of our shared breath. Winnie still wore the yellow flower I had braided into her mane that afternoon. In the morning, I would have to leave her to fly across the continent to my home in Massachusetts.

It was rushed for everyone in the morning, repacking the suitcases, getting them to the porch to be picked up, saying goodbye to the marmots we had enjoyed outside of our guesthouse. When I saw Winnie in the barnyard, I am sure she knew it was the last day for our group to be there. People were scattered around with the horses who had shared their journeys for the week.

Prospera, Winnie and I were in the small area off to the side, as I silently asked Winnie to help me through our parting. As I looked at the two of them, I realized how much they were like my two horses, Burgers and Hawk. Winnie shared the white sock and star, the dark bay color of Burgers, and Hawk shared the black color and arched neck of Prospera. At that moment, I felt pulled into Winnie's heart, felt as if I could turn and see my two horses standing next to us, almost in the twilight space I had been in when I had fallen and had a near-death experience. It was the most present, fully aware of the moment, I had ever felt. I laughed to realize that "in the moment" meant that I was thinking of horses who had long ago passed on, and of the open sky and seemingly endless land around us. There is so much sensory experience within a tiny moment in time.

Carl Safina, in his book *Beyond Words: What Animals Think and Feel*, describes this type of experience: "When I myself look at other animals, I almost never see an otherness. I see the overwhelming similarities; they fill me with a sense of deep relation. Nothing makes me feel more at home in the world than the company of wild relatives. Nothing else except the deepest human love feels as right, as connected, or puts me as much at peace." During my time at Equinisity, once again as I had known with my horses and corgis, I found the deepest peace in Winnie's presence.

As I stroked Winnie's mane, two hairs slipped into my hands. I knew this was a tangible way to always remember her. She had already offered me a hair from her long silky tail the day before. As I thought that these three hairs seemed too much, I could hear Winnie say that I may lose one, and she doesn't need so many. I smiled at her, carefully placing the hairs in my pocket, knowing that 24 hours of flights could indeed cause some losses. Liz reminded me that I could connect with Winnie anytime, and that there are beautiful pictures of her in her books. Winnie nuzzled my sleeve as I let my hands slide away from her neck where I had also left my tears. I told her how much I appreciated our time together here, and how grateful I would be to her always for what we shared.

Being with Hyperion enriched my time at Equinisity. Photo by Liz Mitten Ryan.

Sure enough, I lost one of her hairs in my travels. Winnie was right—it was not too much.

Of peoples' experiences at Equinisity retreats, Liz writes, "There is only one consciousness, one force of love that connects us all. When we experience that, we are instantly and forever changed."

I will be forever changed from my time there, especially from the deep unconditional love Winnie and I felt for one another. Our connection through the one consciousness, the one force of love and life that intertwines all of us, is indeed eternal.

Winnie, on the morning I said goodbye to her. Her daughter prospers in the background.

Afterword

Dances of the Heart
Trystan's Love

The view between a horse's ears ... is very much the same as the view between Trystan's ears.

"The air of heaven is that which blows between a horse's ears."

—Arabian proverb

"Don't try to lead me or to be led by me; just walk beside me and be my friend."

— Il Goldens, *The Dog Gospels*

Trystan, my beloved corgi, even though he has passed the official years of "puppy" status, is full of energy and happiness. Small though he is, he embraces his life with me as an ambassador for the entire world of animals. Each morning, he wakes up when he hears me moving or shifting the blankets on the bed, and he scrambles up from where he likes to sleep under my bed. He makes little "ruff" noises, wiggling his rump and his stubby tail, but not because he wants food, or a walk, as after this ritual he goes back for another nap before those things. He is simply happy for it to be morning, to reconnect with me and get his favorite shoulder rub each morning. When I get out of bed, he optimistically trots behind me into the bathroom and watches as I brush my teeth and tie back my hair before I go to make us both breakfast. And then he flops on his bottom half, hind legs behind him as corgis do (I call it his magic carpet pose because to me corgis are magic), and rests under the bed until he hears his food bowl on the kitchen counter.

I hear the trot of his toenails on the wood floors upstairs before he bounces down the carpeted steps with a big leap onto the kitchen tile. When he sees me in the kitchen, it is as if we have been apart for hours, as he is so happy to see me again, and he sits politely just before I place his bowl before him no matter how squirmy and barking he was before. After his meal, he runs to the living room rug, as has every corgi I've had, and he rolls and scampers in small leaps on the rug, what corgi people call "frapping," something they say corgis do for the shear joy of being a corgi. Then Trystan positions himself next to me, waiting for the customary bit of my breakfast to top off his own breakfast. And after his piece of toast or eggs, he goes off to his favorite sofa in the office to his perch, where he digests and watches the world outside of his personal window. He clearly has his own morning routine before he sees how many games of squeaky toss the day will hold, or where we will go for our walk, or who may be coming over for a craniosacral session, TTouch work, or a visit. It is impossible not to feel joy every moment you are with Trystan, as he has so much happiness himself.

Trystan is about movement. He loves to play on his agility equipment, running fast up his teeter totter,—pausing, like Gene Kelly tipping a chair down when he dances as he is singing in rain—before he tips it down with a whack, and then pauses again at the end as he knows he should, before springing off. He loves his jumps most of all, and I was amazed after a winter off when he graduated from needing treats and directions to play on his agility course, to simply following my hand signals and gaze, springing lightly over the jumps. The tire jump always slows him down a bit as he curls up for a bigger leap, and he is exuberant when he races to jump onto the small bench at the end of our course to wait for praise for a job well done. He does not like his weave poles very much, only doing two or three unless I make an effort to encourage him to do more. Trystan loves to race around the fenced back yard as fast as he can, until you can't see his feet moving, and he becomes a flying corgi.

What are Trystan's particular gifts to me? First, he is a yoga dog. He comes to yoga classes, and with his small size, it easy to have him join me in poses. I can pick him up for a "warrior with a corgi" pose. He can do "corgi on a table" pose and he likes child pose curled under me or "corgi puppy stretch" next to me. Together we do "corgi sitting in a tree" pose. He is completely unaware that yoga-with-your-dog yoga is anything more than a strange way to play with him, or that across the country other people are also working on ways to do yoga with their dogs.

Trystan and I celebrate his love of movement with our version of dog dancing, otherwise known as freestyle to the dog training world. Certainly my freestyle dancing with my horses was polished and accomplished, with the smallest signals of my breath, my weight, the pictures in my mind directing us around the dressage ring. Dog dancing with Trystan combines everything I love—costumes, dancing, music and, most importantly, the connection and communication with my dog. Trystan and I are not fancy competitors; we just dance for fun at small dog shows, or in the living room of our house. The enthusiasm and joy in Trystan's barks as he does his tricks to music, and the feeling of love and connection I sense when Trystan moves towards me, away, and around, with the smallest signals, reminds me of riding my horses in their freestyles.

When Trystan and I go for walks, I watch the world unfold between his upright corgi ears and remember a time when I looked at the world between the bay ears of Burgers or the ears of my other horses. I watch Trystan's rump, shifting right and left as he trots ahead, the same way I have watched countless horses ahead of me on trail rides over the years.

There is a spiritual beauty in watching the world arrive into your senses this way, noticing the squirrels, hearing the rushing stream down the hill, or seeing a chipmunk disappearing into a tree stump, smelling the pine trees in the light breeze. It is the best way to see the world, with an animal as your guide. Even though Trystan is small, we match our footsteps as we observe the world together. I feel his heartbeat travel through the leash as he stops to look intently, ears up, sniffing heavily at some far off deer in the woods. And I know that with him, as with all of my animals, there is the bond of deep love and connection between us. This is what we all want with our animals, to dance with them throughout our shared lives.

With Deep Appreciation and Many Thanks ...

To my mother, Sally Bradway Morgan, whose love for animals and recognition of their intelligence and emotions, started me on my path of understanding and compassion for animals. To Jack Hornor, my beloved ex-husband, who carefully read and edited the first draft, and made diplomatic suggestions for changes, and who told me often to just write, offering unwavering support. I thank him too for his patience and love for all of our shared animals. To my sister, Judy Morgan, DVM, who led by example, encouraging me to tell these stories and guiding me through the publication process, and also for her years of providing the best quality holistic veterinary care for all of my animals. To my many riding students, (especially Katherine, Julia, Sarah, Stacy, Janet, Phoebe, Mara, Kirsten, Jean, Copper, Bramble, Kay, and Rowena) who showed me how to be a teacher and a student. To my equine, canine, feline, lapin and human clients who taught me so much as we shared the process of learning connection and finding health. To Alexandra Kurland for showing me what I knew to be right was indeed a better way. To Sally Swift, for sharing my name and teaching me the balance of a truly independent seat. To Lendon Gray, for believing in small horses.

To Anne Adams for her thorough editing, support, and feedback. To Dan for his overnight thoughtful edits and support. To Bryan for his rescue of text losses and technical assistance. To Deana Riddle for her hard work designing this book with understanding and patience. To Helena Sullivan for her beautiful photographs captured in the last month of Burgers' life.

To Linda Tellington-Jones, for her deep appreciation of animals, and being a lifelong friend who has always supported my journey. My gratitude to her genius and insight informs my life's work. To Bernie Siegel, who believes that stories about animals matter.

And most importantly to all of my animals, who showed me their brilliance and who loved me as much as I loved them. To the horses Blaze, Phantom, Spooky, Goblin, Richard, Boca Kay, Rocky, Smokey, Lucky, Hawk and especially Burgers, I am so grateful to all of you for trying your best every day and for teaching me to dance with you. To my rabbits, Agatha, Candy, Eileen, Hershey, Lily, Rufus, and especially Leo for showing me that big minds and personalities come in small bunny packages. To my dogs, Toby for his patience, Dandy for his love of running, Winston for his genius, Comet for his eternal love, and happy little Trystan for being my newest dance partner, and to all of them for their willingness to always do what I needed, and for showing me that dogs are supremely intelligent, kind, and understanding.

And to all of the animals who bravely share the planet with humans, reminding us of our relationship to nature, for their willingness to make connections with us, and for sharing the dance with us.

Dances of the Heart – Connecting With Animals

Notes

Foreword

p. 4 "you must observe … ": Magali Delgado & Frédéric Pignon, *Gallop to Freedom: Training Horses with the Founding Stars of Cavalia* (Pomfret, Vt: Trafalgar Square Books, 2009), p. 55.

Chapter 1: Dogs and Their Dance of Devotion

p. 14 "morphic field": Rupert Sheldrake, *Dogs That Know When Their Owners Are Coming Home: And Other Unexplained Powers of Animals* (New York: Three Rivers Press, 1999), p. 24–26.

Chapter 2: Finding the Dance With Connection

p. 20 Allison, Barrows, Blake et al., ed., *The Norton Anthology of Poetry* (New York: W.W. Norton and Company, 1983), William Cowper, "Epitaph on a Hare," p. 481.

Chapter 4: Promise of the Dance

p. 43 "Whose woods these are": Allison, Barrow, Blake et al., ed., *The Norton Anthology of Poetry*, shorter ed. (New York: W.W. Norton and Company, 1983), Robert Frost, "Stopping by Woods on a Snowy Evening," p. 542.

Chapter 5: Dedication to the Dance

p. 52 Louise Mills Wilde, *Guide to Dressage* (Millbrook, NY: Breakthrough Publications, 1987).

Chapter 6: The Dance of Faithfulness

p. 62 John W. Pilley, Jr., PhD, *Chaser: Unlocking the Genius of the Dog Who Knows a Thousand Words* (NY: Houghton Mifflin Harcourt, 2014).

Chapter 8: Dancing Beauty

p. 72 "Tellington TTouch® Training Method": Currently this work is referred to as the Tellington Method or Tellington TTouch Training, or Tellington TTouch Training Method, which includes all of the prior names of TTEAM (Tellington Equine Awareness Method), TACT (Tellington Animal Companion Training), and TTouch (Tellington TTouch).

Chapter 9: Dancing With Cooperation

p. 79 Max Gahwyler, *The Competitive Edge: Improving Your Dressage Scores in the Lower Levels* (Middletown, MD: Half Halt Press, 1989).

Chapter 11: The Dance of Touch

p. 87 Linda Tellington-Jones and Carol Lang, *Six Macaques: A Story of Transformation from Lab Primates to Animal Ambassadors* (Kindle Edition, 2016).

p. 88 "we pay a lot of attention ...": Shannon Yewell Weil, *Strike A Long Trot: Legendary Horsewoman Linda Tellington-Jones* (USA: Turtle Rock Press, 2013), p. 102.

p. 92 "photons in living systems ...": Lynn McTaggart, *The Field: The Quest for the Secret Force of the Universe* (New York: HarperCollins Publishers, 2002), p. 43.

p. 92 "a Oneness": Larry Dossey, M.D., *One Mind: How Our Individual Mind is Part of a Greater Consciousness and Why It Matters* (New York: Hay House, 2013).

p. 92 "man is a being of light ...": Fritz-Albert Popp, biontologyarizona.com.

p. 92 "No part of the body ... ": Norman Doidge, M.D., *The Brain's Way of Healing: Remarkable Discoveries and Recoveries From the Frontiers of Neuroplasticity* (New York: Penguin Group, 2015), p. 166–7.

p. 92 "ATM": Feldenkrais.com.

p. 95 "biomagnetic field of the heart,": James L. Oschman, *Energy Medicine: The Scientific Basis* (New York: Churchill Livingstone, 2000), p. 29.

p. 95 "morphic field": Rupert Sheldrake, *Dogs That Know When Their Owners Are Coming Home: And Other Unexplained Powers of Animals* (New York: Three Rivers Press, 1999), p. 24–26.

Chapter 12: The Dance of Freedom

p. 100 "Tellington Training Bit": Linda Tellington-Jones with Roberta Jo Lieberman, *The Ultimate Horse Behavior and Training Book* (Pomfret, VT: Trafalgar Square Books, 2006), p. 291.

p. 100 "theorizes … ": Robyn Hood, "Training Rollerbit," *Staying In TTouch*, vol. 18, issue 3 (July-September 2016): 16-19.

Chapter 14: Purpose in the Dance

p. 114 "their consciousness is mostly pictures": Temple Grandin, *Animals in Translation: Using the Mysteries of Autism to Decode Animal Behavior* (New York: Simon & Schuster, 2005), p. 262.

p. 114 Abigail Witthauer, "No Cue November"(Positively—Victoria Stilwell, positively.com).

p. 114 "one hormone … ": Brian Hare and Vanessa Woods, *The Genius of Dogs: How Dogs Are Smarter Than You Think* (New York: Plume—A Penguin Random House Company, 2013), p. 279.

p. 114 "oxytocin … ": David Grimm, April 16, 2015, sciencemag.org.

Chapter 16: The Dance of Interspecies Communication

p. 126 "the experience was mind altering … " Linda Tellington-Jones with Roberta Jo Lieberman, *The Ultimate Horse Behavior and Training Book* (Pomfret, VT: Trafalgar Square Books, 2006), p. xix.

Chapter 17: Dancing With Horses

p. 132 "amygdala sends projections … to trigeminal and facial nerves … " "Amygdala," Wikipedia.

Chapter 18: To Dance With Confidence

p. 136 When referring specifically to Upledger CranioSacral Therapy, there are capital letters for the "C" and the "S". When I refer generally to this type of work, it is spelled with a small "s". The abbreviation "CST" refers to all craniosacral work.

p. 136 "Work with it …": Norman Doidge, M.D., *The Brain's Way of Healing: Remarkable*

Discoveries and Recoveries From the Frontiers of Neuroplasticity (New York: Penguin Group, 2015), p. 164.

p. 136 "When I have ... ": Magali Delgado & Frédéric Pignon, *Gallop to Freedom: Training Horses With the Founding Stars of Cavalia* (Pomfret, VT: Trafalgar Square Books, 2009), p. 108.

p. 140 Beth Jenkins, *Notes from Riding Through Winter: Or, Classical Dressage in the Real American World* (Janice W. Jenkins, 1990).

Chapter 28: Life Dance

p. 204 "awakened mind state": Anna Wise, *The High Performance Mind: Mastering Brainwaves for Insight, Healing, and Creativity* (New York: Penguin Group, 1997).

p. 206 "heart coherence": HeartMath.org.

Chapter 29: Dance of Magic

p. 207 "awakened mind state in corners of labyrinth": Anna Wise, *The High-Performance Mind: Mastering Brainwaves for Insight, Healing, and Creativity* (New York: Penguin Group, 1997).

Chapter 30: Sharing the Dance With Compassion

p. 213 Candace B. Pert, *Molecules of Emotion: The Science Behind Mind-Body Medicine* (New York: Touchstone, 1997).

p. 220 "obstacles in human relationships with animals ... ": Diane Guerrero, *What Animals Teach Us About Spirituality: Inspiring Lessons from Wild and Tame Creatures* (Woodstock, VT: SkyLight Paths Publishing, 2008), p. 118.

Chapter 31: The Dance of Honesty

p. 226 Masaru Emoto, *The Hidden Messages in Water* (Hillsboro, OR: Beyond Words Publishing Inc., 2004).

p. 226 Jerry and Esther Hicks, *Ask and It Is Given: Learning to Manifest Your Desires* (New York: Hay House Inc., 2004).

p. 226 Wayne Dyer, *The Power of Intention: Learning to Co-Create Your World Your Way* (New York: Hay House Inc., 2004).

Chapter 34: Dancing Creates Wellness

p. 242 Bernie S. Siegel, M.D., *Love Medicine, and Miracles: Lessons Learned About Self-Healing from a Surgeon's Experience with Exceptional Patients* (New York: Harper and Row, 1986).

p. 244 " ... troubles can turn into blessings ... ": Bernie S. Siegel, M.D., *Smudge Bunny* (Tiburon, CA: H J Kramer Starseed Press, 2004).

p. 244 "there is nothing either good or bad, but thinking makes it so": William Shakespeare, *The Tragedy of Hamlet Prince of Denmark*, Louis B. Wright and Virginia LaMar, Ed. (New York: Simon & Schuster, 1958), Act II, scene 2, l. 265, p.48.

p. 246 " ... aware of its interconnection with everything ... ": Robert A. F. Thurman, trans., *The Tibetan Book of the Dead: As Popularly Known in the West: Known in Tibet as the Great Book of Natural Liberation Through Understanding in the Between.* Composed. Padma Sambhaua. Discover. Karma Lingpa. (New York: Bantom, 1994), p. 40.

Chapter 35: Wisdom From the Dance

p. 252 Ted Andrews, *Animal-Wise: The Spirit Language and Signs of Nature* (Jackson, TN: Dragonhawk Publishing, 1999).

p. 252 Ted Andrews, *Animal-Speak: The Spiritual and Magical Powers of Creatures Great & Small* (St. Paul, MN: Llewellyn Publications, 2000).

Chapter 37: Dancing Into Eternity

p. 271 " ... by four days transition is sure to be complete": Robert A. F. Thurman, trans., *The Tibetan Book of the Dead: As Popularly known in the West: Known in Tibet as the Great Book of Natural Liberation Through Understanding in the Between.* Composed. Padma Sambhaua. Discover. Karma Lingpa. (New York: Bantom, 1994), p. 40.

p. 272 Ted Andrews, *Animal-Speak: The Spiritual and Magical Powers of Creatures Great & Small* (St. Paul, MN: Llewellyn Publications, 2000), p. 274.

p. 273 "a graduation, a commencement": Bernie S. Siegel, M.D., *Buddy's Candle* (Victoria, BC Canada: Trafford Publishing, 2008), p. 27.

p. 273 "let your light shine ... ": Bernie S. Siegel, M.D., *Buddy's Candle* (Victoria, BC Canada: Trafford Publishing, 2008), p. 32.

p. 273 Larry Dossey, M.D., *One Mind: How Our Individual Mind is Part of a Greater Consciousness and Why It Matters* (New York: Hay House, 2013).

p. 274 "the greatest story ..." : Carl Safina, *Beyond Words: What Animals Think and Feel* (New York: Holt, 2015), p. 411.

Chapter 38: Spirit Dance

p. 276 "felt like crying, I would think of our love": Bernie S. Siegel, M.D., *Buddy's Candle* (Victoria, BC Canada: Trafford Publishing, 2008), p. 28.

Chapter 39: The Dance of Courage

p. 289 "heart coherence ... ": Shannon Yewell Weil, *Strike A Long Trot: Legendary Horsewoman Linda Tellington-Jones* (USA: Turtle Rock Press, 2013), p. 292.

p. 298 "when a small percentage ...": Gregg Braden, *The Spontaneous Healing of Belief: Shattering the Paradigm of False Limits* (New York: Hay House Inc., 2008), p. 48.

Chapter 40: Miraculous Dance

p. 301 Ginger Kathrens, *Cloud, Wild Stallion of the Rockies* (Irvine, CA: BowTie Press, 2001).

p. 303 "It has always amazed me ... ": Magali Delgado & Frédéric Pignon, *Gallop to Freedom: Training Horses with the Founding Stars of Cavalia* (Pomfret, VT: Trafalgar Square Books, 2009), p. 119.

p. 307 "When I myself ... ": Carl Safina, *Beyond Words: What Animals Think and Feel* (New York: Holt, 2015), p. 362.

Made in the USA
Lexington, KY
01 December 2017